COMPUTER BOOK SERIES FROM IDG

Word 6 For Macs For Dummies

Cheat Sheet

D1552006

The Standard Toolbar

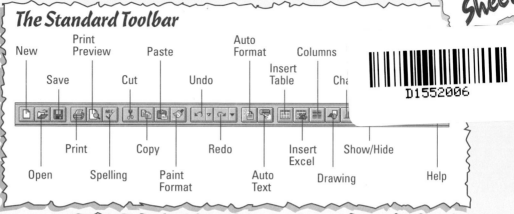

New · Print Preview · Paste · Auto Format · Columns · Insert Table · Ch...
Save · Cut · Undo · Insert Excel
Print · Copy · Redo · Show/Hide
Open · Spelling · Paint Format · Auto Text · Drawing · Help

The Formatting Toolbar

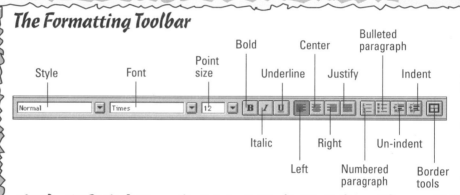

Style · Font · Point size · Bold · Center · Bulleted paragraph
Underline · Justify · Indent
Italic · Right · Un-indent
Left · Numbered paragraph · Border tools

Normal Times 12

Helpful Tips

- Let the computer do the work! Let Word format your pages and insert page numbers, headers, and footers. Don't ever do that stuff "manually" on-screen.
- Always save your documents to disk!
- If a document has already been saved to disk, press ⌘-S to update (save) the document on disk.

Useful Tools

- To check your spelling, press the F7 key or ⌘-Option-L.
- To use the thesaurus, press Shift-F7 or ⌘-Option-R.

Selecting Text

One way to select text is to hold down the Shift key and press keys that move the cursor to extend the selection:

⌘-Shift-→	End of a word	⌘-A	Entire document
Shift-End	End of a line	⌘-Shift-↓	End of a paragraph
Shift-←	Left one character	⌘-Shift-End	End of a document
Shift-→	Right one character		

Getting Around in a Document

Pressing the following keys moves the toothpick cursor as indicated:

↑	Up one line of text
↓	Down one line of text
→	Right one character
←	Left one character
⌘-↑	Up one paragraph
⌘-↓	Down one paragraph
⌘-→	Right one word
⌘-←	Left one word
⌘-Page Up	To top of screen
⌘-Page Down	To bottom of screen
Page Up	Up one screen
Page Down	Down one screen
End	To end of current line
Home	To start of current line
⌘-Home	To top of document
⌘-End	To bottom of document

. . . For Dummies: #1 Computer Book Series for Beginners

COMPUTER
BOOK SERIES
FROM IDG

Word 6 For Macs For Dummies

Cheat Sheet

Word Screen

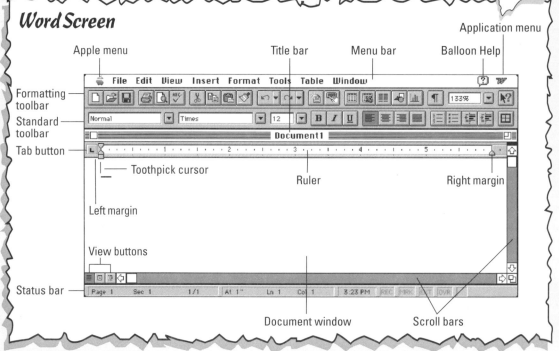

- Apple menu
- Title bar
- Menu bar
- Application menu
- Balloon Help
- Formatting toolbar
- Standard toolbar
- Tab button
- Toothpick cursor
- Ruler
- Right margin
- Left margin
- View buttons
- Status bar
- Document window
- Scroll bars

General Information

To start Word, double-click on the Word icon:

Microsoft Word

- ✔ Use the Ins key (press Shift-Help) to switch between insert and typeover modes.
- ✔ Use the Delete key to back up and erase.
- ✔ Use the Del key to delete the character to the right of the cursor.
- ✔ Press Return to start a new paragraph.
- ✔ Press Tab to indent or align text.
- ✔ Help is the Help key.
- ✔ Press Esc to cancel things and make dialog boxes go away.

⌘-S means to hold down the ⌘ key and tap the S key. Release both keys.

Select the Quit command from the File menu when you're ready to quit Word. Follow the instructions on-screen; save your document to disk.

Always quit Word and then shut down (choose Shut Down from the Special menu) before you turn off your Macintosh.

Common Word Formatting Key Commands

Bold	⌘-B
Italic	⌘-I
Underline	⌘-U
Center text	⌘-E
Left-align	⌘-L
Right-align	⌘-R
Make hanging indent	⌘-T

Common Word Key Commands

Cancel	Esc
Go back	Shift-F5
Help	Help
Mark block	F8
Repeat	⌘-Y
Find	⌘-F
Repeat Find	Shift-F4
Add page break	⌘-Return

The Kindergarten Keys

Copy	⌘-C
Cut	⌘-X
Paste	⌘-V
Undo	⌘-Z

Document Key Commands

Save (Quick)	⌘-S
Save As	F12
Open	⌘-O
New (document)	⌘-N
Print	⌘-P
Print Preview	⌘-F2
Close	⌘-W
Quit	⌘-Q

WORD 6
FOR MACS
FOR
DUMMIES™

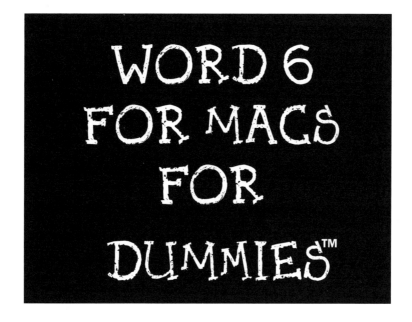

WORD 6 FOR MACS FOR DUMMIES™

by Dan Gookin

author of #1 international best-seller
DOS For Dummies

**IDG
BOOKS**

IDG Books Worldwide, Inc.
An International Data Group Company

San Mateo, California ♦ Indianapolis, Indiana ♦ Boston, Massachusetts

Word 6 For Macs For Dummies

Published by
IDG Books Worldwide, Inc.
An International Data Group Company
155 Bovet Road, Suite 310
San Mateo, CA 94402

Library of Congress Catalog Card No.: 93-080872

ISBN: 1-56884-190-6

Printed in the United States of America

10 9 8 7 6 5 4 3 2 1

1D/QY/TR/ZU

Distributed in the United States by IDG Books Worldwide, Inc.

Distributed in Canada by Macmillan of Canada, a Division of Canada Publishing Corporation; by Computer and Technical Books in Miami, Florida, for South America and the Caribbean; by Longman Singapore in Singapore, Malaysia, Thailand, and Korea; by Toppan Co. Ltd. in Japan; by Asia Computerworld in Hong Kong; by Woodslane Pty. Ltd. in Australia and New Zealand; and by Transworld Publishers Ltd. in the U.K. and Europe.

For general information on IDG Books in the U.S., including information on discounts and premiums, contact IDG Books at 800-434-3422 or 415-312-0650.

For information on where to purchase IDG Books outside the U.S., contact Christina Turner at 415-312-0633.

For information on translations, contact Marc Jeffrey Mikulich, Foreign Rights Manager, at IDG Books Worldwide; FAX NUMBER 415-286-2747.

For sales inquiries and special prices for bulk quantities, write to the address above or call IDG Books Worldwide at 415-312-0650.

For information on using IDG Books in the classroom, or for ordering examination copies, contact Jim Kelly at 800-434-2086.

 is a registered trademark of
IDG Books Worldwide, Inc.

About the Author

Dan Gookin? *DOS For Dummies* author Dan Gookin writing a Mac book? Outrageous! Obviously, he's enslaved some Mac minion to do the work for him.

Surprise! Dan has been a Mac user for a long time. He got his first Mac in 1986 and bought his second in 1993, so he has been at it a while — though stealthily, he admits. First they'd taunt him for having a Mac, then they'd be stunned. And how about the trivia:

- This isn't Dan's first Mac book. He wrote the *Complete SuperCard Handbook* back in 1989.

- Dan has written a guest editorial for *MacWeek*.

- Most of Dan's usual columns (even DOS columns) are written in MacWrite.

- All of Dan's outlines are done using Acta on the Mac — including the outline for *DOS For Dummies*.

- All of Dan's book proposals are done on the Mac.

- Any artwork you see in Dan's books is done on the Mac.

Yes, the closet Mac fanatic is finally out in the open. Though he's written over 30 books on personal computers, Dan still finds himself drawn back to the Macintosh. His ultimate desire is to swipe the PowerBook that IDG Books sent him to help complete this book.

Presently, Gookin still considers himself a writer and computer guru whose job it is to remind everyone that computers are not to be taken too seriously. His approach to computers is light and humorous yet very informative. He knows that the complex beasts are important and can help people become productive and successful. Yet Gookin mixes his knowledge of computers with a unique, dry sense of humor that keeps everyone informed — and awake. His favorite quote is, "Computers are a notoriously dull subject, but that doesn't mean I have to write about them that way."

Gookin's titles for IDG Books include: *DOS For Dummies, MORE DOS For Dummies, WordPerfect For Dummies, WordPerfect 6 For Dummies, PCs For Dummies, Word For Windows For Dummies, C For Dummies,* and the *Illustrated Computer Dictionary For Dummies*. Gookin holds a degree in communications from the University of California, San Diego, and lives with his wife and boys in the as-yet-untamed state of Idaho.

Welcome to the world of IDG Books Worldwide.

IDG Books Worldwide, Inc., is a subsidiary of International Data Group, the world's largest publisher of business and computer-related information and the leading global provider of information services on information technology. IDG was founded more than 25 years ago and now employs more than 5,700 people worldwide. IDG publishes more than 200 computer publications in 63 countries (see listing below). Forty million people read one or more IDG publications each month.

Launched in 1990, IDG Books is today the fastest-growing publisher of computer and business books in the United States. We are proud to have received 3 awards from the Computer Press Association in recognition of editorial excellence, and our best-selling *...For Dummies* series has more than 7 million copies in print with translations in more than 20 languages. IDG Books, through a recent joint venture with IDG's Hi-Tech Beijing, became the first U.S. publisher to publish a computer book in the People's Republic of China. In record time, IDG Books has become the first choice for millions of readers around the world who want to learn how to better manage their businesses.

Our mission is simple: Every IDG book is designed to bring extra value and skill-building instructions to the reader. Our books are written by experts who understand and care about our readers. The knowledge base of our editorial staff comes from years of experience in publishing, education, and journalism — experience which we use to produce books for the '90s. In short, we care about books, so we attract the best people. We devote special attention to details such as audience, interior design, use of icons, and illustrations. And because we use an efficient process of authoring, editing, and desktop publishing our books electronically, we can spend more time ensuring superior content and spend less time on the technicalities of making books.

You can count on our commitment to deliver high-quality books at competitive prices on topics customers want to read about. At IDG, we value quality, and we have been delivering quality for more than 25 years. You'll find no better book on a subject than an IDG book.

John J. Kilcullen

John Kilcullen
President and CEO
IDG Books Worldwide, Inc.

Acknowledgments

I'd like to thank the makers of Xanax for helping me complete this project on time.

I'd like to thank the core crowd at IDG Books: John Kilcullen, David Solomon, Mary "The Bee" Bednarek, Janna Custer, Beth Jenkins, Megg Bonar, and Kathy Day, as well as the hands-on crowd: Laurie Smith, Shawn MacLaren, John Nienart, Chris Collins, Rebecca Forrest, Steve Peake, and Kathie Schnorr.

Thanks also to Matt Wagner, although this book just "came up" and he really didn't do anything other than say how drooling-at-the-mouth anxious IDG was. And thanks to Bill Gladstone, Agent of the Agents at Waterside Productions.

Special thanks goes to Lauren Straub, who helped me with this book's original manuscript. You know, she moved away from Idaho to work at the *L.A. Times.* What a step down!

I'd also like to acknowledge the contributions made by Ray Werner, who assisted with the original *Word For Windows For Dummies,* from which this book is derived.

Finally, warm and fuzzy thanks go to Sandy for her wisdom, calm, and effective dealing with my frustrations about plumbing and electricity. Jordan, Simon, and Jonah helped, too.

(The publisher would like to give special thanks to Patrick McGovern, without whom this book would not have been possible.)

Credits

Publisher
David Solomon

Managing Editor
Mary Bednarek

Acquisitions Editor
Janna Custer

Production Director
Beth Jenkins

Senior Editors
Tracy L. Barr
Sandra Blackthorn
Diane Graves Steele

**Associate
Production Coordinator**
Valery Bourke

Acquisitions Editor
Megg Bonar

Editorial Assistants
Rebecca Forrest
Suki Gear

Project Editor
Laurie Ann Smith

Editor
Shawn MacLaren

Technical Reviewer
John Nienart

Quality Control
Steve Peake

Production Staff
Chris Collins
J. Tyler Connor
Sherry Gomoll
Angela F. Hunckler
Drew R. Moore
Carla Radzikinas
Patricia R. Reynolds
Kathie Schnorr

Proofreader
Alys Caviness-Brosius
Kathleen Prata

Indexer
Anne Leach

Book Design
University Graphics

Cover Design
Kavish & Kavish

Contents at a Glance

Cartoons at a Glance

By Rich Tennant

page 248

page 64

page 261

page 223

page 116

page 7

page 1

page 287

page 101

page 173

Table of Contents

Introduction

Welcome to *Word 6 For Macs For Dummies*, a book that's not afraid to say, "You don't need to know everything about Microsoft Word to use it." Heck, you probably don't *want* to know everything about Microsoft Word. You don't want to know all the command options, all the typographic mumbo jumbo, or even all those special features that you know are in there but terrify you. No, all you want to know is the single answer to a tiny question. Then you can happily close the book and be on your merry way. If that's you, then you've found your book.

This book informs and entertains. And it has a serious attitude problem. After all, I don't want to teach you to love Microsoft Word. That's sick. Instead, be prepared to encounter some informative, down-to-earth explanations — in English — of how to get the job done by using Microsoft Word. After all, you take your work seriously, but you definitely don't need to take Microsoft Word seriously.

The 5th Wave   By Rich Tennant

"THERE! THERE! I TELL YOU IT JUST MOVED AGAIN!"

About This Book

This book is not meant to be read cover to cover. (If that were true, the covers would definitely need to be closer together.) Instead, this book is a reference. Each chapter covers a specific topic in Microsoft Word. Within each chapter are self-contained sections, each of which describes how to do a Microsoft Word task relating to the chapter's topic. For example, in this book, you can encounter the following sections:

- ✔ Saving your stuff
- ✔ Cutting and pasting a block
- ✔ Making italicized text
- ✔ Creating a hanging indent
- ✔ Printing envelopes
- ✔ Cobbling tables together
- ✔ "Where did my document go?"

There are no keys to memorize, no secret codes, no tricks, no pop-up dioramas, and no wall charts. Instead, each section explains a topic as if it's the first thing you read in this book. Nothing is assumed, and everything is cross-referenced. Technical terms and topics, when they come up, are neatly shoved to the side, where you can easily avoid reading them. The idea here isn't for you to learn anything. This book is designed to let you look something up, figure it out, and get back to work.

How to Use This Book

This book helps you when you're at a loss over what to do in Microsoft Word. I think that this happens to everyone way too often. For example, if you press ⌘-F9, Microsoft Word displays a { } thing in your text. I have no idea what that means, nor do I want to know. What I do know, however, is that I can press ⌘-Z to make the annoying thing go away. That's the kind of knowledge you find in this book.

Microsoft Word expects you to push the mouse around and pull down menus to get things done, typical of a Macintosh program. Yet there are times when various *key combinations,* several keys you may press together or in sequence, are required (this you'd expect from Microsoft). This book shows you menu commands, which are listed like this:

File⇨Open

This means that you open the File menu and then choose the Open command. This book also shows you those key combinations, like this one:

⌘-Shift-P

This shorthand means that you should press and hold the ⌘ and Shift keys together, and then press the *P* key. Release all three keys at the same time.

If you look down at your keyboard and find ten thumbs — or, for that matter, scissors and cutlery instead of hands — consider reading Chapter 3, "Using Your Keyboard Correctly," right now.

This book tells you the easiest and best way to perform tasks and offers you alternatives when appropriate. Sometimes it's best to use the mouse, sometimes the keyboard. This book also presents the best keyboard short-cuts. And for those who like to use the toolbars, appropriate toolbar icons show up in the margin.

If you need to type something, I put it in **bold**. If I describe a message or something you see on-screen, it looks like this:

```
This is an on-screen message!
```

This book never refers you to the Microsoft Word manual or to the manualette that came with your Macintosh. I do recommend reading *Macs For Dummies, 2nd Edition,* a companion book in the *...For Dummies* series, published by IDG Books Worldwide.

What You're Not to Read

Special technical sections dot this book like mosquito bites. They offer annoyingly technical explanations, descriptions of advanced topics, or alternative commands that you really don't need to know about. Each is flagged with a special icon or enclosed in an electrified, barbed-wire-and-poison-ivy box (an idea I stole from the *Terwilliger Piano Method* books). Reading this stuff is optional.

Foolish Assumptions

Here are my assumptions about you: You use a computer. You use a Macintosh. Microsoft Word is your word processor. Anything else involving the computer is handled by someone whom I call your *guru.* Rely on this person to help you through the rough patches; when you're hopelessly stuck, wave your guru over or call your guru on the phone. But always be sure to thank your guru. Remember that computer gurus enjoy junk food as nourishment and often accept it as payment. Keep a bowl of M&Ms or a sack of Doritos at the ready for when you need your guru's assistance.

Beyond you, your Mac, and the guru, you also should have a computer worthy of running System 7-dot-whatever. (System 6 isn't covered specifically in this book.) I assume that you have color graphics, though that really doesn't make any difference as far as a word processor is concerned. Just don't be disappointed when I say "this turns your text blue" and you don't see blue on-screen.

One more thing: I call Microsoft Word by its affectionate short form, *Word*. This name is completely unofficial; the publisher even made me (through the miracle of the Replace command) change *Word* to *Microsoft Word* in this introduction. Face it, the program is Word. That's what I call it in the main body of this text.

How This Book Is Organized

This book contains six major parts, each of which is divided into three or more chapters. The chapters themselves have been Ginsu-knifed into smaller, modular sections. You can pick up the book and read any section without necessarily knowing what has already been covered in the rest of the book. Start anywhere.

Here is a breakdown of the six parts and what you find in them:

Part I: Basic Word Stuff

This is baby Microsoft Word stuff — the bare essentials. Here you learn to giggle, teethe, crawl, walk, burp, and spit up. Then you can move on to the advanced topics: moving the cursor, editing text, searching and replacing, marking blocks, spell-checking, and printing. (A pacifier is optional for this section.)

Part II: Formatting — or Making Your Prose Look Less Ugly

Formatting is the art of beating your text into typographic submission. It's not the heady work of creating a document and getting the right words. No, it's "You will be italic," "Indent, you moron!" and "Gimme a new page *here*." Often, formatting involves a lot of yelling. This part of the book contains chapters that show you how to format characters, lines, paragraphs, pages, and entire documents without raising your voice (too much).

Part III: Working with Documents

Document is a nice, professional-sounding word — much better than "that thing I did with Microsoft Word." Besides, *document* is quicker to type. And you sound important if you say that you work on documents, instead of admitting the truth — that you sit and stare at the screen and play with the mouse. This part of the book tells you how to save and shuffle documents.

Part IV: Working with Graphics

PC users, eat your heart out! The Macintosh lives and breathes graphics. This part of the book discusses how you can work art into your document, how you can use Microsoft Word's own *applets* to create your own graphics, and how you can do some things that previously required desktop publishing (or at least a knowledge of what a Mergenthaler was). As in Part II, the idea here is to make your document look oh-so-purty.

Part V: Help Me, Mr. Wizard!

One school of thought is that every copy of Microsoft Word should be sold with a baseball bat. I'm a firm believer in baseball-bat therapy for computers. But before you go to such an extreme, consider the soothing words of advice offered in this part of the book.

Part VI: The Part of Tens

How about "The Ten Commandments of Word" — brought down from Mount Redmond by Bill Gates (CEO of Microsoft). Or consider "Ten Features You Don't Use but Paid for Anyway." Or the handy "Ten Things Worth Remembering." This section is a gold mine of tens.

Icons Used in This Book

 This icon alerts you to overly nerdy information and technical discussions of the topic at hand. The information is optional reading, but it may enhance your reputation at cocktail parties if you repeat it.

 This icon flags useful, helpful tips or shortcuts.

 This icon marks a friendly reminder to do something.

 This icon marks a friendly reminder not to do something.

Where to Go from Here

You work with Microsoft Word, so you know what you hate about it. Why not start by looking up that subject in the table of contents or index? See what this book says about it.

Alternatively, you can continue to use Microsoft Word in the Sisyphean manner you're used to: Push that boulder to the top of the hill, and when it starts to roll back on you, whip out this book like a bazooka and blow the rock to smithereens. You'll be back at work and enjoying yourself in no time.

Part I
Basic Word Stuff

The 5th Wave   By Rich Tennant

"YES, WE STILL HAVE A FEW BUGS IN THE WORD PROCESSING SOFTWARE. BY THE WAY, HERE'S A MEMO FROM MARKETING."

In this part...

Ten thousand years ago, two cavemen named Og and Gronk invented what would soon become the first written human language. Og carved a pictogram of himself hunting a magnificent horned beast and killing it all by himself. "That not way it happened," muttered Gronk. "Beast scare Og. Og run. Beast fall over cliff." And thus the first editor was born. Og quickly smashed his tablet over Gronk's head and then rewrote the tale, but with two beasts.

Today, Og and Gronk's upright descendants use computers and word-processing software to tell their tales. Mr. Ogston drafts a brilliant memo that contains ideas Mr. Gronkstein claims he thought of first. So Mr. Gronkstein hits Mr. Ogston over the head with a lawsuit.

Yes, we've come a long way. So take two ibuprofen and read this part of the book, which describes some interesting things you can do in Word — basic stuff — that you may not have thought of before. Without these knowledge nuggets, you may resort to hitting yourself over the head with a stone tablet.

Chapter 1

Word Processing 101

· ·

In This Chapter

▶ Starting Word

▶ Reading the Word screen

▶ Entering text

▶ Editing a document on disk

▶ Getting Help

▶ Understanding Word's less-than-cuddly way of talking to you

▶ Printing

▶ Saving your stuff

▶ Closing a document

▶ Moving on

▶ Quitting Word

· ·

*T*his chapter offers a stark overview of how Word works — how you can use the program every day to get various word-processing stuff done. *The Basics*. More specific stuff happens in later chapters and is cross-referenced here for your page-flipping enjoyment.

Starting Word

To begin using Word, you must do the following:

1. Prepare yourself mentally.

"Do I really want to do this? You know, those stone tablets were quite good enough for my ancestors, and there really isn't anything wrong with that old typewriter. A computer? Do I have to go out and buy pocket protectors? Tape up my glasses? OK. Deep breath. I will be brave."

2. Turn on the computer, the monitor, and anything else of importance.

You can usually identify the important stuff by the number of lights they have — it's kind of a status symbol in the computer community, you know.

3. **Contend with Mr. Macintosh.**

   This step should be brief. It's the same Mac screen you see every day: folders, happy windows, icons.

4. **Locate the Word icon.**

   Somewhere entombed on-screen — on the *desktop* — is an *icon* that represents Word's heart and soul. You use this picture, shown in Figure 1-1, to start Word.

   This icon may be hidden inside a folder named Microsoft Word 6.0 or maybe just Word; to open that folder, double-click on it. Or you may find Word lying on the desktop like it owns the place.

5. **Start the Word program.**

   Double-click the Word icon with your mouse. Click-click.

Figure 1-1:
The Word
icon, as
seen on-
screen.

Watch in amazement as your computer whizzes and whirs. Before too long, you see a screen that looks like Figure 1-2. It's Word, stumbling into town! The whatzits of the screen are discussed in the section "Reading the Word Screen," later in this chapter.

✔ The first thing you may see on-screen, before it looks like Figure 1-2, is the Tip of the Day. Refer to the following section for information about that phenomenon.

✔ You can set up your Mac to automatically run Word each time it starts. Think of the time that would save! If you want to set up your computer in this manner, grab someone more knowledgeable than yourself — a person I call a *computer guru*. Tell this person, "Make my Mac always start with Word. Put it in the Startup Items folder in the System folder. You know what I mean." If your expert adviser cannot follow simple instructions, frantically grab other people at random until you find someone bold enough to obey you.

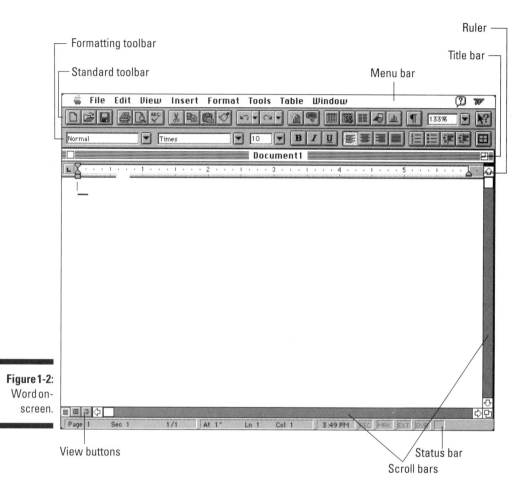

Formatting toolbar

Standard toolbar

Menu bar

Ruler

Title bar

Figure 1-2:
Word on-
screen.

View buttons

Status bar

Scroll bars

TIP

✔ I like to put my popular applications right on the desktop so I can find them easily. If you have System 7, you can create an *alias* of Word and stick it on the desktop while still leaving the original copy cozy in the Microsoft Word 6.0 folder. To create the alias, click once on the Microsoft Word icon and then choose File⇨Make Alias (in other words, choose Make Alias from the File menu). Ta da. A copy, named *Microsoft Word alias*, appears right next to the original. You can then drag the alias out to the desktop and use it to start Word.

✔ It's best to run Word *full screen*, having it hide as much of the distracting desktop as possible. After the program starts, click once on the Zoom box, the postage-stamp doojobbie in the upper-right corner of the document window. This *maximizes* Word to fill the entire screen. Clicking on the Zoom box a second time returns Word to its original size.

> ✔ Additional information about your Macintosh can be found in the fine tome *Macs For Dummies, 2nd Edition,* written by a finer lad, David Pogue, and available from the finest publisher, IDG Books Worldwide. That book does for your Mac what this book does for Word: makes it understandable!

Tip of the Day

Before Word leaves you to your own devices, it attempts to impart some of its silicon-based wisdom in the form of a Tip of the Day. This little window, shown in Figure 1-3, automatically adorns your screen each time you start Word. The value of its advice varies from the obscure ("You can use the style gallery to preview how using a different template will change your document's formatting."), to the inane ("You can undo most actions by clicking on the Undo button on the Standard toolbar."), to the truly useful ("You can hurt yourself if you run with scissors.").

✔ Click the OK button to get to work.

✔ To dispense with the jolly tips each time you start Word, click the mouse in the Show Tips at Startup box. That removes the little X there and enables you to avoid being subjected to this free advice every time you have work to do.

✔ For more tips, or if you feel you've been cheated and want better advice, or if you need a reason to procrastinate, click the Next Tip button.

✔ If you have System 7, whenever you want to just browse the tips, select the Tip of the Day command from Word's Balloon Help menu. The More Tips button in the Tip of the Day box lists all the tips by category if you really want to overwhelm yourself.

✔ At my last count, the Tip of the Day box has only seven truly silly tips (the "Fun and inspirational tips" category). Unfortunately, there is no way to add your own to the list.

Figure 1-3:
The jolly leprechaun Tip O'Day appears each time you start Word.

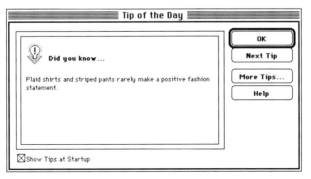

Reading the Word Screen

After Word starts, you face the electronic version of The Blank Page — the idea-crippling concept that induced writer's block in several generations of typewriter users. With Word, it's worse; the blank screen is surrounded by bells, whistles, switches, and doodads that would be interesting if only they were edible.

Figure 1-2 shows the typical, blank Word screen. Three things are worth noting:

✔ Several separate strips of stuff: bars, ribbons, rulers, and other horizontal holding bins for horrendous heaps of hogwash. Each strip performs some function or gives you some information. I warn you not to memorize this list: the *menu bar,* the *Standard toolbar,* the *Formatting toolbar* (also known as the ribbon), the *title bar,* and the *ruler* (who thinks he's the king or something). Refer to the nearby, easily avoidable technical information box, "Forbidden information about strip bars," if you want to load your brain with the details of these strips and bars.

✔ A large empty space. This is where text you type and edit appears. Somewhere in this empty space is the flashing *insertion pointer* — looks like a blinking toothpick — that tells you where the text you type appears.

✔ The bottom of the screen contains the *status bar.* No, this is not a yuppie hangout. It contains a great deal of information that would impress a bureaucrat but that, frankly, makes my eyes glaze over. The gibberish that is usually there explains where you are in your document. Several word fragments are always followed by numbers (like a ninth-grade algebra problem). Table 1-1 explains what this stuff means.

✔ My advice? Ignore the weird numbers on the status bar; concentrate instead on your writing. After all, only the truly disturbed would whip out a ruler and measure a piece of paper in a typewriter as they go along. (The numbers come in handy later to tell you how much stuff you've written or to find your way to a particular spot in a long document. Pretend that they don't exist for now.)

✔ There are also three buttons in the lower-left corner of your document, just above the status bar. Call them Larry, Moe, and Outline. They control how you see your document on-screen, a subject dealt with at length in Chapter 24.

✔ Any weird stuff you see on-screen (a Υ, for example) is a Word secret symbol. Refer to the section "Out, Damn Spots!" in Chapter 23 for more information.

Table 1-1	Stuff on the Status Bar
Algebra Problem	*What It Means*
Page *xx*	The page number you're editing: 1 = the first page, 8 = the eighth page, and so on.
Sec *xx*	The section of the document you're editing: 1 = the first section, 8 = the eighth, and so on. (For most of us, this always reads Sec 1.)
x/x	The page of the document you're editing *over* the total number of pages in the document. So 1/8 means that you're on page one of an eight-page document. (This is not a math problem; 1/8 does not mean .125.)
At *x.xx"*	How far from the top of the document your text is in inches. At 4.89" means that the line you're editing is 4.89 inches from the top of the page.
Ln *xx*	What line you're editing. Ln 5 means that you're working on line 5.
Col *xx*	What column you're in (columns are those vertical support structures for Greek-style architecture). In Word, the first column starts on the left side of the page, and the Col (column) numbers get bigger as you type toward the right side of the page. It's usually the number of characters and spaces you are over from the left margin.
x:xx AM/PM	The current time of day (or what the computer thinks is the current time of day). Here's a helpful aside: Computer biorhythms show enhanced creativity as the clock creeps into the early a.m. hours.
TLA boxes	These boxes contain various TLAs (three-letter acronyms or abbreviations or what-have-you), odd things to stick at the bottom of the screen, anyway. They appear dimmed when the option they represent isn't active. Check out the techy sidebar "What those TLAs mean" for the obscure function each may serve.

✔ The exact spot where the text appears is called the *cursor*. Normally it's also called an *insertion pointer* because traditional computer cursors are underlines that slide under what you type. I prefer the term *toothpick cursor* because "insertion pointer" is just too medically geometric for my tastes. Characters you type appear immediately to the left of where the toothpick cursor is flashing; then the cursor moves forward and waits for the next character.

✔ The bold horizontal line at the end of your text is the *End-of-Text marker*. Below it is a vast, vacuous void of a place. Nothing exists in the white space below this marker, not even blank pages. Only infinite nothingness. The End-of-Text marker is the steel beam that supports your text, holding it from harm's way, keeping it above the evil nothingness that exists below your text.

✔ The *mouse pointer* is different from the toothpick cursor. Normally it's an arrow pointer-like thing. But if you move the mouse around the writing part of the screen, the pointer changes. Over your text, the pointer becomes what's commonly called an *I-beam*. The I-beam means "I beam the insertion pointer to this spot when I click the mouse."

✔ The status bar, on the bottom of the screen, tells what some Word menu commands do. To see how this feature works, hover the mouse over a menu command and press — but don't release — the mouse button. As long as you hold down the mouse button, the status bar tries to explain what the command does.

✔ The status bar also tells you the function of some toolbar buttons. No need to click anything this time — just hover the mouse pointer over a button and voilà! Instant information crystals.

What those TLAs mean

The status bar contains five boxes, the first four of which have strange letter combinations in them. This list tells you what they mean:

REC: Someone, possibly you, is recording a macro. The TLA lets you know that you're recording the macro, which is better than repeating "OK, I'm recording a macro" over and over in your head. Macros are such an obtuse subject that they're not covered in this book.

MRK: The Revision Marking feature is on. This feature enables you to see where someone else has made changes — revisions — to your document. A very useful feature when dealing with editors. See Chapter 28 for information about revision marks and other cool tricks.

EXT: Text is being selected, or *blocked* off, by using the F8 key. Handy thing to know. For more, see Chapter 6.

OVR: Overtype mode is on. Refer to your orthodontist for correction (or look in Chapter 4 for information about deleting text).

Blank!: It's an empty box left over from the PC version of Word, where this box would contain a small chocolate to entice WordPerfect users to switch to Word. No need to bother with that here, though the empty tomb left there is kind of unsettling.

Incidentally, you can switch any option on or off by double-clicking its TLA. Better refer to the chapters mentioned in the preceding list, though, before you mess with such a trick.

Forbidden information about strip bars

This section has nothing to do with strip bars. Instead, the topic here is the information you get from those strips of information on the Word screen. Some of them may be visible, others may not show up at all. Turning them on or off is discussed in Chapter 24.

Menu bar: The first strip contains a list of menus, each of which disguises a pull-down menu you use to select the many Word commands at your beck and call.

Standard toolbar: The second strip holds tools that correspond to the most common Word commands; by clicking on a tool, you quickly choose a command. This strip may or may not be visible on-screen, depending on how Word is set up. The setup is discussed in Chapter 24.

Formatting toolbar: On the third strip, you find the commands that apply styles, type sizes, fonts, attributes (bold, italics, and underline), justifica-tion choices (left, center, right, and full), tabs, and other fun formatting frivolity. As with the Standard toolbar, it's optional whether you see the Format-ting toolbar on-screen. Again, see Chapter 24 for more information about the toolbars.

Title bar: The fourth strip contains the title of the current document.

Ruler: The fifth strip looks like a ruler. It is. And as with the toolbar and ribbon, your screen may not show the ruler — especially if the country you're in despises monarchy.

The visibility of the Standard and Formatting toolbars is controlled by selecting View⇨Toolbars. There you'll discover many more toolbars in addi-tion to these two "standards." Don't bother goof-ing with this stuff until you read Chapter 23. The visibility of the ruler is controlled by selecting View⇨Ruler and clicking the check mark on and off. It's there. It's gone. It's there. It's gone.

Entering Text

To compose text in Word, use your *keyboard* — that typewriter-like thing sitting in front of your computer and below the monitor. Go ahead, type away; let your fingers dance upon the keycaps! What you type appears on-screen, letter for letter — even derogatory stuff about the computer. (Your Mac doesn't care, but that doesn't mean that *Word* lacks feelings.)

New text is inserted right in front of where the toothpick cursor is blinking. For example, you can type this line:

```
"Uncle Cedric," she emphasized. "What were you doing wearing
            my evening gown?"
```

If you want to change the word *emphasized* to *reemphasized*, you move the toothpick cursor to the start of the word *emphasized* and type **re**. Those two letters are inserted into the text and all the text after that falls neatly into place.

✔ You compose text on-screen by typing. Every character key you press produces a character on-screen. This holds true for all letter, number, and symbol keys. The other keys, function keys and keys with words on them, do strange and wonderful things, which the rest of this book tries hard to explain.

✔ If you make a mistake, press the Delete key to back up and erase.

✔ There is no cause for alarm if you see spots — or dots — on-screen when you press the spacebar. These special doohickies let you "see" spaces on-screen. See Chapter 23 for the lowdown.

✔ Moving the toothpick cursor around the screen is covered in Chapter 2.

✔ The *Shift* key produces capital letters.

✔ The *Caps Lock* key works like the Shift-Lock key on a typewriter. After you press that key, everything you type is in ALL CAPS.

✔ The *Caps Lock* light on your keyboard comes on when you're in ALL CAPS mode.

✔ The number keys on the right side of the keyboard are on the *numeric keypad.* To use those keys, you must press Shift-Clear (the Num Lock key). If you don't, the keys take on their "arrow key" function. See Chapter 2.

✔ If you're a former typewriter user, please type 1 for the number one (not an I or a little L), and please type 0 for the number zero, not a capital letter O.

✔ See Chapter 3 for some handy tips on typing and using your keyboard.

✔ No one needs to learn to type to become a writer. But the best writers are typists. My advice is to get a computer program that teaches you to type. It makes a painful experience like Word a wee bit more enjoyable.

Typing away, la la la

Eons ago, a word processor was judged superior if it had the famous *word-wrap* feature, which eliminated the need to press the Return key at the end of each line of text. With Word and all other modern word processors, when the text gets precariously close to the right margin, the last word is picked up and placed at the start of the next line. There's no need to press Return, except when you want to end a paragraph.

✔ You have to press the Return key only at the end of a paragraph, not at the end of every line.

✔ If you want to split one paragraph into two, move the toothpick cursor to where you want the second paragraph to start and press Return.

✔ Don't be afraid to use your keyboard! Word always offers ample warning before anything serious happens. A handy Undo feature recovers anything you accidentally delete. See Chapter 3.

That annoying line of dots

Occasionally, you see a row of dots stretching from one side of the screen to the other — like a line of ants marching straight across your screen. Don't swat at it! That annoying thing, called a *page break*, marks the end of one page and the beginning of another. The text you see above the ants, er, dots, is on the preceding page; text below the dots is on the next page.

✔ You cannot delete the line of dots. C'mon — what good would it even do? Think picnic: you sweep one trail of the little pests away and another trail instantaneously appears. It's insidious insect magic!

✔ You can see how the line of dots works by looking at the scrambled statistics on the status bar. For example, when the toothpick cursor is above the dots, it says Page 5 for page 5. When the cursor is below the dots, you see Page 6 for page 6.

✔ A row of dots close together — very friendly ants — marks a *hard page break*. It even says Page Break right in the middle of the line. This comes from a definite "I want a new page now" command given by the person who created the document. See Chapter 11.

Editing a Document on Disk

You use Word to create *documents*. The documents can be printed or saved to disk for later editing or printing. When a document has been saved to disk, it's considered a *file* on the disk. (You can still refer to it as a document.)

There are several ways to load and edit a document already on disk. Because you are using a Macintosh, why not use the mouse-menu method?

 1. **Choose File⇨Open.**

Using the mouse, click the word File on the menu bar and hold down the mouse button: a drop-down menu, well, drops down. Keeping your finger firmly on the mouse's button, drag the mouse down through the menu and highlight the Open command. Release the mouse button.

Blink! Blink! Blink!

A document opening dialog box appears, as shown in Figure 1-4. (You also can click the Open tool, pictured to the left.)

2. **Select the name of the document (or file) you want to open and edit.**

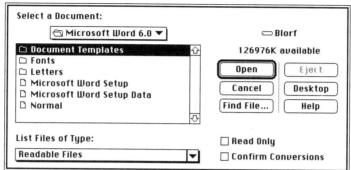

Figure 1-4:
The Open
dialog box
(a.k.a.
"Select a
Document").

Find the document name in the list and double-click it. You can use the controls in the dialog box to whisk yourself around your disk drive and scout out files. Using the Open dialog box is standard Mac stuff. When you find your file, highlight it and click the Open button to open it; or just double-click the filename.

✔ You can open the Open dialog box by using the keyboard shortcut ⌘-O. This method is so primitive, though, that you had better lock the door first. No one wants to be seen using a *keyboard*!

✔ The term *editing* means to read, correct, or add to the text you have composed and saved to disk. This process involves using the cursor keys, which are covered in Chapter 2, "Navigating Your Document." Also see Chapter 4, "Deleting and Destroying Text"; Chapter 5, "The Wonders of Find and Replace"; and Chapter 6, "Text Blocks, Stumbling Blocks, and Mental Blocks."

✔ If you want to edit a file you recently had open, pull down the File menu and look at the list on the bottom of the menu to see whether it is listed. Word "remembers" the last few documents you worked on. If you see what you want there, choose the filename to open it.

✔ When you finish editing a document, you print it, save it back to disk, or do one and then the other. Printing is covered later in this chapter, in the section "Printing"; saving a document to disk is covered in the section "Save Your Stuff!"

✔ Documents must be saved to disk with a filename. Be clever here! It's with this name that you'll later have to identify the document on disk so you can load it again, edit it, print it, and so on.

✔ If you can't find your document, try looking elsewhere on your disk — or on another disk if you have more than one. Also, see Chapter 18, "Managing Files," where I show you how to locate a wandering file.

Getting Help

That group of pocket-protected, bespectacled, Birkenstock-wearing programmers up at Microsoft can make some delightful blunders every once in a while. However, they recently put a wonderful, new-and-improved, technologically advanced, super-duper, ultra-brightening Help system into Word. No matter what else they do, they are forgiven.

Word's Help system is the same Help system you find in just about every Microsoft program. You activate it by pressing the Help key on your keyboard, pressing ⌘-/, or selecting the Microsoft Word Help command from the Balloon Help menu. You can search for helpful topics or, if you're in the middle of something, grab help on only one topic.

The Word Help menu

If you press the Help button on your keyboard, you open the Word Help menu. This displays the Word Help Contents, shown in Figure 1-5, which displays a list of all the topics relevant to Word — including some stuff that borders on being useful.

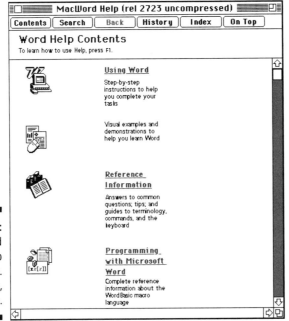

Figure 1-5:
The Word
Help
Contents.
From here,
you get help.

When you're in the Help Contents, you can move the mouse to any of the topics that are shown. When you hover over a "green" topic, the mouse pointer changes into a flying, pointing finger. Click once to select Help for that topic.

- ✔ Click the Using Word green text to display a quick summary of some handy Word Help topics.

- ✔ You can access the Help Index by choosing the Index command from the Balloon Help menu.

- ✔ When you press the Help key while you're doing something else, such as when you're mired in a dialog box, you see helpful information about that topic only. Click the Contents button in the Help system to see the main Contents again.

- ✔ When you're done with Help, you should close its window: click on the close box, located in the window's upper-left corner. Or, if the boss suddenly enters your office, click anywhere outside the Help window to bury the smoking gun. If you act quickly, you can still pretend that you know more than you do.

Context-sensitive help

 The spiffiest thing about Word's Help capability is that it can give you help with what you're doing when you're doing it. If you press Shift-Help (hold down the Shift key while pressing the Help key), the mouse pointer changes into a question mark or arrow. Or just click the question mark/arrow button on the left side of the Standard toolbar for an instant metamorphosis.

Point the question mark/arrow thing at what you want help with and click the mouse. For example, when you point the arrow at the scissors on the toolbar and click the mouse, you find out that the scissors are used to cut text, not to give you a haircut. This button works with just about anything you see on the Word screen — even the really weird stuff.

- ✔ For a briefer, more simplistic, and generally less helpful explanation of what some of the doodads on-screen do, hover the mouse pointer over the icon in question. In a moment, a cryptic couple of words appear, which unfortunately tell you only what the button or tool is and not what it does.

- ✔ A slightly more intelligible explanation simultaneously appears on the status bar.

- ✔ If the computer rudely beeps at you when you click, assume that no help is available for that item.

- ✔ Click the question mark/arrow thing or press the Escape key (labeled Esc) to change the mouse pointer back to normal.

Understanding Word's Less-Than-Cuddly Way of Talking to You

There are times when you try to do some well-meaning thing in Word, and the program, for reasons psychologists are still struggling over, just doesn't get it. Or maybe Word thinks that you're about to do something foolish, and it wants to offer some consoling (or hateful) words of advice. In those cases, you must confront one of Word's famous question dialog boxes, such as the one simulated in Figure 1-6.

Figure 1-6:
A question posed to the humble user.

Don't you really just hate this program sometimes?

| Yes | No | Cancel | Help |

The question in Figure 1-6, which differs depending on what Word is trying to tell you, has four options: Yes, No, Cancel, and Help, one of which is highlighted:

> **Yes** means, "Yes, I agree with you, Word. Couldn't have said it better myself. Please go ahead and do whatever it was I asked you to."
>
> **No** means, "No."
>
> **Cancel** means, "I've changed my mind!"
>
> **Help** begs Word, "Try to help me. I dare you. Double-dog dare."

- Pressing the Return key in a dialog box like this one usually selects the "safe" option. That could be Yes, OK, or even No depending on how the dialog box's warning is worded.

- Press Esc to select Cancel, the never-mind option.

- Sometimes only a few of these four buttons appear — sometimes more!

- The dreaded error dialog boxes usually have only one button in them: OK. So, regardless of whether it's OK, you must press the OK button. OK?

Printing

After entering what you feel is the best piece of written work since Tolstoy, you decide that you want to print it. After all, dragging the computer around and showing everyone what your prose looks like on-screen just isn't practical.

To print your document in Word — the document you see on-screen, all of it — do the following:

1. **Make sure that your printer is on and ready to print.**

   Refer to Chapter 8 if you need additional information about preparing the printer.

 2. **Choose the Print command from the File menu. (You also can choose the Print tool from the Standard toolbar.)**

   The Print dialog box opens. This is the place where printing and related activities happen.

3. **Click the OK button.**

   Zip, zip, zip. The document comes out of your printer. Or whir, crunch, flap-blap-blap, the document comes out of your laser printer all nice and toasty.

   ✔ You also can summon the Print dialog box by pressing ⌘-P. This method is more desirable if you have long fingers or you do needlepoint or the mouse is off eating the cheese again.

   ✔ There is no need to click the OK button when you click the Print tool on the Standard toolbar; your document instantly prints.

   ✔ Detailed information about printing is provided in Chapter 8.

   ✔ To print only part of your document — a paragraph, page, or block — refer to Chapter 6.

Save Your Stuff!

Word doesn't remember what you did the last time you used the computer. You must forcefully tell it to *save* your stuff! The document on-screen must be saved in a file on disk. To do this, you have to use Word's Save command.

 To save a document to disk, choose File⇨Save. (You also can click the Save button on the Standard toolbar, which looks like a wee li'l disk.) If the file hasn't yet been saved, a Save As dialog box appears. In that case, type a name for the file. Click the OK button when you're done.

✔ If the document you created hasn't yet been saved to disk, you have to give Word a filename to remember it by. The name is how you recognize the file later, when you want to edit or print it again. Think of a clever name. Type the document's name in the dialog box. Watch what you type! If you make a mistake, use the Delete key to back up and erase. Click the Save button to save the file.

✔ The fastest way to save a file is to press ⌘-S.

✔ When you save a document, watch the status bar — it is temporarily replaced with a message that Word is saving your document (or fast saving, for our Frequent Fliers).

✔ Save your documents to disk so that you can work on them later! The documents can be reloaded into Word the next time you start it. Refer to the section "Editing a Document on Disk" earlier in this chapter.

✔ After the document has been saved to disk, you see its name displayed on the title bar. This is your clue that your document has been saved to disk.

✔ If you're not in a clever mood, you may decide to name your file with the name of a file already on disk. This is a boo-boo because the newer file *overwrites* the other file with the same name already on disk. For example, if you decide to save your new letter by using the LETTER filename and LETTER already exists on disk, the new file overwrites the old one. There is no way to get the original back, so use another, more clever name instead. Word warns you with this message:

```
Replace existing "whatever"?
```

Click the Cancel button.

✔ If you try to save a document with the name of a document you're already working on (rare and strange, but it happens), you'll see the following techy message:

```
Word cannot give a document the same name as an open
        document. (whatever)
```

Er, uh, Word means you can't use that name. Click the OK button.

✔ See Chapter 18 for more information about files and such.

Closing a Document

If you're finished with a document, you can make it vanish from your screen by *closing* it, which is similar to ripping a sheet of paper out of your typewriter — without the satisfying sound it makes.

To close a document, choose File⇨Close. This step closes the document window and makes it vanish from the screen. Zzzipp! (Of course, you have to say "Zzzipp!" when you do this; Word is mute on the point.)

- ✔ You also can save a document by pressing ⌘-W, the handy keyboard command.

- ✔ Why close a document? Because you're done working on it! Maybe you want to work on something else or quit Word altogether. The choice is yours, and the options are explained in the next section, "Moving On."

- ✔ If you try to close a document before it has been saved, Word displays a warning dialog box. Click the Yes button to save your document. If you want to continue editing, click the Cancel button.

- ✔ If you were working on one document and you close it, Word looks like it has vacated the premises: ribbons and rulers are still there, but through the "hole" in the middle of your screen you can see your Mac desktop peeking through. Don't panic; you've just closed a document and Word has little else to do. Word sits patiently and waits for your next command.

- ✔ If you're working on other documents, another one appears on-screen in place of the document you just closed. See Chapter 16 for information about working with multiple documents.

Moving On

After you close the document, you have several options. I won't mention the "take a break" or "play with the mouse pointer" options. And if you want to play Tetris for a few eyeball-glazing hours, that's up to you as well. But within Word, you have several options.

First, you can start working on another document on disk. Refer to the section "Editing a Document on Disk" earlier in this chapter.

 Second, you can start working on a new document. To do so, press ⌘-N, choose File⇨New and click OK, or click the "I wanna blank sheet o' paper" button on the Standard toolbar. This starts you off again with a clean, blank sheet of "electric" paper. Now it's up to the word-processing muse to get you going again.

Third, you can quit Word and do something else on your Mac. (Tetris looms). Refer to the next section, "Exiting Word."

 You don't have to quit Word when you just want to start working on a new document.

Quitting Word

It is the height of proper etiquette to know when to leave. For example, it's the third act of a monotonous French opera, the stage was lit using Bic lighters, and your date is asleep and drooling on your arm. But you wait until the intermission to get up and leave. It's just proper. Leaving Word is properly accomplished by using the Quit command. This common Mac command is used to quit all applications and programs.

To politely excuse yourself, choose File⇨Quit. Poof! Word is gone.

- ✔ You can also press ⌘-Q to quit Word.

- ✔ If you haven't yet saved your document, Word politely displays a dialog box, asking whether you want to save any changes. Click Yes to save them. This part is important. Then Word peaceably steps aside and lets you do something else, possibly something involving fun. (If the document doesn't yet have a name, Word asks you to think up a name to save your document; refer to the "Save Your Stuff!" section, earlier in this chapter.)

- ✔ Choosing File⇨Quit (or pressing ⌘-Q) is the proper way to exit Word. Do not, under any circumstances, reset or turn off your Mac to quit Word. This is utterly irresponsible and you'll go to Computer Etiquette Jail for life if you're ever caught — and that's in Redmond, Washington! You also run the very real risk of scrambling stuff on your disk so well that you won't ever get it back.

- ✔ Suppose that you don't want to quit, but instead you just want to get rid of a document and start on a new one. Refer to the section "Closing a Document," earlier in this chapter. Then refer to the preceding section, "Moving On," for information about starting over with a new document for editing.

- ✔ Quitting Word returns you to another running application or to the Finder. If you see the Finder, you can start another program; safely shut off your computer; or give up, sell the computer, and start a new hobby, like hatchet throwing.

- ✔ If you want to turn your machine off, choose Special⇨Shut Down. Only when you see the box that says it's safe to turn off your Mac should you do so.

Chapter 2

Navigating Your Document

. . . .

In This Chapter

▶ Using the basic arrow keys

▶ Using ⌘ with the arrow keys

▶ Moving up and down one screenful of text

▶ Moving to the top or bottom of the current screen

▶ Moving to the end of a line

▶ Moving to the beginning of a line

▶ Moving up and down one page at a time

▶ Moving to the end of a document

▶ Moving to the beginning of a document

▶ Using the Go To command

▶ Navigating with the scroll bars

▶ Going back

▶ Using the highly useful Bookmark command

. . . .

*U*nless you're an insanely brief writer, or unless you just write very tiny, an entire letter or document seldom fits on a single computer screen. You need an easy way, therefore, to hop from place to place in your document to see on-screen some other part of your beautiful prose.

How do you get there? Cruise control, of course. To help you navigate, there are various keys on the keyboard plus a few Word commands geared up to get you moving.

Fortunately, this nautical navigation stuff does not go any further than just the name: a document does not have a bow, stern, port, or starboard, and you do not have to learn to tie the cursor into knots. But you *do* have to learn to move easily within your literary creation.

Using the Basic Arrow Keys

The most common way to move about your document is to press the arrow keys, which are called the *cursor-control keys* because they control the tooth-pick cursor on-screen.

You can find the cursor-control keys next to the numeric keypad; they form an upside-down T (see Figure 2-1).

↑	Moves the cursor up to the preceding line of text
↓	Moves the cursor down to the next line of text
→	Moves the cursor right to the next character
←	Moves the cursor left to the preceding character

Cursor-control keys

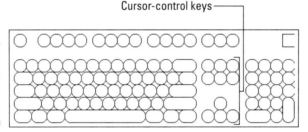

Figure 2-1:
Location of
cursor-
control keys.

✔ You also can use the numeric keypad to move the cursor about. This subject is covered at length in Chapter 3.

✔ The mouse provides a quick and easy way to move the toothpick cursor: First spy a new location for the cursor on-screen. Then move the mouse pointer to where you want the cursor to be and click. The cursor is instantly relocated.

✔ If the cursor is on the top line of the document window (the top line of text) and you press the up-arrow key, the document scrolls to reveal the preceding line of text, if there is one. If not, the computer beeps at you, and the cursor stays put and blinks with that special look it reserves for the mentally impaired.

✔ When the cursor is on the last line of the screen and you press the down-arrow key, the document scrolls up to reveal the next line of text, if there is one. If not, the cursor stays put and blinks at you with that special look it reserves for the soon-to-be-institutionalized.

✔ Moving the cursor does not erase characters.

Using ⌘ with the Arrow Keys

If you press and hold the ⌘ key and then press an arrow key, the toothpick cursor jumps more than one character. This is *cursor afterburner* mode (rumor has it that this is the *only* cursor mode Arnold Schwarzenegger uses):

⌘-↑	Moves the cursor up one paragraph
⌘-↓	Moves the cursor down to the next paragraph
⌘-→	Moves the cursor right one word
⌘-←	Moves the cursor left one word

Press and hold the ⌘ key and then press an arrow key. Release both keys. You don't have to press hard; use the ⌘ key the same as you use the Shift key.

✔ ⌘-← and ⌘-→ always move the cursor to the first letter of a word.

✔ ⌘-↑ and ⌘-↓ always move the cursor to the beginning of a paragraph.

✔ If you press ⌘ and click the mouse, you highlight, or *select,* a sentence in your document. Click again (without the ⌘ key) to move the cursor or to unhighlight the sentence (see Chapter 6 for information about selecting blocks).

Moving up and down one screenful of text

No need to adjust your chair here. The screen does not display an entire document — usually not even a whole page. To see the next or preceding screen, press the Page Up and Page Down keys. These keys move you or your document (I can't tell which) around by the screenful:

Page Up: Moves the cursor up one screen. Or if you're at the tippy-top of your document, it moves you to the top of the screen.

Page Down: Moves the cursor down one screen or to the end of the document, if you happen to be there.

 ✔ The *screen* is also known as the *document window.* I like calling it the screen because it's the most important thing on your Mac's screen when you're writing.

✔ It's funny how Page Up and Page Down moves you up and down a *screen* at a time. You get used to this illogic, if you're not already.

Moving to the top or bottom of the current screen

There are times when you want to zip to the top or bottom of the current screen. This is easy to do:

⌘-Page Up   Moves the cursor to the top of the current screen

⌘-Page Down   Moves the cursor to the bottom of the current screen

Moving to the end of a line

To get to the end of a line of text, press the End key.

- ✔ To move to the end of the current paragraph, press ⌘-↓ and then ←. Pressing ⌘-↓ actually moves to the beginning of the *next* paragraph. Pressing ← moves you back to the end of the current paragraph.

- ✔ Moving to the beginning of a line is accomplished by pressing the Home key, which is covered . . . well, here it is:

Moving to the beginning of a line

To get to the beginning of a line of text, press the Home key.

- ✔ There's no key like Home.

- ✔ To move to the beginning of the current paragraph, press ⌘-↑.

Not-so-moving information about moving the cursor

As you move the cursor around, look at the status bar, on the bottom of your screen. It gives you some valuable information about your location within a document. For example,

    Page 2 Sec 1 2/6 At 2.5" Ln 6 Col 42

The status bar shows which page you are on, which section you are in, your position with regard to the total number of pages in your document, how far down the page you are in inches, the slope of your biorhythm, and number of past lives. Nah, those Microsoft techies aren't that progressive. Actually, the Ln and Col values tell you which line (line 1 is at the top of the page) and column (from the left margin) the cursor is on — useless stuff, but informative.

Moving up and down one page at a time

You knew that there had to be a way to do this. Whereas the loony Page Up and Page Down keys move you up or down a screen at a time, the able assistance of the ⌘ *and* Option keys are required to move you around a page at a time:

⌘-Option-Page Up   Moves the cursor to the beginning of the preceding page

⌘-Option-Page Down   Moves the cursor to the beginning of the next page

A page is actually a printed page of text (the *page break* is delineated on-screen by a line of dots marching from left to right).

The Page thing at the left end of the status bar (on the bottom of the screen) tells you which page you're looking at.

Moving to the end of a document

If you press ⌘-End (hold down ⌘ and press End), you are whisked to the end of your document.

You can use this command to get a feel for how big your document is. Press ⌘-End and then look at the numbers on the status bar. You can see which page you are on, how far down the page you are, which line you are on, and which column you are in. Feel satisfied. Feel accomplished. Take a moment to gloat.

⌘-End is an easy key combination to mistakenly press. It throws you—literally—to the end of your document. If you do this and feel that you have boo-booed, press Shift-F5, the Go Back command, to return from whence you came. (Also see the section "Going Back," later in this chapter.)

Moving to the beginning of a document

To go to the beginning — nay, the tippy-top — of a document, press ⌘-Home.

Using the Go To Command

The ⌘-Home and ⌘-End key combinations let you fly to the beginning and end of a document, but what if you want to get off somewhere in the middle? The Go To command is what you need.

Go To, as in the Shakespearean "Getteth thee outta hereth," enables you to go directly to just about wherever in the document you want to be. To do so, choose Edit⇨Go To and the Go To dialog box appeareth before thine eyes (see Figure 2-2).

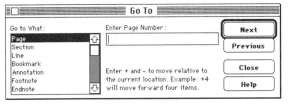

Figure 2-2:
The Go To
dialog box.

You can type a number of things in the Go To dialog box. The most effective use is typing a page number; Word instantly beams you to the top of that page. For example, if you type **14** in the box and press Return, you go to page 14.

- ✔ You also can press the ⌘-G key combination to open the Go To dialog box.

- ✔ You can even press the F5 key to open the Go To dialog box.

- ✔ Some users have been known to summon the Go To dialog box by humming loudly and fluttering their eyelids.

- ✔ If you click twice on the page number on the status bar (muttering "Change, you idiot. Change, change." while you do this helps), the Go To dialog box appears like a genie out of a lamp.

- ✔ To be even more specific in your Go To commands, see the section "Using the Highly Useful Bookmark Command," later in this chapter.

The Go to What part of the Go To dialog box enables you to select a specific whatzit in your document in order to relocate yourself. It's an ugly assortment of items in there, most of which pertain to advanced Word formatting. But if you are inserting graphics or footnotes or using the useful Bookmarks, you can select them from the list, type the proper number or name in the box, and press Return; presto, you're there. Needless to say, this feature is only for the truly bold.

Navigating with the Scroll Bars

If you love your mouse, you can use The Power Of The Mac to help you traverse your documents: use the vertical scroll bar. Located to the right of your document, it looks like a one-lane highway, but you use it like an elevator shaft (see Figure 2-3).

- ✔ To scroll your document up one line of text, click the mouse on the up scroll arrow, at the top of the scroll bar.

- ✔ To scroll down one line of text, click the mouse on the down scroll arrow, at the bottom of the scroll bar.

Up scroll arrow ⌐

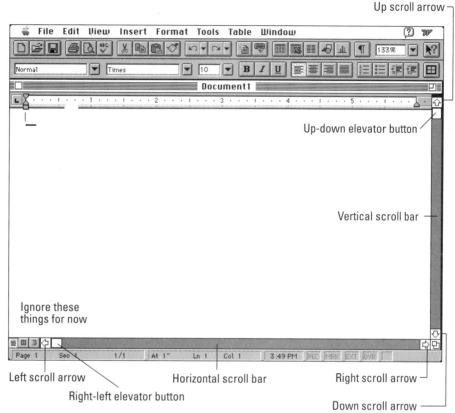

Up-down elevator button

Vertical scroll bar ⌐

Ignore these
things for now

Left scroll arrow

Horizontal scroll bar

Right scroll arrow ⌐

Right-left elevator button

Down scroll arrow ⌐

✔ In the middle of the scroll bar is a scroll box, or elevator button. It gives you an idea of which part of your document you're looking at: if the box is at the top of the scroll bar, you're near the top of your document, and vice versa.

✔ To see the preceding screen of text, click the scroll bar just above the elevator button.

✔ To see the next screen of text, click the scroll bar just below the elevator button.

✔ To move to a specific position in the document, use the mouse to drag the elevator button up or down. The elevator button's position indicates which portion of the document you want to see.

✔ The scroll bar is not where Greek philosophers went to get drunk. Well, OK, maybe they had a *few* drinks there.

Going Back

They say that once you commit, there's no going back. Boy, are they wrong. If you go anywhere you don't want to be, press Shift-F5, and Word carries you back to where you started. The Shift-F5 key command works only in Word; you can't try this command in real life.

 If you keep pressing Shift-F5, you return to where you were before; if you press it again, you're back to where you were before that.

Using the Highly Useful Bookmark Command

Have you ever done this: You're working away on great stuff, but occasionally you need to zip off elsewhere in your document? So you try to fold down the edge of the screen — *dog ear* it, if you will — to remember where you were? I do it all the time. Fortunately, Word has a command that helps save wear and tear on your monitor. It's the highly useful Bookmark command.

Setting a bookmark

To set a bookmark in your document, follow these steps:

1. **Put the toothpick cursor where you want to place a bookmark.**

2. **Select Edit⇨Bookmark (or press ⌘-Shift-F5).**

   The Bookmark dialog box opens, as shown in Figure 2-4.

Figure 2-4:
The
Bookmark
dialog box.

3. **Type a name for the bookmark.**

   Be clever! The name reminds you of where you are in your document. So if you're writing a report on execution styles, the bookmark name *beheading* would be appropriate.

4. **Press Return or click the Add button with the mouse.**

You cannot use certain funky characters in the bookmark name — most disappointingly, you cannot use a space. Word lets you know which characters are taboo; when you type one, the Add button in the Bookmark dialog box becomes dimmed. When that happens, back up and erase the offending character.

Finding a bookmark and moving to that spot in your document

To return to a bookmark, use the Go To command, which I covered in the section "Using the Go To Command," earlier in this chapter. These steps keep you from turning the page and losing your train of thought:

1. **Press F5.**

   The Go To dialog box splats across your screen.

2. **Highlight Bookmark in the Go to What list.**

   It's the fourth item down.

   The Enter Page Number box changes to read Enter Bookmark Name. The bookmark that comes first alphabetically appears in that space.

   If you don't see your bookmark, click the down arrow and you'll see a long list of bookmarks in your document. Highlight the one you want.

3. **Click the Go To button.**

   You're there!

4. **Click the Close button to get rid of the Go To dialog box.**

   A fast way to summon the Go To box is to double-click on the left part of the status bar, on the bottom of the screen.

Chapter 3

Using Your Keyboard Correctly

. . . .

In This Chapter

▶ Using the keys on your keyboard

▶ Pressing and releasing

▶ Inserting and overwriting

▶ Knowing when to press Return

▶ Knowing when to use the spacebar

▶ Using the Undo keys

▶ Using the Kindergarten Keys: Cut, Copy, and Paste

▶ Using the Help key

▶ Using the Repeat key

. . . .

*W*hy the heck do you need to use a keyboard when you can zip around with a mouse? Actually, there's a great deal you can do with a keyboard. Word is, after all, about writing. It's about jotting down notes and making sense with words. That can't be done with a mouse . . . at least not efficiently.

Alas, some people treat their computer keyboards as though land mines lie under half the keys. Fear of losing a digit or a limb keeps these sad souls from taking advantage of the many keyboardish things you can do in Word. Often, these tricks are *quicker* than using a mouse.

If there were a theme to this chapter, it would be "Be bold!" Word doesn't do anything perilous unless you tell it to. Even then, you are asked a yes-no question before the dangerous something happens. You can press the handy Esc key to cancel just about anything before you do it (that's why it's called the "escape" key). And, even better, you can choose Edit⇨Undo to undo your last action. (You also can click the Undo tool or press the ⌘-Z shortcut.) Consider these options to be similar to wearing little high-density uranium thimbles to protect yourself against those keyboard land mines.

Keys on Your Keyboard

Welcome to "Know Your Keyboard 101." Take a look at your keyboard and then at Figure 3-1.

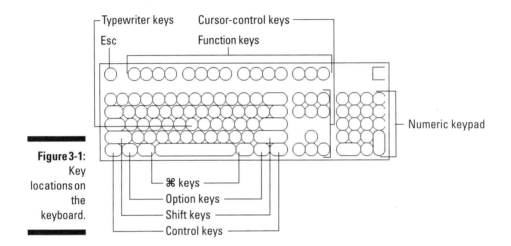

Figure 3-1:
Key
locations on
the
keyboard.

Notice how the keyboard is divided into separate areas; each has a special function. These are keys you use in Word, either alone or in combination with other keys.

Typewriter keys: Standard alphanumeric keys you find on any typewriter: A through Z and 1 through 0, plus symbols and other exotic characters.

Function keys: The top row of the keyboard, labeled F1 through F12 (maybe even F15). These keys are used alone or in cahoots with the various shift keys.

Shift keys: These keys don't do anything by themselves. Instead, the Shift, Control, Option, and ⌘ keys work in combination with other keys.

Cursor-control keys: Arrow keys that move the toothpick cursor around the screen. Also lumped in are Home, End, Page Up, and Page Down. By the way, the Help and ⌧ keys are also cursor keys: Pressing the ⌧ key deletes the character to the right of the toothpick cursor. When you press Control-Help, you activate the Insert key (more on this in a bit).

Car keys: Don't leave these in the car. For added protection, buy The Club.

Numeric keypad: These keys switch between cursor keys and numbers. When Word starts, they're cursor keys, laid out in a pattern shown in Figure 3-2. When you press Shift-Clear, *toggling* the Num Lock key on (the Num Lock light turns on), the keypad produces only numbers. When you press Shift-Clear a second time, you turn off both the Num Lock key and the Num Lock light.

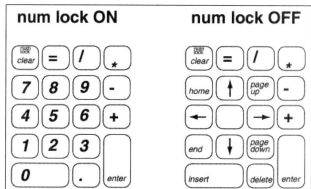

num lock ON   **num lock OFF**

Figure 3-2:
The numeric
keypad's
split
personality.

Three individual keys are worth noting:

Return: Right of the " key, the Return key is marked with the word *Return*. When you are typing text, pressing Return ends the current paragraph.

Enter: The Enter key sits in the lower-right corner of the numeric keypad. Like the Return key, it can be used to end a paragraph of text. In Word, the Enter key also has some unique commands associated with it. You'll be amply warned about them when the time comes.

Escape: The Escape key, labeled Esc, is in the upper-right corner of the keyboard. It's a handy key to use in Word: pressing it generally backs you out of any option or dialog box you may have accidentally wandered into.

✔ Be thankful: a piano has 88 keys, black and white with no labels. It takes years to master. A computer, by comparison, is easy (especially if it's a Macintosh).

✔ Older Mac keyboards have a different layout from the fancy Extended & Enhanced keyboard that is currently popular. Some older models may lack function keys or have cursor keys in a row below the typewriter keys. They all work the same under Word, but this book assumes that you have the Extended & Enhanced keyboard.

✔ The numeric keypad doubles as a cursor keypad. Personally, I find it easier to use than messing with solo-act cursor keys.

✔ Laptop keyboards are all goofed up. Please refer to the special sidebar on using your PowerBook with Word.

Press and Release!

Welcome to Word Aerobic Mania! And press and release and one and two and down on the floor to tighten that tush! OK, lift and squeeze and . . . oh, wait, that's another book. In this section, I help tone those flabby fingers for some fancy Word key combinations.

Word uses key combinations to represent some commands. For example,

⌘-P

If you can lift a basketball with one hand, you can try

⌘-Shift-F5

Each command does something interesting in Word, but no need to trouble your head with that stuff now. Instead, simply remember that a key combination tells you what to press. For example, ⌘-Shift-F5 means "Hold down ⌘ and Shift and then press F5." Then release all three keys.

Key combinations appear all the time. Always press and hold the first key(s) and then press the last key. Press and release.

- ✔ This key combo stuff works just like pressing Shift-F to get a capital F. It's the same thing, but you get to use the odd Control, Option, and ⌘ keys.

- ✔ Yeah, you have to really reach to get some of those key combinations.

- ✔ There's no need to press hard. If you're having trouble working a command, pressing harder doesn't make the computer think, "Oh, lordy, she's pressing really hard now. I think she means it. Wake up, wake up!" A light touch is all that's required.

- ✔ Remember to release the keys. For example, press and hold the ⌘ key, press P, and then release both keys. If you don't know which one to release first, release the second key and then the shift key (that is, Shift, Control, Option, ⌘) last.

- ✔ Ahhh! Feel the burn!

Uh, they forgot some keys on my PowerBook

They had to keep something off the PowerBook to keep the weight down. "Man, dat numeric keypad and all dem function keys had to weigh, oh, at least 40 lbs. Maybe 50."

Nevertheless, you can get around their absence in one of two ways. First, you can use key equivalents or menu commands for the function key commands. For example, Shift-F4 (the Repeat command), my favorite command, is also ⌘-Option-Y. Shift-F5, the Go Back command, is also ⌘-Option-Z.

Second, Word offers a special floating palette (see accompanying figure) for some of the other keys. It contains buttons that approximate the functions of the Home, End, ⌘-Home, ⌘-End, Page Up, and Page Down keys. (Remember that

the Page keys move you a screen at a time.) If you can't figure out the pictograms on each button, hover the mouse over each one and it's oaf-ficial name will pop up.

By the way, you can use this floating palette even if you don't have a PowerBook. Select View ⇨Toolbars and click an X by the PowerBook item. Click OK and you have a toolbar that redundantly repeats something already on your keyboard. Cool.

When to Press Return

On an electric typewriter, you press the Return key when you reach the end of a line. With a word processor, you have to press Return only when you reach the end of a paragraph.

You don't have to press Return at the end of each line because Word *word-wraps* any words hanging over the right margin and moves them down to the next line on the page. Therefore, you have to press Return only at the end of a paragraph, even a short paragraph that is just a line of text by itself.

✔ Some people end a paragraph with two presses of the Return key; others use only one press.

✔ If you want to indent the next paragraph, press the Tab key after pressing Return. This technique works just like it does on a typewriter.

✔ If you want to double-space a paragraph, you have to use a special line-formatting command, covered in Chapter 10, "Formatting Sentences and Paragraphs." You do not use the Return key to double-space lines.

- ✔ If you press Return in the middle of an existing paragraph, Word inserts a new paragraph and moves the rest of the text to the beginning of the next line. This works like inserting any other key in your text.; the difference is that you insert a Return character (¶), creating a new paragraph.

- ✔ You can delete the Return character by using either the ⟨X⟩ key or the Backspace (labeled *Delete*) key; the Backspace key deletes the character to the left of the toothpick cursor. Removing a Return joins two paragraphs together.

When to Use the Spacebar

A major vice committed by many Word users is mistakenly using the spacebar rather than the Tab key. Allow me to clear the air on this one.

Use the spacebar to insert space characters, such as you find between words or sentences. You have to press the spacebar only once between each word or sentence, although some former touch typists (me included) put two spaces between two sentences.

To indent, align columns of information, or organize what you see on-screen, use the Tab key. Tabbing indents text to an exact position. Then when you print, everything is lined up nice and neat. This doesn't always happen when using the spacebar.

- ✔ Use the Tab key to indent; use the spacebar only when you're putting spaces between words and paragraphs. I'm serious: Do not use the spacebar to indent or line up your text. Your stuff will look tacky, tacky, tacky if you do.

- ✔ It is OK, however, to hold your clothes together with safety pins (underwear excluded).

- ✔ As an old touch typist, I'm used to sticking two spaces between a sentence. Period-space-space. The second space isn't necessary when using a word processor; instead, type only one space after a sentence. (I gleaned this information from my managing editor, Mary "The Bee" Bednarek, whose eyes bulged as she screamed at me one day, "Stop putting double spaces between your sentences! It takes me hours to delete them all!")

- ✔ If you want to set tab stops in Word, see Chapter 10.

Trivial information about the Enter and Return keys

Enter or Return? Which is which and why should you care? In PC land, all the keyboards label their keys Enter. On your Mac, it's been traditional to have both an Enter and a Return key, Return living with the typewriter keys and Enter over there on the numeric keypad. So what's the point? (And you really have to be hard up for trivia if you're continuing to read this sidebar.)

The reason has to do with the computer's mixed-up genealogy. On a typewriter, the Return key hearkens back to the pre-electric typewriter days, when you had to whack the carriage return bar to *return* the paper back to the left margin. On a calculator, meanwhile, the Enter key *enters* a formula. So the Mac's typewriter keys have Return and the Mac's numeric keypad (calculator-like) keys have Enter. So there you are.

The Undo Keys

Be bold! Why not? Word has a handy Undo command, which remembers the last several things you did or deleted and unravels any mistakes you made quite easily. Furthermore, there's a Redo command, which is essentially Undo-Undo, though that's too much mental work to bother with right now.

"Now mark me how I will undo myself" — *Richard II, Shakespeare*

What thoust do, thou canst undo

To undelete any text you just accidentally zapped, do any of the following:

- ✔ Press ⌘-Z. This is the quickest way to undo something. ⌘-Z is the handy undo key combination used in almost all Mac applications.
- ✔ Press F1.
- ✔ Choose Edit⇨Undo. When you choose Edit⇨Undo, the last action you did is undone; if you choose Edit⇨Undo again, you undo whatever you did before that.
- ✔ Click the Undo tool, on the Standard toolbar.
- ✔ Yabba-dabba-do.

The Undo item in the Edit menu changes to pertain to whatever needs undoing: Undo Bold, Undo Typing, Undo Boo-boo, and so on.

To undo an Undo, select Redo. See the section "Redo, or 'Take 2'" later in this chapter.

Because the Undo command remembers several things you just did, you can select any one of them for undoing. You do so by clicking the down arrow next to the Undo button, on the Standard toolbar. There you find a terse list of actions (up to 99) that Word remembers and can undo. You can select any *one* of them for undoing, but keep in mind that to do so means undoing an action out of sequence. To undo *everything* up to a point, select the action that you want as well as everything above it.

Can't undo? Here's why

Sometimes it eats you alive that Word can't undo anything. On the menu bar, you even see the message Can't Undo. What gives?

Essentially, whatever it was you just did, Word can't undo it. This can be true for a number of reasons: there is nothing to undo; there isn't enough memory to undo; Word can't undo because what you did was too complex; Word just forgot; and so on.

I know that it's frustrating, but we all have to live with it.

Redo, or "Take 2"

If you undo something and — whoops! — you didn't mean to, you must use the Redo command to set things back. To undelete any text you just accidentally zapped, do any of the following:

- Press ⌘-Y.
- Choose Edit⇨Redo.
- Click the Redo tool, on the Standard toolbar.
- Do-wop-do.

You can't use the Undo command to undo an Undo. (Huh?) This message is primarily for you old hands who are used to it working that way — as you could in previous versions of Word.

Like the Undo command, the Redo command remembers several things you just undid. You can select any one of them by clicking the down arrow next to the Redo button on the Standard toolbar.

If there's nothing to redo, the Redo command becomes the Repeat command. See the section "The Repeat Key," just a few paragraphs away in this chapter.

The Kindergarten Keys: Cut, Copy, and Paste

Cutting, copying, and pasting text are covered in Chapter 6. Three of the key combinations you can press to perform those feats are covered here, however, because by the time you get to Chapter 6, this stuff won't make any sense. The three key combinations are

Cut	⌘-X
Copy	⌘-C
Paste	⌘-V

Now, Copy as ⌘-C I can understand. *C* is for Copy. And Cut is ⌘-X. Sorta like X-ing something out, it disappears from your document right there. But Paste — well, he is a little more complicated. Paste is ⌘-V. It doesn't fit him. It doesn't represent a thing about who he is or the function he performs. It has nothing to do with his dreams or desires. But the V key is near his buddies (go ahead and look), near those he feels are the most similar to himself in all the Word world (See Figure 3-3.) The camaraderie and coziness afforded by this setup are terribly important to Paste at this juncture in his life and are well worth the cost of an unfitting key combination. So, please, just accept it as something that needs to be for right now and let him work it out on his own.

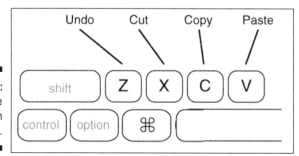

Figure 3-3:
How the Kindergarten Keys line up.

- ✔ The ⌘-Z key is also right there, along with the other kindergarten keys. So maybe ⌘-V isn't so odd, after all.

- ✔ The Cut, Copy, and Paste (and Undo) keys are all related to commands living in the Edit menu.

- ✔ Cut, Copy, and Paste also live on the function keys: F2 is Cut, F3 is Copy, and F4 is Paste. I figure this setup is to make former PC owners feel at home.

- ✔ When you get the hang of them, you'll use these key combos often to save time.

The Help Key

The handiest key on the keyboard is the Help key, also known as the Panic key. Here are some tips for using it:

- ✔ Press the Help key when you're doing something to display help and options available for that something. If you're just editing text, Help displays the Help Index, from which you can select a topic you're interested in.

- ✔ Press Shift-Help to get context-sensitive help. The mouse pointer changes to the question mark/arrow thing. Point and shoot for help!

- ✔ Getting Help in Word really means that you're running another program — the Microsoft Help engine. You should quit this program when you're finished using Help. Do so by clicking on the close box, in the upper-left corner of the Help window.

The Repeat Key

Here's a good one: The F4 key in Word is known as the Repeat key, and it can be a real time-saver. If you press a command, cursor-control, or character key and then press the F4 key, that command, cursor-control, or character key is repeated. (You also can choose Edit⇨Repeat or press ⌘-Y.)

For example, type the following lines in Word:

```
Knock, knock.
Who's there?
Banana.
Banana who?
```

Now press ⌘-Y. Word repeats the last few things you typed, which includes the hours of entertainment from these lines plus anything else you typed before them.

> ✔ ⌘-Y, the Redo command, also acts as the Repeat command — but only when there's nothing to redo. For certain, F4 is the Repeat key.

> ✔ A practical use of this command is creating forms. Type a bunch of underlines on-screen — your form's blank lines — and then press Return. Press the F4 key a few times and the page is soon filled with blank lines.

> ✔ F4 not only echoes text, it's also especially useful when you issue the same command over and over, like when you are doing a find-and-replace, inserting the date, inserting special characters, or extensively formatting a document.

> ✔ If you use the F4 key along with the Shift key, as in Shift-F4, Word repeats your last Find or Go To command (see Chapter 5, "The Wonders of Find and Replace").

> ✔ The F4 key isn't your only access to the Repeat command. It also lives on the Edit menu, although it may be listed as Repeat Typing, Repeat Formatting, or any of a number of Repeat-*blank* options.

Chapter 4

Deleting and Destroying Text

*N*othing gives you that satisfying feeling like blowing away text — especially if it's someone else's document you're "editing." Of course, most of the destroying and deleting that goes on in Word is minor stuff: you ax that extra *e* in *potato,* slay a word here, yank out a sentence there.

 Because you delete text on-screen, it happens quickly and painlessly in the electronic ether. It's much easier than using White Out: no mess, no white goop, and if you change your mind, you can press ⌘-Z (the Undo shortcut key combination) or click the Undo tool to bring your text back to glowing phosphorescent perfection.

Insert and Overtype Modes

The Insert key (press Control-Help) toggles Word's two methods of putting text on-screen. Normally, new text is inserted just before the blinking toothpick cursor; the new text pushes any existing text to the right and down as you type. This is *Insert mode.*

If you press Control-Help, you enter *Overtype* mode. The letters OVR in the lower-right section of the status bar become bold, indicating *over,* as in *Over*type mode or "all of this is *over* your head." Any text you type next over-writes existing text on-screen.

If you press Control-Help again, the TLA OVR returns to its wallflower-gray color, and you're back in Insert mode.

- ✔ The Insert key is really Control-Help.

- ✔ When the numeric keypad light is off (which is normal), the 0 (zero) key acts as the Insert key.

- ✔ New characters in Insert mode appear to the left of the flashing cursor. Then the cursor moves to the right, awaiting the next character you type.

- ✔ The OVR in the status bar indicates that you are in Overtype mode; any new text you type overwrites existing text. If you are typing along and suddenly notice that part of your text seems to be missing, check the status bar to see whether you're in Overtype mode.

- ✔ Leaving Word in Insert mode all the time is a safe bet. If you want to overwrite something, just type the new text and then delete the old.

Your Basic Delete Keys: Delete and Del

You can use two keys to delete single characters of text:

Delete key (labeled Backspace on some keyboards): Deletes the character to the left of the toothpick cursor

Del key (with the ⟨X⟩ symbol on it): Deletes the character to the right of the toothpick cursor

```
C'mon, man. Have a bilte. It tastes just like chicken.
```

In the preceding line, the toothpick cursor is "flashing" between the *i* and the *t* in *bite*. Pressing the Delete key deletes the *i* in *bite*; pressing the Del key deletes the *t*.

- ✔ The Del key is marked with an X in a large, rightward-motivated box, signifying "I'm X'ing out things that-a-way!"

- ✔ When the numeric keypad is off (the light don't shine), the . key on the keypad acts like the Del key. I call this the *period* key, inevitably sparking a furious outcry from the MC (mathematically correct), who prefer to say *decimal.*

✔ After deleting a character, any text to the right or below the character moves up to fill the void.

✔ Even if you're in Overtype mode, the Delete key pulls the rest of the text to the right.

✔ Delete works like the Backspace key on a typewriter. The difference is that when you press Delete in Word, the cursor backs up and erases. (The Word equivalent of the typewriter's Backspace key is the left-arrow key.)

✔ You can press and hold Delete or Del to continuously "machine-gun delete" characters. Release the key to stop your wanton destruction.

The "Delete-Bing" Phenomenon

Word's childlike reaction to something it doesn't like is the *bing,* a nice and brief beep emanating from your computer's speaker. Sometimes you may hear the bing when you press Delete to delete. Nothing is deleted; you hear the bing, bing, bing once for each desperate stab at the Delete key.

The binging is Word's way of warning you that you're trying to delete one of the secret, hidden codes littered about the document — codes that change paragraph formatting and other covert stuff. You can't indiscriminately delete this stuff with the Delete key.

✔ If you really want to delete the codes, press the ← key and then press the Del key. No bing.

✔ Whenever you want to hear the bing, press the End key more than once. Keep holding down the End key to hear Word's equivalent of a raspberry.

✔ The bing can really scare the pee out of you if you have external speakers boosted through an amplifier set up with your Mac.

✔ Don't be surprised by the mystery codes in your document. You put them there as you create and format your text.

✔ If you want your old formatting back, choose Edit⇨Undo or press ⌘-Z or click the Undo tool before you do anything else.

Deleting a Word

Word lets you gobble up entire words at a time by using one of two "delete word" commands:

⌘-Delete	Deletes the word that is to the left of the cursor
⌘-Del	Deletes the word that is to the right of the cursor

To delete a word by using ⌘-Delete, position the cursor at the last letter of the word. Press ⌘-Delete and the word is gone! The cursor then sits at the end of the preceding word, or the beginning of the line if you deleted the first word in a paragraph.

To delete a word by using ⌘-Del, position the cursor at the first letter of the word. Press ⌘-Del and the word is gone. The cursor then sits at the beginning of the next word, or the end of the line if you deleted the last word in a paragraph.

> ✔ If the cursor is positioned in the middle of a word, ⌘-Delete deletes everything from where the cursor is to the last letter of the preceding word.

> ✔ If the cursor is positioned in the middle of a word, the ⌘-Del command deletes everything from where the cursor is to the first letter of the next word.

> ✔ To delete a word, position the mouse pointer on the offending critter and double-click; the word is highlighted. Pressing the Del key erases the word.

Deleting a Line of Text

Word has no keyboard command for deleting a line of text. But you can easily delete a line by using the mouse and pressing a single key. Follow these steps:

1. **Move the mouse into the left margin of your document.**

   The cursor changes into an arrow pointing northeast. The winds of change are a-blowin'. . . .

2. **Point the mouse pointer arrow at the line of text you want to obliterate.**

3. **Click the mouse.**

   The line of text is highlighted, or selected.

4. **Press either the Delete or Del key to send the line into the void.**

When the mouse cursor is pointing northeast, you can drag it down the left margin and select as many lines of text as you care to. They all can then be deleted with one stroke of the Del key.

Northeast = ↗

Deleting a Paragraph

To mark a complete paragraph for destruction, give it the symbolic kiss on the cheek and click three times (quickly) on any word in the paragraph. This action highlights the whole paragraph. Now press either the Delete or Del key and — presto! — vaporizing text!

If you're fond of the northeast-pointing mouse, move the mouse pointer into the left column on the page (where it turns into the northeast pointer) and then double-click. The paragraph to the right of the mouse cursor is selected and primed for deletion.

Deleting a Block of Text

Word can delete characters, words, and lines all by itself. To delete anything else, you have to mark it as a block of text and then delete the block.

To delete a block of text, follow these steps:

1. **Mark the block**.

   To highlight the block by using the mouse, click the mouse at the beginning of the block and then drag to the block's end. To highlight the block by using the keyboard, move the toothpick cursor to the beginning of the block, press F8, and then press the cursor-control keys to highlight the block.

2. **Press the Delete or Del key to remove all the highlighted text.**

Chapter 6 contains more information about selecting, highlighting, and otherwise playing with blocks.

Undeleting

Deleting text can be traumatic, especially for the timid Word user. But editing is editing, and mistakes happen. If you want some of your freshly deleted text back, you can use the Undo key combination, ⌘-Z, to undelete text. It usually works like this:

1. **Panic!**

   "Oh, lordy! I just deleted the best stuff I've ever written and there's no way this brain can ever think of such brilliant prose ever again!"

2. **Press ⌘-Z.**

   This happened to Hemingway all the time.

✔ Don't forget the Undo command in the Edit menu — first item, by the way. If you can't remember ⌘-Z or if you find yourself pressing other keys by mistake, just select Edit⇨Undo *Whatever*. Or you can click the Undo tool.

✔ You can also press the F1 key if you remember that it, too, means Undo.

✔ You can be sloppy with the Undo shortcut because Undo remembers the last several things you just did. But don't get lazy! If you delete something and want it back, press ⌘-Z.

Chapter 5
The Wonders of Find and Replace

*L*ittle Bo Peep has lost her sheep. Too bad she doesn't know about Word's Find and Replace commands. She could locate the misplaced ruminants in a matter of microseconds. Not only that, she could find and replace all the sheep with frequent-flier miles. It's all a cinch after you force the various purposes of Find and Replace into your head.

Sadly, only words and other literary stuff can be replaced. If Word could find and replace real things, there would be at least one more wonderful house with a swimming pool and sauna in this world, I bet you.

Finding Text

Word can locate any bit of text anywhere in your document. The command used to find text is called, surprisingly enough, the Find command. It lurks in the Edit menu.

Follow these steps to use the Find command and locate text in your document:

1. **Think of some text you want to find.**

   For example, "sheep."

2. **Choose Edit➪Find.**

   You see the Find and Replace dialog box, shown in Figure 5-1.

```
┌─────────────────────────────────────────────────────┐
│ ▣▭▭▭▭▭▭▭▭ Find and Replace ▭▭▭▭▭▭▭▭▭                 │
│ Find What:  [|                          ▼] [Find Next]│
│             [                            ] [ Cancel  ]│
│ Search:  [All      ▼]  □Match Case                    │
│                        □Find Whole Words Only [Replace...]│
│                        □Use Pattern Matching  [  Help  ]│
│                        □Sounds Like                   │
│ ─Find                                                 │
│      [No Formatting] [Format ▼] [Special ▼]           │
└─────────────────────────────────────────────────────┘
```

Figure 5-1:
The Find and
Replace
dialog box.

3. Type the text you want to find.

Enter the text into the box titled Find What. For example, **sheep**. Type lowercase letters.

4. Click the Find Next button to start the search.

Or you can press Return.

If any text is found, it is highlighted on-screen. The Find dialog box does not go away until you click the Cancel button, press Esc, or click the close box (in the upper-left corner of the dialog box). As a result, you can keep searching for more text, if you're so inclined.

✔ The shortcut key combo for finding text is ⌘-F (the *F* stands for Find).

✔ Type the text you want to find exactly. Do not end the text with a period unless you want to find the period, too.

✔ If the text isn't found, you see this message:

```
Word has finished searching the document.
```

Oh, well. Try again and check your typing.

✔ To find any additional occurrences of the text, click the Find Next button.

✔ After you close the Find and Replace dialog box, you can use the handy, timesaving Shift-F4 key combination to repeat finding the next matching bit of text in your document.

✔ You can search for a variety of things by using the Find command: text, spaces, the Return character (¶), and formatting codes. This subject is covered in the section "Finding secret codes," later in this chapter.

✔ Typing lowercase letters helps you find just about any text in the document. But when you want to find text that matches case the way you type it, be sure to select the Match Case check box. This box makes the Find command know the difference between *Mr. Sheep* and a plain old *sheep*.

✔ You also may select the nifty Sounds Like option so that Word notifies you of all instances in the document where anything sounding like the text you're looking for occurs. So if Miss Peep gets distracted in her task and starts looking for her *ship* to come in, Word says

```
Wrong fairy tale.
```

Seriously, it looks for and matches *ship* for *sheep*.

Searching up, down, left, and right

This one may toss you for a loop: Word typically looks for text from the tooth-pick cursor's position to the end of the document. It's like looking for an oncoming train by facing only one direction down the track. To get Word to turn around and look up your document (your faithful program deserves a cheap thrill every so often), click the Search drop-down box in the Find and Replace dialog box. You find three options:

Down: Searches from the toothpick cursor to the end of the document

Up: Searches from the toothpick cursor to the beginning of the document

All: Damn the toothpick cursor — searches the *entire* document!

I was just kidding about searching left and right. Left is actually up, or before the toothpick cursor; right is down, or after the toothpick cursor.

TIP

Finding or not finding bits and pieces of words

Word finds *any* matching text in your document. It can find things so well that it can drive you crazy. For example, if Miss Peep no longer cares about sheep but wants instead to find the *ship* that holds her destiny (there is just no future for a young lady in the sheep business, y' know), Word shows her ships in places she hadn't yet thought of: friend*ship*, court*ship*, and relation*ship*, not to mention the *ship*shape *ship*ment of *ship*mates waiting down at the *ship*yard.

To make Word more precise — to locate only a whole *ship*, for example, the type that sails on the ocean blue — select the Find Whole Words Only check box in the Find and Replace dialog box. When that box is checked, Word logically locates only words and not things nestled in other words.

Finding secret codes

Laced throughout a document are secret codes and printing instructions. You don't see these codes on-screen, but they affect the way your document looks and prints. Basically, you can search for the secret commands — bold, underline, center, and special paragraph formatting, for example — just like you can look for text.

To search for a secret code, choose Edit⇨Find and then click the Format button; a menu drops down, asking whether you want to search by font, paragraph, language, or style. Click Font to open the Find Font dialog box, shown in Figure 5-2.

With this dialog box, you can find a bunch of character-related stuff. If you want to search a document for italicized words in 9-point Times, for example, select each of these things from their menus and click OK. The dialog box closes, and you can then select Find Next from the Find and Replace dialog box to look for any of this highly stylized stuff.

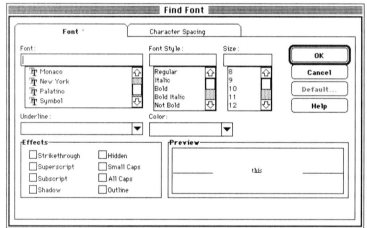

Figure 5-2:
You can find a bunch of character-related stuff by using this dialog box.

- ✔ You can use the Find Font dialog box to look for specific occurrences of a font, such as Courier or Zapf Dingbats, by selecting from the Font selection list. Scroll through the font menu to see what you can choose.

- ✔ You can look for a particular size of type (24 point, for example) by selecting from the Size selection list. See Chapter 9 for information about character formatting.

- ✔ You can look for occurrences of anything (or any combination of things) shown in this box by selecting what you want to look for.

✔ You also can search for paragraph formatting: select Paragraph from the Format drop-down menu in the Find and Replace dialog box. See Chapter 10 for information about paragraph formatting.

✔ You also can search for styles: select Style from the Format drop-down menu in the Find and Replace dialog box. Refer to Chapter 14 for a discussion of styles.

✔ For those of you who often find yourselves slipping back and forth between more than one language (it's tough being fluent in so many different tongues, I'm sure), you can also search for text by language. Word even discriminates between the English used by Aussies, the Brits, and us Yanks. Woo-hoo.

✔ A box between the Find What and Search boxes contains formatting information you may have just searched for. Word doesn't forget this information, and it's possible for a whole mess of formatting stuff to accumulate. So if Find refuses to locate some text that you *know* is in your document, click the No Formatting button. That way, Word finds only text and forgets about any formatting stuff.

Finding unprintable, unmentionable characters

No, this isn't a censorship issue. There are just some characters that you can't properly type in the Find What part of the Find and Replace dialog box. Try finding a Tab character, for example; press the Tab key and — whoops! — nothing happens. That's because the Tab character is special, and you must force-feed it (and a few others) into the Find and Replace dialog box.

To find a special, unprintable character, click the Special button. You see a pop-up list of various characters that Word can search for but that you would have a dickens of a time typing. Choose one and a special, funky shorthand representation for that character appears in the Find What box (such as ^t for tab). Click the Find Next button to find that character.

✔ The special characters appear in the Find What box in secret code. This code starts with a caret (^) and then includes some letter. Please don't try to make sense of it.

✔ The Paragraph Mark special character (¶) looks the same as the Return character — what you press to end a paragraph.

✔ Any Character, Any Digit, and Any Letter represent, well, just about anything. These buttons are used as wild cards for matching lots of stuff.

✔ The caret is a special character. If you want to search for it, be sure to select Caret Character from the Special button's pop-up list.

Replacing Stuff

Replacing is the art of finding a bit of text and replacing it with something else. This happens all the time. For example, you can replace the word *goat* with *caprine*. You can do it in a snap by using the Replace command.

1. **Choose Edit⇨Replace.**

   The Replace dialog box, shown in Figure 5-3, appears on-screen. It looks seriously like the Find and Replace dialog box, but notice that it has an extra box for the replacement text. (Actually, you can get here from there by clicking the Replace button in the Find and Replace dialog box.)

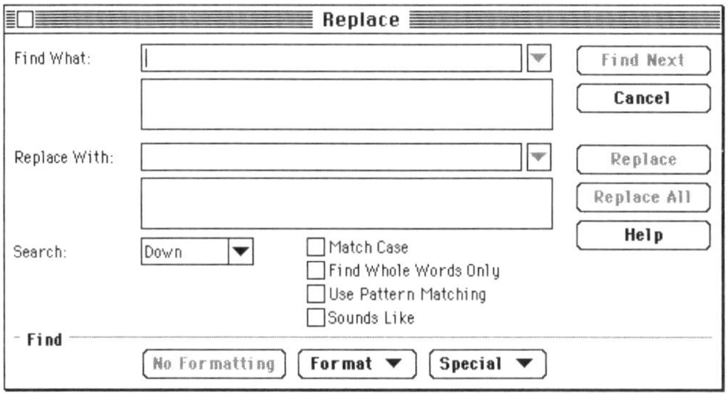

Figure 5-3: The Replace dialog box.

2. **In the Find What box, type the text you want to find.**

   This text is the text you intend to replace with something else. For example, you could type **goat**. Press the Tab key when you're done typing.

3. **In the Replace With box, type the text you want to use to replace the original text.**

   For example, type **caprine**, which is the fancy-schmancy, biologically dooded-up term for the goat family — neighbors you definitely want to have downwind.

4. **Ask yourself, "Do I want the chance to change my mind before replacing each bit of found text?"**

   If so, click the Find Next button. This is a good idea. If not, you can click the Replace All button; text is found and replaced automatically, giving you no chance to change your mind.

5. **If you selected Find Next, Word pauses at each occurrence of the text.**

   The found text is highlighted on-screen, just like in the regular Find task. When this happens, you can click the Replace button to replace it or click Find Next to skip and find the next matching bit of text. Click the Cancel button or press Esc when you tire of this.

When the Replace operation is over, Word announces that it's done by displaying the following message:

```
Word has finished searching the document.
```

✔ Word replaces the same way it finds text: either up or down or all over the document. If you want to replace every instance of some text in your document, click the Search button's drop-down list and select All.

✔ If you select Replace All, Word displays a dialog box telling you how many items were replaced. Interesting trivia.

✔ Always type something in the Replace With box. If not, you systematically delete all the found text: a wanton round of wholesale slaughter. This process is called "Finding and deleting," and it's covered later in this chapter, in a section by the same name.

✔ The shortcut key combo for the Replace command is ⌘-H. Uh-huh. *H* means what? Hunt and replace?

✔ My advice is to select Find Next most of the time. Only if you're replacing something and you're certain (a rare occurrence, at least in my book) should you select Replace All.

✔ The Undo command restores your document to its previous condition if you foul up the Replace operation. Refer to Chapter 4 for more information about undoing things.

Finding and Replacing Spaces

Here's a practical use for the Replace command. Too many Word users litter their documents with excessive spaces. The most harmless of all these spaces come at the end of a line of text, after the period but before you press Return. I do this, too.

These extra spaces serve no purpose, and you can't scare them away easily (stringing garlic around your neck and screaming "Be gone with ye" does nothing, for example). To get rid of them, follow these steps:

1. **Choose Edit⇨Replace.**

   Or press ⌘-H. Either way, the Replace dialog box appears.

2. **Open the Special pop-up list.**

   Click the Special button, at the bottom of the dialog box.

3. **Select White Space.**

4. **Repeat Steps 2 and 3 and select Paragraph Mark rather than White Space.**

   This step tells the Replace command that you're looking for a space followed by a ¶ (which you inserted in your text by pressing Return). The following code appears in the Find What box:

   ```
   ^w^p
   ```

   These characters are the secret codes for a space and ¶ — essentially, extra space (that no one needs) at the end of a paragraph.

5. **Press Tab to move to the Replace With box.**

6. **Click the Special button and select Paragraph Mark.**

   So you're replacing ^w^p with ^p, which is just getting rid of the ^w — excess spaces — which is the end to this madness.

7. **Click Replace All.**

   It's OK to click Replace All here. Or if you're not the daring type, select Find Next. You're telling Word to replace the space-¶ with just ¶. The end result is to remove the spaces before the Return characters in your document.

   ✔ To confirm whether any spaces exist before trying this exercise, use the Find command to search for space ^p.

   ✔ To replace double spaces between sentences with single spaces, stick two White Space characters in the Find What box (^w^w) and only one (^w) in the Replace With box. Then try to wean yourself from the double-spacing-after-period habit they taught you in typing class.

   ✔ A quick way to transform extra spaces into a tab is to search for five spaces in a row and translate them into tabs. In the Find What box, enter White Space (^w) five times. In the Replace With box, select Tab Character (^t). Any grouping of five spaces is replaced with a tab, which is much easier to align. See Chapter 10 for more information about using and setting tabs.

Finding and Deleting

If you don't type anything in the Replace With box, Word's Replace command systematically deletes all the Find Whats. This process can be a scary thing, so be sure to select Find Next. Otherwise, you may zap parts of your document and, boy, would you be bummed (until you used the Undo command, of course).

Suppose, however, that Miss Peep wants to get rid of her sheep. (Now she wants to be a truck driver.) These steps show you how to delete the *sheep* from a Word document:

1. **Choose Edit⇨Replace.**

   Or press ⌘-H (if that ever makes sense to you).

2. **In the Find What box, type the text you want to find.**

   For example, **sheep**. Enter the text exactly. Any previously searched-for text appears at the prompt. Edit it or type new text, secret codes, or whatever you want Word to search for.

3. **Don't type anything in the Replace With box — leave it blank.**

   You're deleting text here and replacing it with nothing — a bold concept I wish they would have addressed in a "Star Trek: The Next Generation" episode.

4. **Click the Replace All button.**

   In moments, your text is gone. Bo Peep's sheep go pop, pop, popping away! If you were timid and selected the Find Next button instead of Replace All, it takes a bit longer because you have to squint at the screen and then press the Replace button at each occurrence.

Let's all wish Miss Bo Peep good luck in her new profession.

The 5th Wave — By Rich Tennant

"SO THIS GUY SAYS HE NEEDS TO GET RID OF HIS APPLE PC BECAUSE ITS GETTING TOO OLD, AND THE OTHER GUY SAYS 'HOW OLD IS IT?' AND THE FIRST GUY SAYS, 'THIS APPLE'S SO OLD, IT'S STARTING TO ATTRACT FRUIT FLYS!' AAAAAHH HAHAHAHAHA HA THANK YOU THANK YOU!'"

Chapter 6

Text Blocks, Stumbling Blocks, and Mental Blocks

· ·

In This Chapter

▶ Marking a block

▶ Copying and pasting a block

▶ Cutting and pasting a block

▶ Pasting a previously cut or copied block

▶ Deleting a block

▶ Formatting a block

▶ Spell-checking a block

▶ Using Find and Replace in a block

▶ Printing a block

· ·

A major advantage of a word processor over, say, a stone tablet is that you can work with blocks of text. You can break stone tablets up into blocks, but gluing them back together again is *très gauche.* Hand such a thing with a report on it to your boss and she'll shake her head and mutter, "Tsk, tsk, tsk. This is tacky, Jenson."

A Word block is a marvelous thing. You can rope off any old odd section of text — a letter, word, line, paragraph, page, or a rambling polygon — and then treat the grouping as a unit. You can copy the unit (or *block*), move it, delete it, format it, spell-check it, use it to keep the defensive line from getting to your quarterback, and on and on. Think of the joy: years after childhood, Word has made it OK for us to play with blocks again.

Marking a Block

You can't do anything with a block of text until you *mark* it. Marking a block is telling Word, "OK, my block starts here. No, *here!* Not over there. Here, where I'm looking, where the cursor is." You can mark a block two ways in Word: by using the mouse or by using the keyboard.

Marking a block by using the mouse

To mark a block by using the mouse, follow these rodent-like steps:

1. Position the mouse pointer where you want the block to start.

2. Hold down the mouse button and drag the mouse over your text.

As you drag, the text becomes highlighted, or *selected,* as shown in Figure 6-1. Drag the mouse from the beginning to the end of the text that you want to mark as a block.

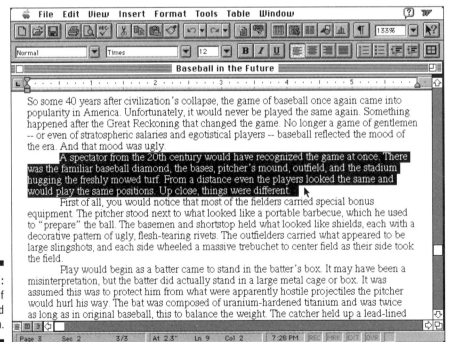

Figure 6-1:
A block of text marked on-screen.

3. **Release the mouse button — stop the dragging — to mark the block's end.**

   ✔ If you drag above or below the text that appears on-screen, the screen scrolls up or down.

   ✔ To quickly mark a word, position the mouse pointer over that word and double-click.

   ✔ To quickly mark a sentence, press and hold the ⌘ key while clicking the mouse.

   ✔ To mark a line of text, move the mouse pointer to the left margin. The pointer becomes an arrow that points northeasterly. Click the mouse to highlight one line of text; drag the mouse to select several lines at a time.

   ✔ To mark an entire paragraph, place the insertion pointer anywhere in the paragraph and click three times.

Marking a block by using the keyboard

Dragging over the screen with the mouse is great for selecting small portions of text. Marking anything larger than a screenful, however, can get a bit out of hand when using the mouse — which tends to think that there's a cat around or something whenever you scroll-drag and move too fast to control. In those instances, it's much better to mark text by using the keyboard. Follow these steps:

1. **Press F8.**

   This is the Start Block command. The F8 key "drops anchor," marking one end of the block.

2. **Use the cursor-control keys to move to the other end of the block.**

   The cursor-control keys are discussed in Chapter 2.

Word highlights text from the point where you drop anchor to wherever you move the toothpick cursor. Text appears in white-on-black. After the block is marked, you're ready to do something with it.

   ✔ After you press F8, you see EXT (for Extend Selection) on the status bar. The block-marking mode is active until you enter a block or formatting command or press Esc to cancel.

   ✔ To quickly mark a word, position the toothpick cursor on the word and press F8 twice.

- To quickly mark a sentence, position the toothpick cursor somewhere in the sentence and press the F8 key three times.

- To quickly mark a paragraph, position the toothpick cursor in the paragraph and press the F8 key four times.

- To mark your whole do-dang document, press the F8 key five times. Or press ⌘-A.

- Press Esc to cancel the block-drop-and-chop F8 method of marking text. The block still is marked; move the cursor to unhighlight it.

- You can use the mouse *and* the F8 key to get real fancy. Position the cursor at either end of the block you want to mark and press the F8 key. Then position the mouse cursor at the other end of the block and click. Everything between the block's ends is marked.

- After a block has been marked, you're ready to enter a block command. You can copy the block, cut it, paste it elsewhere, format it, print it, spell-check it, or a dozen more interesting things, all covered in this chapter.

- Rather than press the cursor keys to mark a block with the keyboard, you can type a character. Word locates the next occurrence of that character and includes all the text between it and the beginning of the block inside the block. You can do this several times to make the block as large as you want.

- Get used to using the keyboard commands to block your text and you will be much happier, believe me.

Another keyboard way: the Shift key

Using the Shift key in combination with any of the cursor-control keys also marks a slab of text on-screen. Refer to Chapter 2 for information about the keys that you can use to move around your document. Just press and hold the Shift key with those keys to mark text as you move the cursor. (This method may tie your fingers in knots, so be careful.)

Marking a block by using the Find command

Marking a block can get sloppy when using the mouse or the cursor-control keys — especially if you're pressing the Page Up and Page Down keys to mark acres of text. A better way is to use the Find command to locate the end of the block. Do this:

1. **Position the toothpick cursor at the beginning of the block.**

   The cursor must be blinking right before the first character to be included in the block. Be precise.

2. **Press F8.**

   This step turns on the EXT word-fragment message on the status bar. You're in block-marking mode.

3. **Choose Edit⇨Find.**

   Or just press ⌘-F. You see the Find and Replace dialog box open on-screen. Yes, you're still in block-marking mode, but now you can use the Find command to locate the end of your block.

4. **Type the text that you want to locate, which marks the end of the block.**

   After typing the text, press Return. Word stretches the block highlight down to that point in the text and includes the found text in the block.

5. **Press Esc to blow away the Find and Replace dialog box. Then get ready for true block action.**

   When the cursor is at the end of the block, you're ready to use a block command. Refer to the proper section later in this chapter for additional details.

✔ Until you enter a block command, the block remains highlighted and EXT continues to stare at you from the status bar. Remember to press Esc to cancel block-marking mode.

✔ If text isn't found by using the Find command, you see an appropriate not found error message box displayed — but you're still in block-marking mode. Click the OK button to tell Word what a good little program it is and that you are sorry it was unsuccessful.

✔ To find the next occurrence of the matching text, you can click the Find Next button in the dialog box. Or . . . .

✔ If you don't see the dialog box on-screen, pressing the Shift-F4 key combination does a Find Next for you.

✔ Although you're using the Find command to help mark your block, you still can use the cursor-control keys. Heck, you can even use the mouse if you press and hold the Shift key first. Blocking is a liberal thing; you're not limited to any one method when marking a block.

✔ More details about the Find command are in Chapter 5, in the section "Finding Text."

Marking the whole dang-doodle document

To mark everything, choose Edit⇨Select All. The commonly accepted Macintosh key equivalent for this command is ⌘-A.

Copying and Pasting a Block

After a block is marked, you can copy it and paste that block into another part of your document. The original block remains untouched by this operation. Follow these steps to copy a block of text from one place to another:

1. **Mark the block.**

   Locate the beginning of the block and select text until you've highlighted to the block's end. Detailed instructions about doing this task are offered in the first part of this chapter.

2. **Conjure up Edit⇨Copy.**

    Choose Copy from the Edit menu. Or if you're adept at such things, press ⌘-C. Or click the Copy tool.

   Word places a copy of the marked block on the *Clipboard* — a storage area for text or graphics that you've cut or copied.

3. **Move the cursor to where you want the block copied.**

   Don't worry if there isn't any room there; Word inserts the block into your text, pushing aside any existing text — just as though you had typed the block there manually.

4. **Choose Edit⇨Paste.**

    ⌘-V is the Paste shortcut; you also can click the Paste tool. Either way, you now have two copies of the block in your document.

   ✔ You also can copy blocked text with the mouse. Position the mouse cursor anywhere in the blocked text, hold down the Option key and click the mouse to drag the block to the location where the copy will be placed. The mouse pointer changes to an arrow-with-square-lasso design while you're dragging. Release the mouse button to paste in the block copy.

   ✔ After a block has been copied, you can paste it into your document a second time. This subject is covered in the section "Pasting a Previously Cut or Copied Block," later in this chapter.

Cutting and Pasting a Block

Cutting a block is like deleting it — but nothing is really gone. Instead, the cut block can be pasted into your document at another location. This process is technically called a *move;* you move a block of text from one spot to another in your document. (Talk about writing moving text!)

Cutting a block of text works similarly to copying a block. Follow these steps:

1. Mark the block of text you want to move (cut).

Locate the block's start by using the cursor and press F8 to turn on block-marking mode. Then press the cursor-control keys or use the mouse to highlight the block.

2. Choose Edit⇨Cut.

 You also can press ⌘-X, the Cut shortcut. Or click the Cut tool. Either way, the block disappears. That's OK — it's been sent to the Clipboard, an electronic storage place nestled deep in your computer's memory.

3. Move the toothpick cursor to where you want the block pasted.

Don't worry if there isn't any room for the block; Word makes room as it inserts the block, pushing aside any existing text — just as though you had typed the block there manually.

4. Summon Edit⇨Paste.

 To paste in your block, you also can press ⌘-V or click the Paste tool.

✔ You can read additional information about marking a block in the first two sections of this chapter.

✔ Copying a block works just like moving a block, although the original isn't deleted. Refer to the preceding section, "Copying and Pasting a Block."

✔ Moving a block is not the same as deleting a block; the block can be recovered only by positioning the cursor and pasting it back in.

✔ Pressing ⌘-Z (the Undo shortcut) undoes a block move.

✔ After a block has been cut and moved, you can repaste it into your document a second time. This subject is covered in the next section, "Pasting a Previously Cut or Copied Block."

✔ You also can move blocked text by dragging the mouse — although I recommend using this tip only when the move is just a short distance away. (Scrolling the screen while dragging can be unwieldy.) To do so, position the cursor anywhere in the blocked text and hold down the mouse button while you drag the soap bar-looking cursor to where you want the block moved. This dance step is particularly useful when you are rearranging stuff on a page.

Pasting a Previously Cut or Copied Block

Whenever a block of text is cut or copied, Word remembers it. You can yank that block back into your document at any time — sort of like repasting text after it's already been pasted in. You use ⌘-V, the Paste shortcut.

To paste a previously cut block of text, follow these exciting steps:

1. **Position the toothpick cursor at the spot where you want the block of text to be pasted.**

   This step should always be done first. The block appears right at the cursor's position as though you had typed it in yourself.

2. **Choose Edit⇨Paste.**

    You also can press ⌘-V, the Paste shortcut. (⌘-V equals paste? Uh-huh.) Or click on the Paste tool.

3. **Whoomp. There it is.**

   ✔ If nothing has been copied or cut by using the other block commands, nothing is pasted by this command. Duh.

   ✔ Word has a small brain. It remembers only the last cut or copied block. Anything cut or copied before that is gone, gone, gone.

Deleting a Block

There are two ways to delete a block: the complex way and the easy way. What say we do the easy way, eh?

1. **Mark the block.**

   Refer to the first section of this chapter for the best block-marking instructions in any computer book.

2. **Press either the Delete or Del key.**

    Thwoop!

   ✔ This time, the block can be recovered by using the EditÍUndo command (or clicking the Undo tool). This step is what makes deleting a block different from cutting and pasting a block. When you undo, however, the block appears in the same position it was before you so rudely deleted it.

   ✔ Chapter 4 covers the vast subject of deleting and destroying text. Turn there to quench your destructive thirsts.

Formatting a Block

When you've roped off a section of text as a block, you can format the text and characters as a single unit. Formatting is covered in detail in Part II of this book, "Formatting — or Making Your Prose Less Ugly." So instead of going over the details, here are the various formatting things you can do to a block:

- ✔ You can make the text bold, underlined (two different flavors), italicized, superscripted, or subscripted by using various ⌘-key combinations, all of which are detailed in Chapter 9.

- ✔ You can change the font for the block's text (also covered in Chapter 9).

- ✔ Any formatting changes affect only the text roped off in the block.

- ✔ Information about changing the text style — such as bold, underlining, italics, and all that — is offered in Chapter 9. Information about shifting between upper- and lowercase is presented in the same chapter.

- ✔ Information about changing the position of a block — its *justification* — is covered in Chapter 10.

Spell-Checking a Block

If you want to spell-check a small or irregularly sized part of your document, you can block it off and then use Word's Spelling command. Doing this is much quicker than going through the pains of a full spell-check.

To see whether your spelling is up to snuff, follow these steps:

1. **Mark the block.**

   Refer to the first section in this chapter.

   The highlighted area marked by the block is the only part of your document that is spell-checked.

2. **Select Tools⇨Spelling.**

    No muss, no waiting — the block is spell-checked. (You also can click the Spelling tool.)

3. **Word compares all words in the block with its internal dictionary.**

   If a misspelled or unrecognized word is found, it is highlighted and you are given a chance to correct or edit it. If you tire of this, click the Cancel button.

4. **After the block has been spell-checked, Word asks whether, by the way, you want to continue checking the rest of your document. Click No.**

   Or Click Yes if you really want to see how poor your spelling is outside the block.

Chapter 7 covers using Word's spell-checker in glorious detail. Refer there for additional information about changing or correcting your typos.

Using Find and Replace in a Block

You cannot find text in a marked block, but you can use Word's Replace command. When a block is marked, Replace finds and replaces only text in that block. The rest of your document is unaffected (unless you tell Word to replace outside the block when it's done).

- ✔ A full description of this operation is offered in the Chapter 5 section "Find and Replace." I'm too lazy to rewrite all that stuff here.

- ✔ The Find command cannot be used in a block because the Find command is used to mark the block; see the section "Marking a block with the Find command," earlier in this chapter.

Printing a Block

Word's Print command enables you to print one page, several pages, or an entire document. If you want to print only a small section of text, you have to mark it as a block and then print it. Here's the secret:

1. **Make sure that your printer is on and ready to print.**

   See Chapter 8 for additional printer setup information.

2. **Mark the block of text that you want to print.**

   Move the cursor to the beginning of the block and press F8 to turn on block-marking mode; move the cursor to the end of the block or use the mouse for wrist-action block marking.

3. **Choose File⇨Print.**

   You also can press ⌘-P.

4. **Click in the Print Selection Only box.**

   This action tells Word that you want to print only your highlighted block.

5. **Click the OK button**

   Or press Return. In a few moments, you see the hard copy sputtering out of your printer.

↙ The Print tool on the Standard toolbar is used only to print the entire document, not your selected block. If you need a shortcut, press ⌘-P to print your block instead.

↙ Additional information about marking a block of text is in the first section of this chapter.

↙ Printing is covered in full in Chapter 8. Look there for information about printing options and setting up your printer.

↙ The Print Selection Only item is available only when you have a block selected.

Chapter 7
The Electronic Mrs. Bradshaw

- -

In This Chapter
▶ Checking your spelling

▶ Checking only one word

▶ Adding words to the dictionary

▶ Using the miraculous AutoCorrect

▶ Checking your grammar (woe is I)

▶ Using the thesaurus

▶ Counting your words

- -

*E*veryone should have a fourth-grade teacher like Mrs. Bradshaw. The woman was a goddess in the annals of proper English pronunciation and, of course, spelling. Nothing pleases a 10-year-old more than a smile from Mrs. Bradshaw: "Very good, Danny. There is no *e* at the end of potato." The woman could probably correct the Queen.

Whatever happened to Mrs. Bradshaw? The folks at Microsoft somehow scooped the essence out of her brain, sliced it thin, and distributed it on the Word disks. Every copy of Word comes with a spelling checker that's as efficient and knowledgeable as Mrs. Bradshaw (but lacks her red check marks). Somehow, her vast English vocabulary has been included as well: Word's thesaurus offers alternative word suggestions quicker than Mrs. Bradshaw could frown disapprovingly over my misuse of the word *boner.* And to top it all off, Word can correct your grammar quicker than Mrs. Bradshaw could say, "Me, Danny. Woe is me."

Checking Your Spelling

One of the miracles of modern word processing is that the computer knows how to spell better than you do. Thank goodness. I really don't know how to spell. Not at all. The rules are obtuse and meaningless. There are too many exceptions. Besides, I like to give my editors something to do. But thank the guardians of fourth-grade golden rules: with Word, you needn't worry about being accurate. Just be close and the Spelling command does the rest.

To spell-check the words in your document, follow these steps:

1. Choose Tools➪Spelling.

You also can click the Spelling tool or press F7, the Spelling shortcut.

Word scans your document for offensive words — those that would debun Mrs. Bradshaw's hair. When a misspelled word is found, the Spelling dialog box appears and the misspelled or unknown word appears highlighted in your text on-screen. The dialog box displays the misspelled word and suggests alternative spellings — most of them correct. Figure 7-1 shows an example.

Figure 7-1:
A misspelled
word.

2. Pluck the correct spelling from the list.

Highlight the correct word and click the Change button. If the word isn't listed, you can type it in the Change To box. Or if the word is OK (sheesh, what was Word thinking?), you can click the Ignore button; Word then skips over the word without making any changes.

3. Word continues to check every word in your document.

When it's done, you see a dialog box proclaim

    The spelling check is complete

✔ Click the Ignore All button if your word is really a word (such as your name) and you don't want Word to stop every time it encounters the word in this document.

✔ Select Change All if you want to change every instance of a misspelled word to whatever is in the Change To box. If you have the annoying habit of typing *breif* rather than *brief,* for example, you can click Change All so that Word automatically makes the substitution without bothering you.

✔ If you find yourself making a number of consistent mistakes — *teh* for *the*, *fi* for *if*, *alright* for *all right* — take advantage of Word's AutoCorrect tool. Refer to the section "Correcting Stuff As You Type," later in this chapter.

✔ You can click the Add button to place words that Word doesn't know into its dictionary. For example, your last name, street name, city, and other frequently used words probably aren't in Word's dictionary. When the word is flagged as misspelled, click the Add button and it becomes a part of Word's dictionary for life.

✔ Undo Last undoes your last spelling change, most of the time. This option is great for those sleepy nighttime spell-checks: when you think that you may have mistakenly selected the wrong replacement word, just click Undo Last and check out the last word again. (Undo Last may not work all the time; don't count on it.)

✔ To check the spelling of only one word — which does come in handy — see the next section, "Checking Only One Word."

✔ To check the spelling of a paragraph or other block of text, refer to the section "Spell-Checking a Block" in Chapter 6.

✔ The Word dictionary is not a substitute for a real dictionary. Only in a real dictionary can you look up the meaning of a word, which tells you whether you're using the proper word in the proper context. No computer writer works with an electronic dictionary alone; there's usually a good, thick Webster's sitting within arm's reach.

✔ If two identical words are found in a row, Word highlights them as a Repeated Word. Error, error! Click the Ignore button to tell Word to forget about the double word, or click the Delete button to blow the second word away, or click the Suggest button if you meant to type something similar but your fingers didn't respond.

✔ My, but this is a long list of check marks.

✔ The Spelling command also locates words with weird capitalization. For example, *bONer*. You're given an opportunity to correct the capitalization, just as though the word were misspelled.

✔ The Word dictionary is good but definitely not as good as Mrs. Bradshaw. For one thing, it doesn't check your words in context. For example, *your* and *you're* can be spelled correctly in Word's eye, but you may be using them improperly. The same thing goes for *its* and *it's*. For that kind of in-context checking, you need something called a *grammar checker*. Lucky for you, Word has one. Its use is discussed later in this chapter.

✔ The word *spell* here refers to creating words by using an accepted pattern of letters: it has nothing to do with magic. Many people assume that a spell-check instantly makes their document better. Wrong! You have to read what you write and then edit, look, and read again. The Spelling command doesn't fix your document; it simply finds rotten words and suggests replacements.

Checking Only One Word

There's no need to spell-check an entire document when all you want to check is one word. Actually, this is a great way to deal with English spelling: go ahead and spell the word how you think that it *should* be spelled. Then check only that word. Word looks up the accurate, wretched English spelling and you're on your way. And the cool part is that you don't have to learn a thing!

To check the spelling of a single word, do the following:

1. **Put the cursor somewhere on the word or just before it.**

2. **Highlight the word.**

   Press F8 twice.

   Or if you double-click the word with the mouse, you can skip Steps 1 and 2.

3. **Spell-check it!**

    Choose Tools⇨Spelling. Better yet, click your Spelling tool or press F7, the Spelling shortcut.

4. **Word checks that word.**

   If you spelled the word correctly (the way I spell, the odds are 50-50), Word reports that it has finished checking the selection. Then, with a great deal of reverence and respect, it politely asks whether you want it to check the remainder of the document. If you misspelled the word, however, Word sighs that exhausted sigh of saints, martyrs, and elementary school-teachers everywhere and displays the Spelling dialog box, listing possible alternative spellings.

5. **Click a word from the suggested spellings.**

6. **Press the Change button.**

   Word replaces the word you misspelled with its proper (and decidedly nonintuitive) spelling.

   ✔ Refer to the first section of this chapter for additional information about working with Word's Spelling feature.

   ✔ Single-word checking is often a good way to immediately tackle a word that looks hopelessly wrong. Of course, my philosophy (or "filosofy") is to spell any old which way and then use a document spell-check to catch everything at once.

Adding Words to the Dictionary

Some common words don't appear in Word's dictionary — my last name, for example. If your name, city, business, and so on all are unknown to Word, Word will suggest alternative spellings for those words every time you spell-check a document. You can avoid this tautological conundrum in two ways:

✔ The first, and more stupid, option is to click the Ignore button when the spell-checker finds the word. Word ignores that word during the rest of the spell-check, but you again have to tell Word to ignore the word the next time you spell-check. Dumb, dumb, dumb.

✔ The second, and wiser, option is to add said word to your supplemental dictionary. Word then skips these unique words every time you spell-check.

To add a word to the supplemental dictionary, follow these steps:

1. **Start your spell-check.**

   Refer to the first section of this chapter for the persnickety details.

2. **Lo, Word stumbles upon a word unbeknownst to it yet beknownst to you.**

   And you know that the word is spelled just fine.

3. **Select the Add button.**

   This step stuffs the word into the supplemental dictionary; you never have to mess with it again.

✔ When a word is in the supplemental dictionary, Word knows and recognizes it as if it resided in the real dictionary — the one they made from Mrs. Bradshaw's brain.

✔ Be careful when you decide to add a word to the dictionary because it isn't easy to un-add a word from the dictionary. In other words, watch out that you don't inadvertently put a seriously misspelled word in the dictionary. (I once added *fo* to the dictionary and spent three weeks in the Word penalty box — and that's in Seattle, of all places!) To get the word out, you need to check the technical information box (optional reading) sitting nearby.

> ✔ You actually can maintain several supplemental dictionaries on disk. To select a new dictionary, select the Add Words To text box in the spelling dialog box and pick a new dictionary name. Word adds the word and uses the supplemental dictionary (along with the real one) for the spell-check. You can create new dictionaries by clicking the Options button, which I explain next.

What? The Add Button Is Dimmed!

This happens because you haven't set up a personal dictionary. To do so, follow these steps:

1. **Fire up the Options for the Speller.**

   If you're in the Spelling dialog box, click the Options button. Otherwise, choose Tools⇨Options and then click the word *Spelling*, located on one of the tabs in the top of the Options dialog box.

2. **Click the New button to create your own dictionary.**

   The Create Custom Dictionary dialog box appears.

3. **Type CUSTOM and press Return.**

4. **Click the OK button in the Options dialog box.**

   You can now use the Add button in the Spelling dialog box to stick words into your own personal dictionary.

No need to bother with this trivial drivel about the supplemental dictionary

The supplemental dictionary is a text document on disk. It contains, in alphabetic order, all the words you added. And as a special bonus, you can edit the list and remove any deleterious words you may have added.

The standard Word supplemental dictionary is found in the Microsoft® folder on your hard drive, and it's named Custom Dictionary. Here is its cutesy icon: 🔲

The dictionary file is really a special type of document that you can edit by using Word. You can open it just like any other document and then change it — for example, remove extra words from the supplemental dictionary. Suppose, for example, that you accidentally stuck *fo* in the dictionary. Only by editing the Custom Dictionary file can you get *fo* out *fo* there.

My advice is to make a copy of the file before you edit it. That way, if the edited copy gets fouled, you can restore the duplicate. Needless to say, this isn't something for the timid, which is why I wisely stuck it in this box, out of the way, where only the true Word goof-offs bother to read.

Correcting Stuff As You Type

One of the handy things Word can do is correct your foul spelling as you type. The feature is called AutoCorrect and 'tis truly amazing stuff. You type *teh* and Word quickly and quietly corrects it. So if you know how to spell a word but find out that your fingers just don't have a clue, AutoCorrect comes to your rescue.

Activating AutoCorrect

To ensure that AutoCorrect is on, choose Tools⇨AutoCorrect. The AutoCorrect dialog box appears, as shown in Figure 7-2.

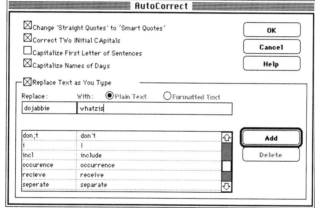

Figure 7-2: The AutoCorrect dialog box.

About midway down the left side of the box, you see the words *Replace Text as You Type* next to a wee box. If the box is empty, click the mouse in it. That sticks an X in the box, turning AutoCorrect on.

AutoCorrect's main role in life is to replace words that you commonly flub automatically. It also has four other functions, each of which is listed at the top of the AutoCorrect dialog box (and described in the following check mark items). To activate or deactivate any function, click it with the mouse. An X in an item's box means that it's on and working.

✔ The Change 'Straight Quotes' to 'Smart Quotes' item directs Word to automatically insert the friendly curly quotes when you press the double-quote or single-quote keys in your documents. This is definitely *trés chic* and something PC owners will have to howl over eternally.

✔ The Correct TWo INitial CApitals item directs Word to correct this common typing faux pas by switching the second uppercase letter to lowercase.

✔ The Capitalize First Letter of Sentences item controls whether Word automatically capitalizes the first letter in a sentence when you forget to. e. e. cummings leaves this item unchecked.

✔ The Capitalize Names of Days item capitalizes Monday, Tuesday, and so on. Thank goodness Word can do this for you automagically because half the class was absent and missed Mrs. Bradshaw's capitalization lesson.

Adding words to AutoCorrect's repertoire

The bullies at Microsoft inserted a few common typos into AutoCorrect's brain. These are listed at the bottom of the AutoCorrect dialog box, in a scrolling list. The dojabbie on the left is the way you often spell something. The whatzits on the right is what Word replaces it with.

From Figure 7-2, you can see the common *recieve-receive* combination; type **recieve** and Word automatically corrects it to **receive**.

To add a new item to the list, follow these steps:

1. **Choose Tools⇨AutoCorrect.**

   The AutoCorrect dialog box appears.

2. **Focus in on the Replace box.**

   Click the mouse in the Replace box.

3. **Type the word you often goof.**

   Don't worry if you can't think of words to add; it's also possible to add words to AutoCorrect's repertoire by using the Spelling command. See the checklist following this numbered list for information.

4. **Press Tab.**

   This step moves you over to the With box, where you type the proper way the word goes.

5. **Type the proper way the word goes.**

6. **Click the Add button.**

7. **To add more AutoCorrect words, repeat Steps 2 through 6.**

8. **Click the OK button when you're done.**

✔ You can remove words from AutoCorrect that you don't want repaired automatically. Just highlight the word in the list and click the Delete button. Poof! It's gone.

✔ You may notice the (r) thing in AutoCorrect's word list: it's an abbreviation for a special symbol that AutoCorrect automagically inserts into your document. To specify a special symbol, type that character in the With box. To make *(c)* equal to the copyright symbol (©), for example, type **(c)** in the Replace box, press Tab, and then press Option-G in the With box. (See the section "Inserting Oddball and Special Characters" in Chapter 9 for more information about such characters.)

✔ It's entirely possible to be cruel with AutoCorrect. For example, inserting a meanie like **thier** for **their** would drive some people nuts. Remember, AutoCorrect is subtle. If you type looking at the keyboard, you never know what it's up to.

✔ An easier way to get words into AutoCorrect's list is to click the AutoCorrect button in the Spelling dialog box (refer to Figure 7-1). But be careful! Clicking the AutoCorrect button sticks the misspelled word and the highlighted replacement into AutoCorrect's list. Make sure that you have the proper replacement word highlighted *before* you click the AutoCorrect button.

Checking Your Grammar (Woe Is I)

Word's grammar checker is a wonderful tool, and I hate it. It keeps telling me how far I have strayed from the boring writing style that the folks who gave the checker life think is the "one true path." Don't get me wrong — it does a great job of distinguishing between *I* and *me, neither* and *nor,* and other similar stuff. I just think it's snooty.

For example, I think we all agree that Henry David Thoreau was no slouch as a writer. Aaah, but check out the dialog box in Figure 7-3: perfect little Word can assume an air of condescension even with one of America's great literary treasures. Obviously, the grammar checker values a senseless adherence to the narrow strictures of socially ordained dialogue over the untamed spirit of inspired prose.

Figure 7-3:
The
grammar
checker
sizes up
Henry David
Thoreau.

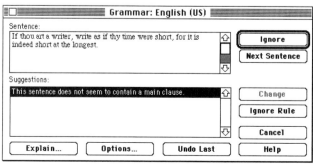

Anyway, regardless of the results, if diagramming sentences didn't burn out enough of your creative brain cells, select Tools⇨Grammar. Your document is spell-checked (because the Grammar checker has a sense of spell) and then the Grammar dialog box opens — unless you're computer perfect.

- ✔ If you are going to run the grammar checker, don't bother spell-checking first. The grammar checker checks your spelling as well as your grammar.

- ✔ The grammar checker works much like the spell-checker; it tells you what's wrong and then suggests, in a patronizing tone, how to fix it.

- ✔ By clicking the appropriate button in the Grammar dialog box, you can ignore the grammar checker's suggestion, make the changes, move on to the next sentence, ignore the offending rule (my favorite), demand an explanation from Word about why it didn't like what you did, or get out.

You can select the Options button to set the way the grammar checker works:

- ✔ Word sets some rather rough parameters, enabling you to select between three sets of writing rules: Strict, Business, and Casual.

- ✔ You can turn off the Check Spelling button so that Word doesn't tell you that, yes, once again, you misspelled February when all you really wanted to know was whether that preposition could live at a sentence's end.

- ✔ You also can check the box that presents the grammar statistics after the checker is done. You should probably check this box because it's one of the few ways to get a word count.

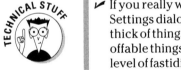

- ✔ If you really want to get into the grammar thing, open the Customize Settings dialog box. Yea, verily, although you're several dialog boxes in the thick of things, the one you see on-screen contains many switchable-offable things that you can set or reset to control the grammar checker's level of fastidiousness.

Using the Thesaurus

If you think that I'm smart enough to use all the big words in this chapter, you're grievously mistaken. Witness: *tautological conundrum.* That ain't me talkin'; that's Word's thesaurus in action. An amazing tool, astounding utensil, or marvelous implement. You get the idea. With the thesaurus, you can look up synonyms or other words that have the same meaning but more weight or more precision.

Here's how to instantly become a master of big, clunky English words:

1. **Hover the cursor over a simple word, such as *big*.**

   The thesaurus works best with adjectives, although the Word Statistical Department tells me that the thesaurus contains more than 120,000 words.

2. **Do Tools⇨Thesaurus.**

   Or press the Thesaurus shortcut, Shift-F7. Instantly, the Thesaurus dialog box opens (see Figure 7-4). Word displays several alternatives for the word. They're grouped into categories: by meanings (the box on the left) and synonyms (right).

Figure 7-4:
Looking up a
word in the
thesaurus.

3. **To replace the word in your document, highlight your choice and select Replace.**

   After selecting a word, you return to your document. If you don't find a better word, select Cancel to return to your document.

   ✔ A thesaurus is not a colossal, prehistoric beast.

   ✔ If one of the words in the left column is close but not exactly what you want, select it and click the Look Up button. The new word's synonyms appear in the right column.

   ✔ If the word that you select has no synonym, the thesaurus displays an alphabetic list of words. Type a new, similar word or select Cancel.

   ✔ After inserting a new word, you may have to do a bit of editing: perhaps you may need to add *ed* or *ing* to the word or maybe change its article (that's a Mrs. Bradshaw's highfalutin word for the li'l word —*a* or *an*— that precedes your word).

Pulling a Word Count

Mrs. Bradshaw — and her counterparts on up through 16th grade — were big on papers of a certain length. "I want you to write a five-page dissertation on why ketchup isn't green," she'd announce.

Five pages! Are you nuts? Didn't Strunk and White stress brevity and clarity of thought over ghastly verbiage? But I digress.

Some of us get paid by the word. "Dan, write a 1,000-word article, evaluating 17 different tape backup systems for the Mac." I need to know when to stop writing. Also, curiosity generally gets the best of any writer, and you want to get a good feel for how many words and such you have in your document. To find out, select the Tools⇨Word Count. (The Word Count command is far more accurate than a page count. Pages can be fudged: larger fonts and wider margins have saved many a student from turning in too short a paper and facing Mrs. Bradshaw's wrath.)

The Word Count dialog box displays a summary of your document's pages, words, characters, paragraphs, and lines. How impressive. OK. Click the Close button and get back to work.

Chapter 8

Send *This* to the Printer!

*O*h, you can get into a lot of trouble when it comes to printing. For example, the phrase *sending something to the printer* means nothing until you explain that a *printer* is a device connected to a computer that enables you to print things. Noncomputer people think that a printer is a person who prints stuff. For computer people, the printer is a nifty device tethered to the computer that lets us produce that all-important hard copy — physical proof of our toil on-screen.

Of course, sending something to the printer isn't magic. If you've been messing with your printer for a while, you'll discover that it's a stubborn little guy, rarely cooperative, and hard to tame.

In this chapter, I give you some tips for using your printer so that you can make it give you Word documents that look exactly as you imagined — or at least professional enough to fool those who think that printers wear inky aprons.

Getting the Printer Ready

Before printing, you must make sure that your printer is ready to print. Unfortunately, this involves more than flipping on a power switch.

Start by making sure that your printer is plugged in and properly connected to your Macintosh. The cable that connects them should be firmly plugged in at both ends. (This cable has to be checked only if you're having printer problems.)

Laser printers should have a good toner cartridge installed. If the laser printer's "toner low" message appears or a "toner low" light is on, replace the toner at once! If you have a nonlaser printer, make sure that it has a good ribbon. Old, frayed ribbons produce faint text and are bad for the printing mechanism. Trying to save a few bucks now by using a ribbon longer than necessary will cost you more later in repair bills.

There must be paper in the printer for you to print on. The paper can feed from the back, come out of a paper tray, or be fed manually one sheet at a time. However your printer eats paper, make sure that you have it set up properly before you print.

Finally, your printer must be *on-line* or *selected* before you can print anything. Somewhere on your printer is a button labeled *On-line* or *Select,* and it should have a corresponding light. You have to press that button to turn the option (and the light) on. Even if your printer is plugged in, its power switch is on, and it has finished its warm-up stretching exercises, it won't print unless it's on-line or selected.

✔ Before you can print, your printer must be plugged into a power outlet; plugged into your computer; turned on; full of paper; and *on-line* or *selected.* (Most printers turn themselves on when in the *on-line* or *selected* mode.)

✔ Never plug a printer cable into a printer or computer that is on and running. Always turn your printer and computer off whenever you plug anything into them. If not, you may damage the internal electronic components.

✔ If you're printing to a network printer — and it makes me shudder to think of it — *someone else* is in charge of the printer. It should be set up and ready to print for you. If not, though, there's usually someone handy whom you can complain to.

✔ Some additional information about setting up, or *installing*, your printer for use with Word is covered in Chapter 25, "The Printer Is Your Friend." That chapter also contains troubleshooting information. I also provide a detailed anatomical guide to popular printers so that you know where to shoot your printer for a quick death or a lingering, slow, and painful one.

Selecting a Printer

One of the joys of printing with any Macintosh application is its capability for using many different printers. Word even remembers the capabilities of several different printers and automatically formats your work to show you, on-screen, what it will look like when it gets to paper. This feature is called *WYSIWYG* (pronounced "wizz-i-wig"), or *what you see is what you get* (more or less).

After the joy, depression sets in when you realize that you can only select a printer that has been formally introduced to your Mac. This is definitely Mac guru time, although you should rest happy in the knowledge that if your printer works with other Mac programs, it works swell with Word, too. This is perhaps the only redeeming quality your Macintosh has over a DOS Computer. That, and it isn't as ugly.

To select a printer — if you *really* want to — follow these steps:

1. Select the Chooser command from the Apple menu.

This command runs the Chooser program, which displays a list of printers known to your Macintosh (see Figure 8-1).

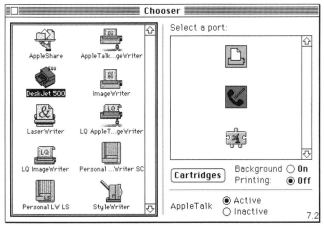

Figure 8-1:
The Chooser program is how you pick a printer for use with your Mac and Word.

2. Click on whichever printer is connected to your Mac.

So I don't have a LaserWriter. Boo-hoo! I have a nifty DeskJet 500. So I click on its icon.

3. Select a printer or port.

My printer uses the modem port, so I highlight that one. If you're on a network, you may see a gaggle of printers in the list. Click on one that's near your office or one you've been forbidden to use. I mean, encouraged to use.

4. **Close the Chooser by clicking in it's close (also known as its go-away) box.**

   You're done. That's it.

   ✔ Selecting a printer is necessary only if more than one printer is connected to your Mac.

   ✔ If you're using a network printer, an appropriate section for your needs is hidden in Chapter 25.

Previewing Printing

Printing something 1,000 times to get it right sure doesn't make Mr. Bunny feel good. Not that I have anything against slaughtering trees. I own a few myself. It's a cash crop! But that's not an excuse to waste paper. Instead you can take the more environmentally conscious route — and save yourself time as well — by employing Word's fancy Print Preview command, which lets you see what your document will look like printed before you print it.

 To sneak a peak at how your document will print, choose File➪Print Preview. Or click on the handy Print Preview button (on the Standard toolbar). This command switches Word's display to a rather standoffish perspective.

   ✔ I don't really use Print Preview much for standard fare. But if you're printing something that contains heavy-duty formatting — footnotes, strange columns, and stuff like that — Print Preview can be a godsend.

 ✔ Click on the Close button if you want to return to your document for editing.

 ✔ Use the Page Up and Page Down buttons to peruse various pages of your document in Print Preview mode.

 ✔ Click on the Print button to print your document right here and now! See the next section for details.

   ✔ No, you can't edit anything in Print Preview mode. Sniff.

Printing a Whole Document

If you think that your work is worthy enough to be enshrined on a sheet of paper, follow these steps. They print your entire document — from top to bottom, head to toe, from *Once upon a time* to *happily every after.*

1. **Make sure that the printer is on-line and ready to print.**

   What's that noise? Is Bobby at it again with the Playskool Li'l Plumber Kit? No, it's the printer humming its ready tune.

2. **Summon File⇨Print.**

    You also can click the Print tool or press ⌘-P. A Print dialog box magically appears (see Figure 8-2). Your print dialog box may look different, depending on which type of printer you're using. Most of the major buttons are the same.

```
┌─────────────────────────────────────────────────────────────┐
│ PowerPrint                    DeskJet 500 v2.0.1  ( Print  ) │
│                                                              │
│ Print Mode:  ● Graphics  300 ▼  ○ Draft        ( Cancel )   │
│ Quality:     ● Best          ○ Fast            (Options)    │
│ Pages: ● All  ○ From: [    ] To: [    ]  Every page ▼ (Help)│
│ Copies: [1]     Feed: ● Automatic  ○ Manual                 │
│ Print: [ Document      ▼]  [All Pages in Range ▼] (Word Options)│
│ (Range...)  ☐ Print Selection Only         (Word Help)      │
│                                     ⊠ Collate Copies        │
└─────────────────────────────────────────────────────────────┘
```

Figure 8-2:
The Print
dialog box.

3. **Click Print or press Return.**

   No need to do this if you click the Print tool.

4. **The printer warms up and starts to print.**

   Printing may take some time. Really. A long time. Have patience. Gutenberg didn't do a Bible an hour, after all.

Fortunately, Word lets you continue working while it prints in "the background." To ensure that it works this way, refer to the techy sidebar, "Printing and getting on with your life."

✔ If nothing prints, don't hit the Print command again! There's probably nothing awry; the computer is simply still thinking or sending (*downloading*) fonts to the printer. If you don't get an error message, everything will probably print, eventually.

✔ If you have a manual feed printer, the printer itself will beg for paper. Your printer says, "Beep, feed me!" You must stand by, line up paper, and then shove it into the printer's gaping maw until your document is done printing. Refer to the section "Printing Envelopes" later in this chapter to figure this one out.

Printing and getting on with your life

Word has the capability to print while you do something else. If this capability isn't coddled to life, you have to wait a dreadfully long time while your document prints. To ensure that it's on, select the Word Options button in the Print dialog box. The Options dialog box appears, with the Print area up front.

In the upper-left corner of the Print area is the Printing Options corral. The last item is Background Printing. Make sure that it has an X in its little box. If not, click in the box. Press Return or click the OK button when you're done; then press Esc to banish the Print dialog box.

✔ Before you print, consider saving your document to disk and — if we're talking final draft here — do a spell-check. Refer to the Chapter 7 section "Checking Your Spelling" and the Chapter 16 section "Saving a document to disk (after that)."

✔ While Word prints, the time on the status bar changes to a little printer spewing out pages.

Printing a Specific Page

Follow these steps to print only one page of your document:

1. **Make sure that your printer is on and eager to print something.**

2. **Move the toothpick cursor so that it's sitting somewhere in the page you want to print**.

   Check the Page counter in the lower-left corner of the screen to make sure that you're at the page you want to print.

3. **Choose File⇨Print.**

   Or press ⌘-P. The Print dialog box appears.

4. **Click the Range button.**

   A dialog box appears with three options.

5. **Click Current Page.**

6. **Click OK or press Return.**

7. Click Print or press Return.

Word returns you to your document when that sole page is printed on your printer.

The printed page should have a header, footer, and all other formatting — even a page number — just as though you had printed it as part of the complete document.

Printing a Range of Pages

Word enables you to print a single page, a range of pages, or even some hodgepodge combination of random page numbers from within your document. To print a range or group of pages, follow these steps:

1. Make sure that the printer is on-line, happy, and ready to print.

2. Conjure up File⇨Print.

Or press ⌘-P. You see the Print dialog box.

3. Click the Range button.

An Amana Radar Range dialog box appears!

4. Click on Pages.

The cursor's attention moves to the box by Pages. To print pages 3 through 5, type **3-5**. To print pages 1 through 7, type **1-7**.

5. Choose OK.

6. Choose Print.

The pages you specified — and only those pages — are printed.

You can get very specific with the page ranges. For example, if you want to print page 3, pages 5 through 9, pages 15 through 17, and page 19 (boy, that coffee went everywhere, didn't it?), type **3, 5-9, 15-17, 19**.

Printing a Block

When a block of text is marked on-screen, you can beg the Print command to print only that block. Refer to the section "Printing a Block" in Chapter 6 for the down-and-dirty details.

Printing Several Documents

It may seem that the best way to print several documents at a time is to load them one at a time and print them one at a time. There is a better way, however: it's hidden in the Find File command, tucked away in the File menu. You can use this command to tell Word which files you want to print. This process is rumored to be easier than loading each file into Word, printing it, putting the file away, and then loading another file. You be the judge.

To print several files at a time, follow these steps:

1. **Make sure that the printer is on, selected, and rarin' to print.**

2. **Choose File⇨Find File.**

   The Search dialog box, shown in Figure 8-3, opens. If you've already used the Find File command to search for files, the Find File window itself opens. Move down to Step 5 and continue or click the Search button to activate the Search dialog box.

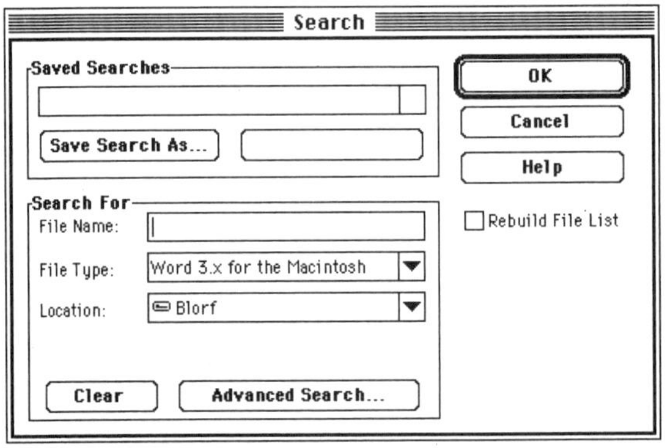

Figure 8-3:
The Search
dialog box.
Don't let its
simplicity
fool you.

If you are the one person in a thousand who is familiar with the Find File dialog box, skip ahead to Step 4. If this is the first time you have used it, you have to tell it where to look for your files. To do this, continue with the next step.

3. **Tell Word where to look for your files.**

   Make sure that the File Name box is blank.

   Click the down arrow next to the File Type box and select Readable Files from the list.

Click the down arrow by the Location box and select the disk drive where you want to hunt for the files to print.

Make sure that the Rebuild File List has an X in it. If not, click on it and the X appears.

4. Click the OK button.

This step tells Word to search for Word files all over the drive that you specified. This may take a while. Be patient.

5. The Find File dialog box appears (finally).

If you know Window's File Manager, this box looks familiar (see Figure 8-4).

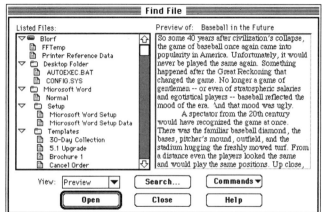

Figure 8-4:
The Find File dialog box in all its glory.

6. Scroll through the file list, looking for the files you want to print.

7. When you find a file, Command-click it.

Press and hold the ⌘ key and click on the file. This action highlights the file. Keep Command-clicking until you've marked all the files you want to print.

8. Click the Commands button, at the bottom of the Find File dialog box.

A list of commands appears in a pop-up list. The one you want is the second one down, Print.

9. Click the Print command.

10. The Print dialog box appears.

At last, familiar territory.

11. **Click OK to print the many documents**.

    Word happily prints all the documents that you selected.

- ✔ This is perhaps the most obtuse way of printing multiple files that I've ever encountered in any word processor.

- ✔ Yes, as with printing a single document, printing multiple documents takes a while.

- ✔ The Find File dialog box is officially tackled in Chapter 18, "Managing Files."

Printing Envelopes

Yes, Word can print envelopes. Yes, it can even be a snap. A special Word command is specifically designed for this purpose. (Alas, Word does not print the stamp as well.)

To print an envelope, follow these steps:

1. **Make sure that your printer is oh-so-eager to print something.**

2. **Choose Tools⇨Envelopes and Labels.**

   This step opens the Envelopes and Labels dialog box, shown in Figure 8-5. If an address had been selected in your document or if Word has somehow magically located the address near the toothpick cursor, it appears in the Addressed To box. If Word didn't automatically fill in the address, type it now.

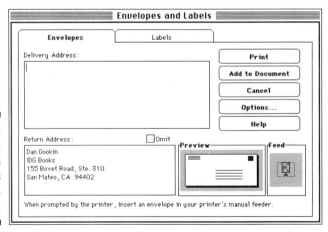

Figure 8-5: The Envelopes and Labels dialog box, please.

3. Stick an envelope in your printer.

I mention this step because most printers must be spoon-fed envelopes one at a time. (Mine works like this.) In some fancy-schmancy offices, printers may have *envelope feeders*. La-di-da.

By the way, you can click the Feed part of the Envelopes and Labels dialog box to tell Word how the envelope will arrive through the printer. This really depends on how your printer sucks in envelopes. Mine has a special slot for them that takes 'em face up in the middle.

4. Choose Print.

A Print dialog box appears.

5. Choose Print again.

This time it means it. Your printer may beep or otherwise prompt you to insert the envelope, or it may just print it right then and there.

✔ Check the envelope to make sure that you didn't address the backside or put the address on upside-down — as I so often do. If you goof, just repeat these steps to reprint your envelope.

✔ Place the envelope in your laser printer's manual-feed-slot-thing. The envelope goes in face up with the top side to your left. Draw a picture of this or print the preceding two sentences on a piece of paper and tape it to the top of your laser printer for future reference.

✔ On a dot-matrix printer, the envelope goes into the feeder upside-down and faces away from you. It helps to wedge it in there a bit to make sure that the printer grabs it. Or you may have a newfangled printer that has a special envelope slot. And if you do, well, la-di-da.

✔ Printing envelopes on a dot-matrix printer like the Imagewriter is a study in frustration. The envelopes usually wind up looking like something a 4-year-old did in preschool, all smeared up and illegible. You may be able to reduce the amount of smear by increasing the distance between the paper and the roller; you have to experiment.

✔ If you don't want the return address to print, check the Omit box in the upper-right part of the return address space in the dialog box. I do this routinely because my printer munges the top part of the envelope and the return address never prints right.

Part II

Formatting—or Making Your Prose Look Less Ugly

The 5th Wave   By Rich Tennant

5th Wave Power Tip: To increase application speed, punch the Command Key over and over and over as rapidly as possible. The computer will sense your impatience and move your data along quicker than if you just sat and waited. Hint: This also works on elevator buttons and cross walk signals.

In this part...

*F*ormatting makes your documents shine. It's what makes you boast when you show your printed labors to some — dare I say it — PC user, who snivels, "Gosh, how'd you get it to look so good?" Few other things in life make you swell with such pride.

Yet formatting isn't without its dark side. It involves a great deal of key pressing and other secret rituals. This part describes the intricacies of how formatting works in Word and how to make your documents look oh-so-purty.

Chapter 9
Formatting Characters

- -

- -

The most basic thing you can format in a document is a character. *Characters* include letters (which form words, sentences, and paragraphs) and weird Uncle Lloyd, who trims the hair in his ears with a butane lighter. You can format characters to be bold, italicized, underlined, little, big, in different fonts, or in an Easter bunny suit at Thanksgiving dinner. Word gives you a magnificent amount of control over the appearance of your text, enabling you to generate documents that are truly professional in quality — and fool everyone in the process.

Making Bold Text

To emphasize a word, you make it bold. Bold text is, well, bold. It's heavy. It carries a lot of weight, stands out on the page, speaks its mind at public meetings, wears a cowboy hat — you know the type.

To make new text stand out, follow these steps:

1. Press the ⌘-B key combination.

This step activates bold mode, in which everything you type is bold. Go ahead—type away. **La-la-la.** (You also can click the Bold tool, in the Formatting toolbar, to turn on bold mode.)

2. Press ⌘-B again.

This step turns off the bold mode. All new text looks normal. (Click off the Bold tool.)

If you already have text on-screen and you want to make it bold, you have to mark it as a block and then make it bold. Follow these steps:

1. Mark the block of text you want to make bold.

Move the toothpick cursor to the beginning of the block; press F8 to turn on block-marking mode; move the cursor to the end of the block. Or you can use the mouse to drag and select the block. The block appears highlighted on-screen.

2. Press ⌘-B.

The block turns bold. (You also can click the Bold tool.)

✔ Everything you type after pressing ⌘-B appears in boldface on-screen and in your printed document. However, if you wander with the toothpick cursor, you may turn off the bold command. My advice is to do this: Press ⌘-B, type bold stuff, press ⌘-B, and type normal stuff.

✔ When the Bold **B** tool (on the Formatting toolbar) is depressed (it's crying or bemoaning something trivial), the character to the left of the toothpick cursor has the bold attribute. (This feature helps when you can't tell whether text on-screen is already bold.)

✔ You can mix and match character formats; text can be bold and italicized or bold and underlined (or, heaven help you, bold and italicized and underlined). To do so, you have to press the proper keys to turn on those formats before typing the text. Yes, this means that you may have to type several Word character-formatting commands before typing your text: ⌘-B, ⌘-I, and ⌘-U for bold, italicized, and underlined text all at once, for example. It's a hassle, but everyone has to do it that way.

✔ You can turn off all character formatting with one stroke by pressing the ⌘-spacebar key combination. Granted, it helps to have a block of format-ted text marked first.

✔ Refer to the section "Marking a Block" in Chapter 6 for more information on marking blocks.

Making Italicized Text

Italics are replacing underlines as the preferred text-emphasis format. I'm not embarrassed to use italics to emphasize or highlight a title because it looks so much better than shabby underlines. Italics simply jump off the page; they're light and wispy, poetic and free. Underlining is what the DMV does when it feels creative.

To italicize your text, follow these steps:

1. Press the ⌘-I key combination.

 Italics mode is on! (You also can click the Italic tool.)

2. Type away to your heart's content!

Watch your delightfully right-leaning text march across the screen. Pat Buchanan, eat your heart out!

3. Press ⌘-I when you're done.

Italics mode is turned off! (Click off the Italic tool.)

If the text you want to italicize is already on-screen, you must mark it as a block and then change its character format to italics. Follow these steps:

1. Mark the block of text you want to italicize.

Do the block-marking thing here. Detailed instructions are offered in Chapter 6 and earlier in this chapter.

2. Press ⌘-I.

 This step italicizes the block. (You also can click the Italic tool.)

> ✔ If you want to double up on a character font — make something italic and bold, for example — you can press both character-formatting keys while you hold down the Control key. Holding down the Control key and pressing I and then B seems to be easier than doing the ⌘-I and ⌘-B dance.
>
> ✔ You also can press ⌘-spacebar to turn italics off, but then you turn off all other formatting as well.

Making Underlined Text

Underlined text just isn't as popular as it used to be. Instead, people now use italicized text for *subtle* emphasis — unless they are writing a paper on <u>War and Peace</u> for that stodgy professor who thinks that all modern influence is of the devil. In that case, underline the title of major literary texts (or at least those by Tolstoy). And always, *always,* italicize titles by Danielle Steele. Everything in between is pretty much a judgment call.

To underline your text, follow these steps:

1. Press the ⌘-U key combination.

This step turns on the underline mode. (You can also click the Underline tool-button thing, on the Formatting toolbar.)

2. Type!

You're now free to type the text you want underlined.

3. Press ⌘-U again.

This step returns you to typing normal text. (Or click off the Underline tool.)

If you already have text on-screen that you want to underline, you have to mark the text as a block and then change its character format to underlined. Here are the steps you take:

1. Mark the block of text you want to underline.

Refer to Chapter 6 or the first section of this chapter for exciting block-marking rules and regulations.

2. Press ⌘-U.

The block is underlined. (Or click the Underline tool.)

✔ After you finish typing underlined text, you can press ⌘-U or click the Underline tool to turn off underlining. You also can press ⌘-spacebar, but then you turn off all other formatting as well.

✔ Chapter 6, the king of the block chapters, contains a section called "Marking a Block," which tells you more about — you guessed it — marking blocks.

Text-Attribute Effects

Bold, italics, and underlining are the most common ways to dress up a character (see the previous sections). However, they are only the beginning of what Word can do for your character formatting. You can use a whole slew of other ⌘-key combinations to slap a different look on your text. Most of this stuff is rather esoteric, so I stuck it in a boring old table (Table 9-1) instead of writing about it with sharp wit in a traditional paragraph.

Table 9-1	Text-Format Samples and Commands
Key Combination	*Applies This Format*
⌘-Shift-A	ALL CAPS
⌘-B	Bold
⌘-Shift-D	<u>Double Underline</u>
⌘-Shift-H	Hidden Text (it doesn't print — shhh!)
⌘-I	*Italics*
⌘-Shift-K	SMALL CAPS
⌘-U	<u>Continuous underline</u>
⌘-Shift-W	<u>Word</u> <u>underline</u>
⌘-=	Subscript
⌘-Shift-=	Superscript
⌘-Shift-Z	Undo character formatting

To apply one of these weird text formats to a character you type or blocked text, refer to the preceding section, "Making Underlined Text," and substitute the proper shortcut from Table 9-1.

Any of these neat-o formatting tricks can also be achieved by opening a dialog box. if you are feeling reckless, powerful, able to leap tall terminals in a single bound, skip ahead to the end of this chapter and read "Doing it the hard way — Taking a Yellow Line bus tour of the Font dialog box." Fair warning: Tying your fingers in knots with key combinations is much safer.

Pressing ⌘-spacebar is the easiest way to recover when your character formatting seems to have gotten rambunctiously encumbered.

Hidden text — what good is that? It's good for you, the writer, to put down some thoughts and then hide them when the document prints. Of course, you don't see the text on-screen either. To find hidden text, you must use the Find command to locate the special hidden-text attribute (see the Chapter 5 section "Finding secret codes"). You have to press the Format button, choose Font, and then click the Hidden box. (This information really should have been hidden to begin with.)

Text-Size Effects

Attributes — bold, italics, underline, and so on — make up only half the available character formats. The other half deal with text size. By using these commands, you can make your text teensy or humongous.

Before getting into this subject, you must become one with the official typesetting term for text size — *point*. It's not point as in *point your finger* or *the point on the top of your head*; it's a measurement of size. One point is equal to $1/72$ inch. Typesetters....

To change the size of text as you type, follow these steps:

1. Get to the point size box on the Formatting toolbar.

Two ways to do this: Click the mouse in the point size box or press ⌘-Shift-P.

2. Type the new point size and press Return.

The text you type from that moment on is in the new size.

If you'd rather not use the keyboard at all, follow these steps:

1. Click the mouse on the down arrow by the font size box.

A list of available font sizes appears, arranged from smallest to largest.

2. Drag through the list and release the mouse button over the size you want.

The text you type from that moment on is in the new size.

Here are some things to remember about setting the point size:

✔ To display the entire gamut of point options for your current font, click on the drop-down button next to the font size box.

✔ Bigger numbers mean bigger text; smaller numbers mean smaller text.

✔ The average point size is 12, or sometimes 10.

✔ TrueType or Adobe Type 1 fonts can be sized from 4 points to 127 points.

✔ The author is 5,112 points tall.

If you want to change the size of text that is already on-screen, you have to mark those characters as a block before modifying the size.

To quickly change the size of a marked block, you can use the following short-cut keys:

⌘-]: Makes text one point size larger

⌘-[: Makes text one point size smaller

There really is no good mnemonic for this feature; you just have to commit it to memory.

Some fonts look ugly in certain point sizes. To ensure that the font looks good, you can use the following shortcut keys:

⌘-Shift->: Makes the font larger in the next "look good" size

⌘-Shift-<: Makes the font smaller in the next "look good" size

Making superscript text

Superscript text sits above the line (for example, the *10* in 2^{10}). To produce this effect, press ⌘-Shift-= (the equal key) and then the text you want to superscript. Or mark a block of text and then press ⌘-Shift-= to superscript the text in the block. To return your text to normal, press ⌘-spacebar.

Here's a reason to be glad for Pepto-Bismol: ⌘-Shift-= is the art of pressing the ⌘ and Shift keys at the same time — which anyone can do after a light lunch — and then pressing the equal key. Actually, Shift-= is the plus key. So this key combination is really ⌘-+. Ugh. I bet that if they made a bigger keyboard, the folks at Microsoft would find things to do with all the keys, no sweat.

Making subscript text

Subscript text sits below the line (for example, the 2 in H_2O). To subscript your text, press ⌘-= (the equal key) and then type away. If you mark a block of text and then press ⌘-=, all the text in the block is subscripted. To return your text to normal, press ⌘-spacebar (the long, bony key under your thumb).

Making Normal Text

Sometimes you have so many character attributes going that you don't know what to press to get back to normal text. This situation can be very frustrating. Fortunately, Word has bent a tiny ear to the cries of help. You can use the Reset Character text-formatting command to shut off everything — size and attribute formats — and return the text to normal. Here's how:

Press ⌘-spacebar, the Reset Character shortcut.

Everything you type from that point on is normal (or at least has the normal attributes).

If you mark a block and then press ⌘-spacebar, all text in the block is returned to normal. Refer to the section "Marking a Block" in Chapter 6 for more information on marking blocks of text.

Pressing ⌘-spacebar does not work on cousin Melvin.

Changing the Font

One of the fun things about Word is its capability to use lots of different fonts. Sure, text can be made bold, italic, underlined, big, little, and on and on, but adjusting the font to match your mood takes expression to an entirely new level.

To switch to a different font, follow these steps:

1. **Arouse the font box, on the Formatting toolbar.**

   Click the down arrow by the box with the mouse or press ⌘-Shift-F.

2. **Type the name of the font your want.**

Of course, sometimes you don't know the name. In that case, you need to drop down the list-o-fonts. Here's how:

1. **Click on the down arrow by the font box.**

   A list of fonts appears in alphabetic order. Any fonts you've recently chosen appear at the top of the list, before the double bar (see Figure 9-1).

2. **Scroll down to the font you want.**

3. **Release the mouse over the font you want.**

Everything you type after choosing a new font appears on-screen in that font. It should print and look the same as well.

If you know the name of the font you want, you can save time by toggling directly to the font window and typing the name of the font in which you want your text to appear. *Caveat:* Word is not lenient on spelling mistakes.

Figure 9-1:
A list of
fonts you
can use in
Word.

You can change a font for text already in your document by first marking the text as a block (refer to Chapter 6) and then choosing the font you want.

The section "Doing It the Hard Way," later in this chapter, contains information on previewing certain fonts, so you can see how they will look before you use them.

Fonts are the responsibility of your Macintosh, though Word does come with a few of its own interesting fonts. You install new fonts by dragging their little suitcase icon into the Fonts folder in your System folder. Thousands of fonts are available, and they work in all your applications. (Some users trade fonts like characters in cheesy sitcoms trade insults; contact a local computer club or scour the back of a computer magazine to look for some cool fonts.)

Changing Case

Upper- and lowercase effects aren't usually considered part of a character's formatting. But still, the geniuses at Microsoft found room in their bustling bag o' Word tricks for a two-fingered command that lets you mix around in the case conversion of your text. And it doesn't even sound like procrastination, huh?

To play with, er, I mean convert the case of a block of text:

1. **Mark the text to convert as a block.**

   Refer to Chapter 6 for the best block-marking advice since the ancient Babylonians.

2. **Press Shift-F3.**

   This step capitalizes the first letter of each word or capitalizes every character in the block or returns them all to their humble, lowercase origins.

3. **Continue pressing Shift-F3 until you have settled on the case you like most.**

   Yes, a veritable cornucopia of case conversion lies at your fingertips. Genie-in-a-key-combo, I like to call it.

Inserting Oddball and Special Characters

Look over your keyboard. Yeah, it contains the letters of the alphabet plus numbers and some weird symbols. Word can display all those characters just fine; you see them on-screen every day.

But there are several dozen to several hundred additional, interesting characters you can display. These Word oddball characters seem to accumulate like coat hangers.

Oddball characters are inserted by using the Insert⇨Symbol command. Here's how you work it:

1. **Position the toothpick cursor where you want the oddball character to appear.**

2. **Choose Insert⇨Symbol.**

   You see the Symbol dialog box, as shown in Figure 9-2. (If the Special Characters panel appears, click the Symbols tab.)

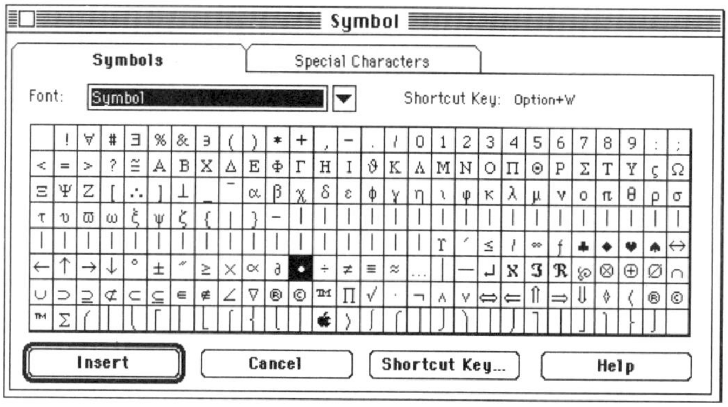

Figure 9-2:
The Symbol
dialog box.

3. Choose the symbol you want.

Point the mouse at the symbol that interests you and then double-click that character. Or you can press the cursor-control keys to move a highlight box around; when you reach the desired symbol, press Return.

4. The oddball character is inserted into your text.

Well, I'll be ©%_&_d!

Here are some tips for inserting special characters:

- ✔ To get a good look at a particular symbol, point the mouse cursor at it and click (and hold down) the mouse button. That one symbol is magnified until you release the mouse button.

- ✔ Some of the fonts that you have installed may appear in the drop-down list at the top of the Symbol dialog box. Typically, only the interesting, symbol-laced fonts show up. To look at other symbols, click the down arrow next to the Font box and choose a different symbol set by clicking on its name. The best symbols can be found in the various Wingdings fonts.

- ✔ Peeking out from behind the Symbol card is the Special Characters card. This card contains more things, kinda like symbols, but more of the kind of stuff an English teacher might use (as opposed to a cursing cartoon character). To access the card, click on the Special Characters tab; then find the symbol you want. Or if you can remember such things and have long, spindly fingers, refer to each character's special key combination.

Doing it the hard way—Taking a Yellow Line bus tour of the Font dialog box

Too many choices can overwhelm you. Most people prefer simple, straightforward information—all the options explained right on a menu, for example, with pictures of what the stuff looks like. Or a smell may waft from two tables over, and you'll point and say, "I want what the nun is having."

Then again, there are times when—if you know what you're doing—you want all the options right there at once. You know which levers you want pulled—the salad dressing and potato fixings and how burnt the meat should be—all at once. For those times, Word offers the rather imposing Font dialog box, a place where you can do almost all your character formatting simultaneously. This dialog box is definitely not for the timid. But exciting and exotic things await. You can make all sorts of text settings there; click OK to apply them to your text (that's any new text you type or text already highlighted on-screen).

To open up the Font dialog box, select Format➪Font, or press ⌘-D. All sorts of interesting things happen here, depending on where you get off the bus:

Day 1	Font	If you click on the drop-down list under the word Font, you see the name of every font known to your copy of Word. There may be anywhere from a handful to a kabillion of them. If you highlight the name of one, a sample appears in the Preview (or *sneak-peak*) box.
Day 2	Font Style	Choose from Regular, *Italic,* **Bold**, **Bold Italic,** and, if you're in Seattle, Double-Decaffeinated Latté!
Day 3	Size	If you click on the drop-down list under Size, you see all available sizes of the font in question. The available sizes usually run from 4 points to 127 points, or from teensy-weensy to awfully big.
Day 4	Underline	Choose either <u>a single continuous underline</u>, a <u>double continuous underline</u>, a dotted continuous underline, or <u>to underline</u> <u>only the words</u>.
Day 5	Color	Create text in living color by choosing a new color from the Color drop-down list. The color shows on-screen only if you have a color monitor, and it prints only if you have a color printer.
Day 6	Effects	~~Strikethrough~~, Superscript, Subscript, Hidden text, SMALL CAPS, or ALL CAPS.

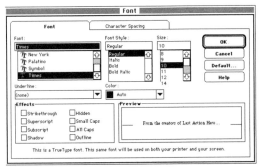

A bonus afternoon excursion to the Character Spacing panel

If you're willing to pay extra, click on the Character Spacing tab to see the panel that is hiding behind the main Font panel. (This panel stuff is really batty. If you're new to it, get used to it. It's a preview of how all Microsoft applications will look in the future. O, aren't we lucky?)

1:35 p.m. Spacing   Enables you to condense or expand the letters in your text as necessary.

2:15 p.m. Position   Your text may ^{rise} above the crowds or $_{sink}$ to new depths. Sounds pretty much like superscripting and subscripting, huh? But it's not. It's brand-new technology thought up by those genius developers over at Microsoft. Brand-new. Really!

3:10 p.m. Kerning   *Kerning* is the process of making juice drinks. In Word, it refers to how snugly letters hug each other — really advanced typesetter stuff, but WHOOMP! — there it is. If you're willing, you can make the kerning for fonts above the indicated Points and Above size automatic. Big deal. My advice is to leave well enough alone.

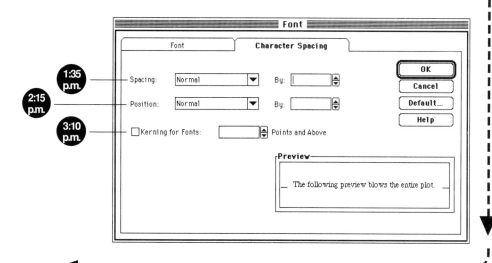

The 5th Wave   By Rich Tennant

THAT'S RIGHT, THE UPPER CASE BUTTON WORKS ON-SCREEN, BUT THEY'RE NOT COMING OUT ON THE DANG PRINTER! HOLD? SURE, I'LL HOLD.

Poet e.e. cummings makes his last service call.

Chapter 10
Formatting Sentences and Paragraphs

. . . .

In This Chapter

▶ Centering text

▶ Flushing text right

▶ Changing line spacing

▶ Indenting a paragraph

▶ Double-indenting a paragraph

▶ Making a hanging indent

▶ A paragraph-formatting survival guide

▶ The tab stops here

▶ The fearless leader tabs

▶ Doing it the hard way — taking a Yellow Line bus tour of the Paragraph dialog box

. . . .

A character is the most basic thing that you can format. But with Word, you also can format sentences and paragraphs: you can center them, shove them to the left or right, riddle them with tab stops, and space them far enough apart so as not to offend anything.

This stuff can be done on the fly, but I recommend doing it just before printing (along with page formatting — see Chapter 11) or by including the formatting in a style sheet (see Chapter 14). That way, you will pull out only half your hair while you struggle with spelling and grammar and getting your ideas on paper.

Of course, when the document is perfect, you usually wind up pulling out the rest of your hair and sending your blood pressure through the roof while you struggle anew with line and paragraph formatting. (Ugh. Will it never end?) Look at the bright side: No more tedious trips to the barber.

If you want to learn to access all sentence and paragraph formatting through menus, turn to "Doing it the hard way — taking a Yellow Line bus tour of the Paragraph dialog box," at the end of this chapter.

Centering Text

Word lets you *center* a single line of text or an entire block of text. If you do this, your text is miraculously centered down the middle of the page on-screen and when printed. Another miracle of modern computing.

If you want to center just a single line, follow these steps:

1. **Start on a new line, the line you want to be centered.**

   If the line is already on-screen, no doubt waiting impatiently, skip to the next set of numbered instructions.

2. **Press ⌘-E, the Center command.**

   I know that *E* doesn't mean *center* in your brain. But the word *center* does have two *es*. How about *E* means *equator?* Nah, that goes side to side. I give up.

    You also can center text by clicking the Center tool, on the Formatting toolbar. The tool looks like the thing you yell into when you order burgers at a drive-thru.

3. **The cursor zips over to the center of the screen (or thereabouts).**

4. **Type your title or heading.**

5. **Press Return when you're done.**

 If you want to center more than a line (a paragraph or more, for example), keep typing. When you tire of seeing your text centered, press ⌘-L to return to *left justification* (or click the Align Left tool). (Left justification is the way text normally appears in Word: everything aligns at the left margin.)

Follow these steps to center text that's already in your document:

1. **Mark as a block the text you want to center.**

   Refer to Chapter 6 for the best block-marking directions you'll ever read in a computer book.

2. **Press ⌘-E.**

    The blocked text, along with any paragraph it is in, is promptly centered. (You also can click the Center tool.)

- ✔ The Center command, ⌘-E, centers paragraphs only. If you want to center just one line at a time, you must end each line by pressing Return — making that single line a paragraph.

- ✔ The easiest way to accomplish quick paragraph formatting, such as centering, is to use the tool buttons, on the Formatting toolbar (also known as the ribbon). Just click one instead of pressing ⌘-E, ⌘-L, or whatever and your text will be formatted accordingly.

- ✔ To _justify_ text — that's when text aligns at the left _and_ right margins — click the Justify tool or press ⌘-J.

Flushing Text Right

Flush right describes text that aligns at the right margin. In other words, _flush right_ is when all the text is slammed against the right side of the page — like what happens when you pick up a piece of paper and jerk it wildly until the text slides over. (You'll soon discover that a lot of flushing occurs in paragraph formatting.) Text is usually _flush left_, with each line aligning at the left margin.

You can right-align a single paragraph of text (even if it's only a single line) or mark any size of text as a block and flush it right. If you want to flush a single paragraph, follow these steps:

1. **Position the toothpick cursor where you want to type a paragraph flush right.**

   The cursor is on the left side of the screen; this is OK. Don't press the spacebar or Tab key to move the cursor; the Flush Right command moves everything in just a second. If the text you want to flush right is already on-screen, skip to the next set of numbered instructions.

2. **Press ⌘-R, the Flush Right command.**

   Golly, _R_ equals _right._ This is amazing.

   The cursor skips on over to the right margin, on the right side of the screen. (You also can click the Align Right button, on the Formatting toolbar.)

3. **Type your paragraph and then press Return.**

   The characters push right, always staying flush with the right side of the document. It's like writing in Hebrew!

4. **Press ⌘-L to return to left-justified text when you're done.**

   Or press the Align Left tool.

For flushing right more than a single paragraph of text that you already have in your document, you have to mark it all as a block. Follow these steps:

1. Mark as a block the text you want to flush right.

Chapter 6 has block-marking details to soothe your furrowed brow.

2. Press ⌘-R.

You see the text zip over to the right margin. Og say block flush right. Block good. (You also can click the Align Right tool.)

✔ Be careful not to flush large objects, cardboard, or other foreign objects when you're adjusting your text. Do not flush while the train is parked at the station.

✔ *Flush right* is a design term that means the same thing as *right aligned* or *right justified*.

✔ Typographers use words other than *justification*. They occasionally use the word *ragged* to describe how text fits. For example, left justification is also *ragged right*; right justification is also *ragged left*. A *rag top* is a convertible with a soft top, and a *rag bottom* is any child still in diapers.

Flushing your dates right

A good thing to flush right is the date. Most people start their letters this way. To flush right the date at the top of a document, follow these handy steps:

1. Move the toothpick cursor to the line where you want to put the date. This must be a blank line.

2. Press ⌘-R, the Flush Right command. The cursor zooms over to the right side of the page.

3. Press Control-Shift-D to insert the current date into your document. (No need to memorize this command; just flag this page.)

4. Press Return.

5. Press ⌘-L to go back to left justification.

As you continue writing, the current date sits proudly flushed right at the top of the page.

Changing Line Spacing

On a typewriter, you change the line spacing with a double or triple whack of the carriage return. Sadly, although whacking your computer twice or thrice helps your attitude, it doesn't do diddly for your document's line spacing. Instead, you have to use Word's Line Spacing command.

To change the line spacing for new text, you have three options:

1. **Press ⌘-1 (that's a one, not an L) for single-spaced lines.**

1¹/₂. **Press ⌘-5 (that's a five, not an S) for 1¹/₂-spaced lines.**

   The 1¹/₂-spacing means that your lines are between single- and double-spacing — which gives editors and teachers less room to mark up your stuff but still lets in all that "air" that makes the text readable.

2. **Press ⌘-2 (that's a two, not a Z) for double-spaced lines.**

   Double-spacing is often required by fussy editors who, without enough room in their precious 1-inch margins, want to write under, over, and between what you write.

You can quickly change the spacing of a paragraph that is already on-screen by placing the toothpick cursor anywhere in the paragraph and pressing the magical key combinations!

The ⌘-1, ⌘-2, and ⌘-5 shortcuts also affect any block marked on-screen. Refer to Chapter 6 for information on marking a block.

⌘-5 means 1¹/₂-line spacing, not 5-line spacing.

Unnecessary, more-specific spacing stuff

If you want line spacing other than single, double, or 1¹/₂, choose Format➪Paragraph. The Paragraph dialog box opens (which I detail at the end of this chapter). Make sure that the Indents and Spacing panel is in front. Choose Exactly in the Line Spacing box and enter the measurement you want in the At box.

To triple-space lines, for example, choose Exactly under Line Spacing and type 3 li in the At box. This action sets the spacing to 3 lines ('cause in Word a *li* is the same as a *line*). If you don't type li, Word may use pt (which stands for *points*) or maybe even some other aggravating typesetting measurement. My advice is to keep it in your brain to type li for line; leave the points for the seller to worry about.

Indenting a Paragraph

To make a paragraph of text feel good about itself, you can indent it, making it stand out on the page. It says: "Hey, notice me! Can I talk here? Please stop interrupting, Mr. Vice President." Naturally, all paragraphs clamor for this recognition, but you have to be selective.

Indenting a paragraph doesn't mean just indenting its first line, which you can do with the Tab key. Instead, you can indent, or *nest,* the entire paragraph by aligning its left edge against a tab stop. Here's how you do it:

1. **Move the toothpick cursor anywhere in the paragraph.**

   If the paragraph hasn't been written yet, move the cursor to where you want to write the new text.

2. **Press ⌘-M, the Indent shortcut.**

   Ummm — indent! Ummm — indent! Say it over and over. It kinda works. (You also can click the Increase Indent button, on the Formatting toolbar.)

3. **Type your paragraph (if you haven't already).**

   If the paragraph is blocked, it is indented to the next tab stop.

Keep these tips in mind when you're indenting paragraphs:

✔ To return indented text to its original margin, Press ⌘-Shift-M or, heck, ⌘-Z, the Undo command (which is why it's there). You also can click the Decrease Indent tool.

✔ To indent the paragraph to the next tab stop, press ⌘-M again.

✔ Although the ⌘-M and ⌘-Shift-M shortcuts aren't mnemonic, the only difference between them is a Shift key. So when you get used to using them, they're easy to remember.

✔ To indent both the right and left sides of a paragraph, see the following section, "Double-Indenting a Paragraph." Also check out the section "Making a Hanging Indent," later in this chapter.

If you're in a fair mood, refer to the section "The Tab Stops Here," later in this chapter, for information on setting tab stops.

Double-Indenting a Paragraph

Sometimes an indent on the left just isn't enough. There are those days when you need to suck a paragraph in twice: once on the left and once on the right. You may want to double-dip, for example, when you lift a quote from another paper but don't want to be accused of plagiarism. I do this to Abe Lincoln all the time.

When I quote ol' Abe, I follow these steps:

1. **Move the toothpick cursor to the beginning of the paragraph.**

   If the paragraph hasn't been written yet, move the cursor to where you want to write the new text.

2. **Choose Format⇨Paragraph.**

   The Paragraph dialog box appears. Make sure that the Indents and Spacing panel is in front. In the upper-left region is the Indentation area, which contains three items: Left, Right, and Special.

3. **Enter the amount of left and right indentation.**

   Click in the Left box. Type a value, such as **.5** (to indent the paragraph $\frac{1}{2}$ inch). Then click in the Right box (or press Tab once) and type **.5** again. This step indents your paragraph $\frac{1}{2}$ inch from the left and right.

   You also can click the up and down arrows that cling to the right side of the Left and Right boxes to spin numbers up and down.

4. **Click OK or press Return.**

5. **Type your paragraph if you haven't already.**

✔ The Paragraph dialog box is given a shave and a haircut at the end of this chapter.

✔ Obviously, a double-indented paragraph should be inhaled equally from the left and right sides of the page; the numbers in the Left and Right boxes should be the same.

✔ When you modify a paragraph in the Paragraph dialog box, check out the Preview box, at the bottom of the panel. Your paragraph's format is shown in dark ink on the sample page.

✔ To indent only the left side of a paragraph, refer to the preceding section, "Indenting a Paragraph."

Making a Hanging Indent

A hanging indent has committed no felonious crime. Instead, it's a paragraph in which the first line sticks out to the left while the rest of the paragraph is indented — the paragraph looks like an upside-down baseball cap or a side view of a high-diving board. To create such a beast, follow these steps:

1. **Move the toothpick cursor into the paragraph you want to hang and indent.**

   Or you can position the cursor to where you want to type a new, hanging-indent paragraph.

2. **Press ⌘-T, the Hanging Indent shortcut.**

   Ta-da! The Hanging Indent shortcut keeps the first line in place but moves the rest of the paragraph over to the first tab stop.

   ✔ 'Tis easy to remember ⌘-T because the Brits always hang felons a tad before Tea Time.

   ✔ If you want to indent the paragraph even more, press the ⌘-T key more than once.

   ✔ See the section "Indenting a Paragraph," earlier in this chapter, for more information on indenting paragraphs.

   ✔ To undo a hanging indent, press ⌘-Shift-T (that's the unhang key combination); your paragraph's neck will be put back in shape.

   ✔ Hanging indents depend on the placement of tab stops. See the following section, "The Tab Stops Here," for help with tabs.

The Tab Stops Here

When you press the Tab key, indent a paragraph, or make a hanging indent, Word moves the cursor or text over to the next *tab stop.* Normally, the tab stops are set every half inch. You can change this setting to any interval or even customize the tab stops. Follow these steps:

1. **Position the toothpick cursor to a place in the document before the position where you want to change the tabs.**

   If you want to change the tab stops in more than one paragraph, mark the paragraphs you want to change. Refer to Chapter 6 for block-marking instructions.

2. **Click on the ruler where you want a new tab stop.**

   The mouse pointer changes into an arrow shape when it's not hovering over text. Point that pointer at the spot on the ruler where you want your new tab stop to appear.

   After clicking, a little, bold corner — a plump L — appears and marks the tab-stop location.

3. **Modify or fine-tune the tab-stop position by dragging the tab indicator to the left or right with the mouse.**

   ✔ If you don't see the ruler on-screen, choose View⇨Ruler.

   ✔ If you decide that you don't want the new tab stop after all, drag it off the ruler altogether; that is, grab it with the mouse and drag it up or down. Thwoop! It's gone.

   ✔ When I'm working with a lot of tabs, I usually press the Tab key only once between each column of information. Then I select all the paragraphs and drag the tab indicators around so that each of my columns aligns. Using one tab instead of two or three is much easier to edit. And it lets me do fancy stuff, like sorting and math. You can read more about this neat-o stuff in Chapter 12.

Paragraph-formatting survival guide

This table contains all the paragraph-formatting commands you can summon by holding down ⌘ and pressing a letter or number. By no means should you memorize this list.

Key Combo	Does This to Paragraphs	Key Combo	Does This to Paragraphs
⌘-E	Centers	⌘-T	Makes a hanging indent
⌘-J	Fully justifies	⌘-Shift-T	Unhangs the indent
⌘-L	Left-aligns (flush left)	⌘-1	Single-spaces lines
⌘-R	Right-aligns (flush right)	⌘-2	Double-spaces lines
⌘-M	Indents	⌘-5	Makes 1½-space lines
⌘-Shift-M	Unindents		

Meddlesome nonsense about tab types

Word uses four different types of tabs, as depicted by four different icons that can appear on the far left side of the ruler. Whichever one you see determines which types of tabs are set. This list shows what each type does:

The most common tab is the left tab, the plump L. This tab works like the Tab key on a typewriter: Press Tab and the new text appears at the next tab stop. No mental hang-ups here.

The right tab causes text to line up right-justified at that tab stop. This tab gives you leeway to do some fancy paragraph justification on a single line, which you can read about in Chapter 23.

The center tab stop centers text on the tab stop. Good for one-word columns.

The decimal tab aligns numbers by their decimals. The number is right-justified before you press . and then left-justified on the decimal.

The Fearless Leader Tabs

The leader tab, which is interesting but not required for most writing, produces a row of dots when you press Tab. You see this all the time in indexes or tables of contents. Word lets you choose from three different leaders:

To choose from among the different types of tabs, follow these steps:

1. Position the toothpick cursor on the line where you want a leader tab.

For example, you're just starting your table of contents for this year's family-reunion newsletter.

2. Set a tab stop.

This step is important. Follow the steps outlined in the section "The Tab Stops Here," earlier in this chapter. Stick the tab where you want it. For example, to put a tab under the 3 on the ruler — sticking a tab in just about the middle of the page — click under the 3 with the mouse. You see a left tab stop appear there on the ruler.

3. Choose Format⇨Tabs.

You see the Tabs dialog box, shown in Figure 10-1. Door number 3, Leader, is where you need to focus.

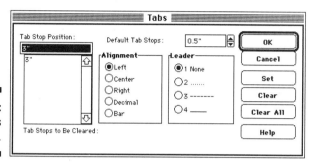

Figure 10-1:
The Tabs
dialog box.

4. Choose the style of fearless leader tab you want.

Click on the appropriate style. Or, to choose a style by using the keyboard, press ⌘-1 through ⌘-4.

5. Click the OK button or press Return.

6. Type the text to appear before the tab stop.

For example, type **Ugly baby pics from the '50s.**

7. Press Tab.

Zwoop! The toothpick cursor jumps to your tab stop and leaves a trail of, well, *stuff* in its wake. Stuff is the technical term for dot leader (or dash leader or underline leader).

8. Type the reference, page number, whatever.

9. Press Return to end the line.

✔ Setting the dot leader tabs doesn't work unless you manually stick in your own tab stops, as discussed in the section "The Tab Stops Here," earlier in this chapter.

✔ You can adjust the tab stops after setting them if some of the text doesn't line up.

✔ Using the right tab right-aligns your dot-leader-tabbed items. (The right tab is the backwards L dojobbie; refer to the "Meddlesome nonsense about tab types" sidebar.)

Doing it the hard way — Taking a Yellow Line bus tour of the Paragraph dialog box

It's possible to get all your paragraph formatting done in one place, just as I'm sure that the Lord Almighty has this one control panel from which He directs the universe. And like that control panel, the Paragraph dialog box is a complex and dangerous place in which to loiter.

To summon the Paragraph dialog box, choose Format⇨Paragraph. It should open up with the Indents and Spacing panel on top. A panel to help you unravel the mysteries of Text Flow lies underneath. To flip back and forth between panels, click on the tabs.

Most of the stuff that happens in the Paragraph dialog box is described elsewhere in this chapter; I also point out the shortcut key combos that enable you to avoid this dialog box. Still, I'll be sent to Word prison and, worse, laughed at during the next Word Book Authors' Convention (WOBAC) if I don't take you on a whirlwind bus tour of this dialog box. We begin with the Indents and Spacing card:

Day 1 — Indentation: Here's where you can enter the formatting for nested paragraphs and hanging indents. Left indicates how far from the left margin your paragraph will be in inches. Right is how far from the right margin your paragraph will be in inches. You can choose Special to either indent or hang the first line of your paragraph. You can type values in the boxes or use the tiny up or down triangles to "spin the wheels."

Day 2 — Spacing: Hmmm, you hum. "OK, I press Return at the end of a *paragraph*. But how can I put extra space between paragraphs?" This is the place. Before and After allow you to stick extra lines before or after your paragraphs. If you type .5 li in the Before box, for example, Word puts an extra half line before each paragraph. The same process applies for After. The Line Spacing box controls the line spacing for a paragraph; type the proper spacing value in the box or use the up or down triangles to wheel through the values.

Day 3 — Alignment: You can apply any of the following alignments to selected text or to the paragraph where the cursor is currently located: Left, Center, Right, or Justified. Each alignment is discussed earlier in this chapter.

Day 4 — Preview: The Preview window shows you how your paragraph will look after you click the OK button; your text changes are shown as black lines, and current text is shown in gray.

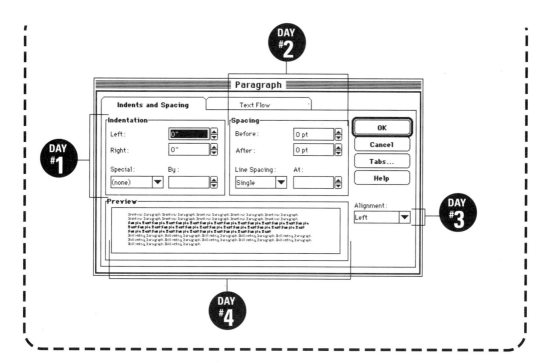

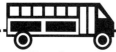

Optional walking tour (trail gear recommended)

"How do you get to the Text Flow panel?" "Practice, practice, practice." Or click on the Text Flow tab, shyly peering out from behind Indents and Spacing.

During this part of the trip, please keep within sight of your trail guide. (He was once named Outback Hunk of Montana, and rumor has it that he's part Sasquatch.) I say this for your own safety.

Trail 1 — Pagination: These sophisticated commands tell Word where it is allowed to start a new page. Page Break Before tells Word to start a new page before this paragraph. Keep With Next tells Word that it can't start a new page just yet. Keep Lines Together tells Word not to start a new page in the middle of the paragraph. Widow/Orphan control keeps the last/first line from being stranded alone on the preceding/next page.

Trail 2 — Misfits: Suppress Line Numbers prevents Word from numbering the lines in a given paragraph if you've ordered the rest of a document to have numbered lines. Don't Hyphenate tells Word not to hyphenate that particular paragraph when you've directed Word to hyphenate the rest of a document.

(continued)

(continued)

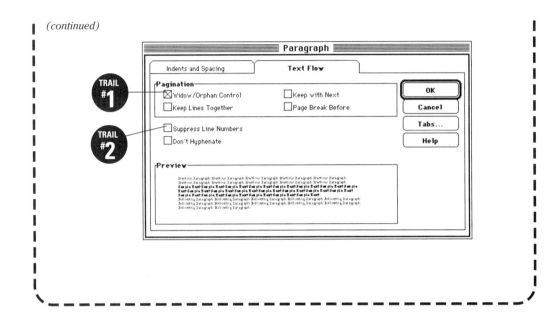

Chapter 11

Formatting Pages and Documents

*A*t last, the formatting three-ring circus has come to this. Formatting pages and documents isn't as common as formatting characters or even formatting paragraphs. This major-league stuff affects your entire document, and it can be really handy: headers and footers, page numbers, even footnotes. This is the stuff of which professional-looking documents are made. This chapter explains it all so carefully that even we amateurs fool them.

Starting a New Page — a Hard Page Break

There are two ways to start a new page in Word:

✔ Keep pressing the Return key until you see the row o' dots that denotes the start of a new page. Needless to say, this method is tacky and wrong.

✔ Press Shift-Enter, the hard page break key combination: you see a tighter row of dots, also denoting the beginning of a new page. And, in case you can't tell the difference between rows of dots, Word adds the notation *Page Break* to remind you that the hard page break is artificial (see Figure 11-1). This is the preferred method for starting a new page.

Figure 11-1:
A Word hard
page break.

·······························Page Break·······························

Keep these things in mind when you're dealing with hard page breaks:

- ✔ The hard page break works just like a regular page break does, except you control where it falls in your document.

- ✔ To insert a hard page break, press Shift-*Enter*, not Shift-Return. You must use the Enter key here. This is one of those rare instances when Enter and Return behave differently.

- ✔ Pressing Shift-Enter inserts a hard page break *character* in your document. That character stays in place, always creating a hard page break — no matter how much you edit the text on previous pages.

- ✔ You can delete a hard page break by pressing the Delete or Del key. If you do this accidentally, just press Shift-Enter again, or you can press ⌘-Z to undelete.

Taking a Break — a Section Break

Books have chapters and parts to break up major plot lines. Formatting has something called a *section break* that serves the same function. Word uses several kinds of breaks: page breaks, column breaks, and section breaks, but not lunch breaks.

You can use a section break when you want to apply different types of formatting to several different parts of a document. You may want different margins to appear in different places, a banner headline, different numbers of columns, whatever. You can ensure that parts of your document are formatted differently by inserting a section break. It's kinda like building an island: All types of weird formatting can live on it, isolated from the rest of the document.

No, this isn't a common, everyday thing, but if you get heavily into formatting pages, you'll be thankful for it.

To insert a section break, do this:

1. **Position the toothpick cursor where you want the break to occur.**

2. **Choose Insert⇨Break.**

    The Break dialog box opens, as shown in Figure 11-2.

Figure 11-2:
The Break
dialog box.

3. Choose your section break.

Click on Next Page if you want the new section to start on a fresh page. Choose Continuous if you want the break to happen wherever you happen to be. Choose Next Page, for example, to center text on a title page (see the section "Centering a page, top to bottom," later in this chapter). Continuous is used for all other circumstances.

4. Choose OK.

A double line of dots appears on-screen with the notation End of Section in the middle (see Figure 11-3). Lo, you have your section break, and new formatting can begin.

Figure 11-3:
A Word
section
break.

=================================End of Section=================================

Section breaks also provide a great way to divide a multipart document. For example, you can format the title page, the introduction, Chapter 1, and Appendix A as different sections.

You can use Word's Go To command to zoom to a section. Refer to Chapter 2 for more information on the Go To command.

Here are some tips for dealing with section breaks:

✔ The key combination for doing a Next Page section break is ⌘-Enter.

✔ You can delete a section break with the Delete key. When you do this, however, you lose any special formatting that you applied to the section. If you delete a section break accidentally, press ⌘-Z, the Undo command, before you do anything else.

✔ You can also use the Break dialog box to insert a Page Break, but pressing Shift-Enter is much quicker; refer to the preceding section.

Adjusting the Margins

Every page has margins. This is the "air" around your document — that breathing space that sets off the text from the rest of the page. Word automatically sets your margins at 1 inch from the right, left, top, and bottom of the page. Most English teachers and book editors want things like this because they love to scribble in margins. But you can adjust the margins to suit any fussy professional.

You have two basic choices when setting margins: from here on and change it all.

To change the margins, follow these steps:

1. **If you want to change "from here on," move the toothpick cursor to the place in your text where you want the new margins to start. (If, on the other hand, you want to "change it all," it doesn't matter where you place the cursor.)**

   It's best to set new margins at the top of the document, top of a page, beginning of a paragraph, or beginning of a section.

2. **Choose File⇨Document Layout.**

   The Document Layout dialog box appears, as shown in Figure 11-4.

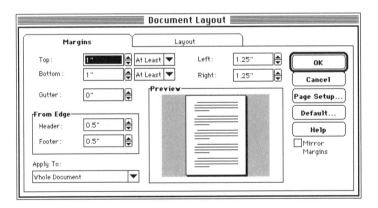

Figure 11-4: The Document Layout dialog box with the Margins panel up front.

3. **Click on the Margins tab if the Layout panel is in front.**

4. **Enter the new measurements for the margins by typing new values in the appropriate boxes.**

   For example, typing **1** in all boxes sets all margins to one inch. Entering a value of **2.5** sets a 2 1/2-inch margin. There's no need to type the inch symbol (").

5. From the Apply To drop-down list, choose Whole Document or This Point Forward.

Whole Document applies the new margins to your document ("changes it all"). This Point Forward applies new margins from the toothpick cursor's position to the last jot or title you typed ("from here on").

6. Choose OK.

Your new margins appear.

Yo! Check it out! You have visual feedback on-screen regarding your new margin settings. The Preview window shows you what the document will look like when the changes are finally made.

You don't have to change all the margins every time. If you want to adjust only one or a few values, leave the other items alone; Word remembers the old values and keeps using them until they're changed.

What's in the gutter? The Gutter box applies to documents intended to be bound in a booklike format. It's a bonus margin that appears on the left side of right-facing pages and vice versa. No need to put your mind in the gutter.

Here are some tips to keep in mind when you're setting margins:

- ✔ If you want to change the margins to a different value later and leave the current settings in place for the first part of your document, move to where you want new margins. Start at Step 1 in the preceding numbered list and choose This Point Forward from the Apply To drop-down list. A single document can have several margin changes, just as a single driver on the freeway may change lanes several times.

- ✔ Laser printers cannot print on the outside half inch of a piece of paper — top, bottom, left, and right. This half inch is an *absolute margin*: although you can tell Word to set a margin of 0 inches right and 0 inches left, text still does not print there. Instead, choose .5 inches minimum for the margins.

- ✔ If you want to print on three-hole paper, set the left margin to 2 or 2.5 inches. This setting allows enough room for the little holes, and it offsets the text nicely when you open up something in a three-ring notebook or binder.

- ✔ If your homework comes out to three pages and the teacher wants four, bring in the margins (but don't tell Mrs. Bradshaw). For example, set the left and right margins to 1.5 inches each. And then change the line spacing to 1 $1/2$. Refer to the section "Changing the Line Spacing," in Chapter 10. (You also can choose a larger font; check out the section on text size effects in Chapter 9.)

Setting the Page Size

Most printing takes place on a standard, 8 1/2-by-11-inch sheet of paper. But Word lets you change the paper size to anything you want — from an envelope to some weird-size sheet of paper. The following steps describe how you change the paper size to legal size (8 1/2-by-14 inches):

1. **Position the toothpick cursor at the top of your document or at the top of a page for which you want to start using the new paper size.**

2. **Choose File⇨Page Setup.**

   The Page Setup dialog box appears.

3. **Choose the Paper Size from the list at the top of the dialog box.**

   Four sizes are shown right away: US Letter, US Legal, and the funky A4 and B5 European paper sizes. A drop-down list enables you to choose other sizes. Click on the paper size you want.

   Printing on legal paper? Click that button. It's legal.

4. **Choose Whole Document or This Point Forward from the Apply Size and Orientation To drop-down list.**

   Well, which do you want?

5. **Choose OK.**

   OK. Type away on the new size of paper.

Here are some tips to keep in mind when you're setting page size:

✔ The Paper Size drop-down list may not contain the measurements for your paper (for example, when you want to print a love letter on that new, pretty, and perfumed, albeit odd-sized, stationery). In that case, click on the Custom button; then get out your trusty old ruler and type the paper's proper measurements in the Width and Height boxes.

✔ In the following section, I tell you how to print sideways on a sheet of paper. This technique really fools the relatives into thinking that you're a word-processing genius.

✔ If you're printing on an odd-sized piece of paper, remember to load it into your printer before you start printing.

✔ Refer to Chapter 8 for information on printing envelopes. There's a special command for doing that.

Landscape and Portrait

Word usually prints up and down on a piece of paper — which is how we're all used to reading a page. However, Word can print sideways also. In this case, the page's *orientation* is changed. The technical "I'm an important word-processing expert" terms for the two orientations are *Portrait mode* (up-down) and *Landscape mode* (sideways). A portrait picture is usually taller than it is long to accommodate our faces — my Aunt Bette and her offspring excepted. Landscape is for those lovely oil paintings of seascapes that are wider than they are tall.

To make Word print in Landscape mode, do the following:

1. Choose File⇨Page Setup.

The Page Setup dialog box appears.

2. Look for the Orientation buttons.

They're shown in Figure 11-5.

Figure 11-5:
The orientation buttons tell Word which way the paper goes.

3. Choose Portrait or Landscape.

The Sample document and the tiny icon in the Orientation area change to reflect your perspective.

4. Click OK.

Avoid printing standard documents in Landscape mode. Scientists and other people in white lab coats who study such things have determined that human reading speed slows drastically when people must scan a long line of text. Reserve Landscape mode for printing lists and items for which normal paper is too narrow.

Centering a page, top to bottom

Nothing makes a title nice and crisp like having it sit squat in the middle of a page. That's top-to-bottom middle as opposed to left-to-right middle. To achieve this feat, follow these steps:

1. **Move the toothpick cursor to the top of the page where you want the title and type the text (or move to the top of the page that contains the text that you want centered from top to bottom).**

   A title should be on a page by itself — actually, a section by itself.

2. **Create a new section break.**

   If the text that you want centered isn't on the first page of the document, press ⌘-Enter to insert a section break (you see a double line on-screen).

   You also have to mark the end of the text you want centered with a section break: move the toothpick cursor to the end of the text and press ⌘-Enter again. Then move the cursor back to the text you want centered.

3. **Choose File⇨Document Layout.**

   The Document Layout dialog box appears.

4. **Click on the Layout tab.**

   This action brings forward the Layout panel if it's not up front to begin with. You should focus your laser beams on the upper-right corner, in the area roped in and named Vertical Alignment.

5. **Select Center from the Vertical Alignment drop-down list.**

6. **Click OK.**

In Normal view, you get no visual feedback that you've centered a page on-screen. Choose View⇨Page Layout to get a sneak peak at the centered page. (You may have to Zoom out to see the titled centered; see Chapter 23 to learn about the Zoom command.) Choose View⇨Normal to return to Normal view.

All text on the page is centered from top to bottom with the Center Page command. It's a good idea to keep as little text on the page as possible — a title, description, and so forth.

Refer to the section "Taking a Break — a Section Break," earlier in this chapter, for more information on section breaks.

Refer to Chapter 9 for more information on formatting characters, such as making text big and fancy or whatnot.

If you also want your title text centered from left to right, refer to Chapter 10 for information on centering a line.

Where to Stick the Page Number

If your document is more than a page long, you should put page numbers on it. Word can do this for you automatically, so stop putting those forced page numbers in your document and follow these steps:

1. **Choose Insert⇨Page Numbers.**

   The Page Numbers dialog box appears (see Figure 11-6).

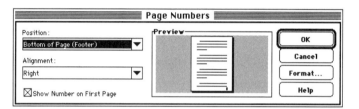

Figure 11-6:
The Page
Numbers
dialog box.

2. **Where doest thou wantest thine page numbers?**

   From the Position drop-down list, choose Top of Page (Header) or Bottom of Page (Footer). From the Alignment drop-down list, choose Left, Center, Right, Inside, or Outside. There are many different possible placements for your page numbering. Ponder this situation carefully and keep an eye on the Preview box — a slight change can alter drastically the power of your document.

3. **Choose OK.**

   The page numbers are inserted.

You also can create page numbering by sticking the page number command in a header or footer. See the following section, "Adding a header or footer." If you put the page number in a header or footer, you do not have to use the Page Numbers command.

If you want to employ fancier page numbers, click the Format button in the Page Numbers dialog box. This step opens the Page Number Format dialog box. From there, you can select various ways to display the page numbers from the Number Format drop-down list — even those cute little *ii*s and *xx*s.

To start numbering your pages with a new page number, click the Format button in the Page Numbers dialog box. This step opens the Page Number Format dialog box. Click the Start At radio button and then type in the corresponding box the number that you want to begin with or press the arrows to wheel up and down. This procedure is something that you may want to do for the second, third, or later chapters in a book. By setting a new page number, the page numbers in all chapters are continuous.

Adding a header or footer

A *header* is not a quickly poured beer. Rather, it's text that runs along the top of every page in your document; it may include title, author, date, page number, even dirty limericks. For example, the top of each left-hand page in this book has the part name and the top of each right-hand page has the chapter name.

A *footer* is text that appears on the bottom of every page. A great footer is "Turn the page, dummy." Some footers include page numbers, chapter title, document title, and what-have-you. You add a footer in exactly the same way as you create a header.

To add a header or footer, follow these steps:

1. **Choose View⇨Header and Footer.**

   The document window changes and you're given a sneak peek at your document's header (or footer), roped off with the title Header (or Footer) in the left corner. Also visible is the floating Header and Footer toolbar. Witness Figure 11-7 for an example.

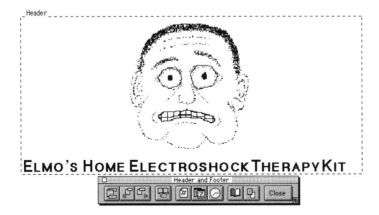

Figure 11-7: A sample header with graphic.

2. **Click the Switch Between Header/Footer icon to toggle between the Header and Footer for editing.**

3. **Enter your header or footer text.**

   The text can also be formatted just as though it were a separate document by using most of the tools in the Standard and Formatting toolbars.

4. **Use the buttons in the Header and Footer toolbar for adding special items.**

   Hover the mouse pointer over each one to see a brief explanation of its function (just like in the big toolbars!). These buttons are described in detail in the sidebar "The Header and Footer toolbar unbuttoned."

5. Click the Close button when you're done.

 You're back in your document. The header and/or footer are/is there, but you can't see it/them until 1) you print, 2) choose the Print Preview command from the File menu (or click the Preview button, on the Standard toolbar), or 3) view your document in Page Layout view.

 You can put anything in a header or footer that you can put in a document, including graphics. This capability is especially useful if you want a logo to appear on each page. See Chapter 20 for a discussion of inserting graphics.

Here are some tips for adding headers or footers:

 ✔ If you want to insert the page number in the header or footer, put the toothpick cursor where you want the page number to appear and click the Page Numbers button, on the Header and Footer toolbar. The current page number appears in the header text.

✔ If you're a kind author, you probably will want to put some text in front of the page number because a number sitting all by itself tends to get lonely. You can get real creative and type the word **Page** and a space before you click the Page Numbers button, or you can come up with some interesting text on your own.

✔ To insert the current date or time into the header or footer, click the Date or Time buttons, on the Header and Footer toolbar.

 ✔ To see your header or footer displayed on-screen, choose View⇨Page Layout. In Page Layout view, you can see your header or footer, but they appear washed out—in not very appealing gray text. Choose View⇨Normal to return to the normal way you look at Word.

You can have two headers, odd and even, running on different pages — and the same with footers. To do this, from the Header and Footer toolbar, click the Document Layout button. The Page Setup dialog box opens. On the Layout panel, check Different Odd and Even and then click OK. Create an odd and an even header (or footer) in turn, according to the preceding steps, and they print differently on odd and even pages. Cool.

 To prevent the header or footer from appearing on the first page of text, which usually is the title page, click the Page Setup button, on the Header and Footer toolbar. Then check Different First Page and click OK. In your document, move to the first page header (it says *First Page Header*) and leave it blank. This procedure places an empty header on the first page; the header appears on all the other pages as ordered. You also can use this option to place a different header on the first page — a graphic, for example. See Chapter 20 to learn about placing graphics in a document.

A header is a section-long thing. You can change parts of a header, such as chapter name or number, from section to section, without changing other parts of the header, like the page number. Refer to the section "Taking a Break — a Section Break," earlier in this chapter, for more information on sections.

I've always hated all that fuzz on top of a stein of beer. But recently I was in Germany and had a beer connoisseur tell me that it is an imperative part of a good beer. Hmm. Of course, this from a nation where they drink their beer *warm*. Yech.

Editing a header or footer

To edit an already created header or footer, follow these steps:

1. **Go to the page that has the header or footer you want to edit.**

   If you want to change the odd-page header, go to an odd page; if you want to edit the first-page footer, go to the first page.

The Header and Footer toolbar unbuttoned

One little, two little, ten little buttons on the Header and Footer floating palette of button joy. This table lists the official picture, title, and function for each:

Button	Official Name	Purpose in Life
	Switch Between	Header/Footer Like the name says
	Show Previous	View preceding header or footer
	Show Next	View next header or footer
	Same as Previous	Copy preceding header or footer to this header
	Page Numbers	Insert page number into the header or footer
	Date	Insert current date into header or footer
	Time	Insert current time into header or footer
	Page Setup	Grant you access to Word's Page Layout dialog box
	Show/Hide Document	Allow you to view the document's text along with the header or footer
Close	Close	Return you to your document and close the Header and Footer screen

The Show Previous, Show Next, and Same as Previous buttons are necessary because Word allows you to have several different headers and footers in the same document. Want a new header on page 17? Create it. Actually, you can have dozens of different headers and footers (though that's kind of impractical); the Show Previous, Show Next, and Same as Previous buttons let you switch between them.

2. Choose View⇨Header and Footer.

The Header and Footer screen appears.

 3. If necessary, click the Switch Between Header/Footer button to move to what you want to edit.

4. Make any changes or corrections.

Do this as you would edit any text on-screen.

5. Choose Close when you're done.

Editing a header or footer changes how it looks for your entire document. You don't have to move the cursor to the tippy-top of your document before editing.

 You also can edit a header or footer from Page Layout view: Choose View⇨Page Layout or click the Page Layout button. This command adjusts the way Word displays your document and exposes the thinly veiled text sequestered in your headers or footers.

Using Footnotes

Some folks seem to think that footnotes are pretty advanced stuff. Pooh! A lot of people need them in their documents. I mean, academics use them all the time and look how many people consider them "experts."

To create footnotes, follow these handy steps:

1. Position the toothpick cursor in your document where you want the footnote to be referenced.

This spot displays the tiny number and refers to the footnote. For example[1].

2. Choose Insert⇨Footnote.

You see the Footnote and Endnote dialog box. It's kind of boring, so I'm not putting a figure of it in this book.

If this is the first footnote for a document, you have to decide where you want your footnotes placed. Choose Options from the Footnote and Endnote dialog box, and you see the Footnote Options dialog box (I'm not showing it to you either). Choose where you want the footnotes to appear: on the bottom of the page where the footnote is referenced or beneath the text that contains the reference. (Endnotes — open the other panel — can be placed at the end of the current section or at the end of the document.) After you make this selection, you don't have to open this dialog box again unless you change your mind. Click OK.

---

[1]Made you look!

3. **If you want Word to number footnotes for you (and who wouldn't?), leave AutoNumber selected and then click OK.**

   The toothpick cursor magically appears in the sub-bottom of your page.

4. **Type your footnote.**

   You can place in a footnote anything you can place in a document — charts, graphs, pictures, even text.

5. **Choose OK.**

Figure 11-8 shows what a footnote can look like. If you find traditional text-only footnotes dreary, remember that you can add graphics in your footnotes.

Figure 11-8:
A footnote, such as you'll find in any government document.

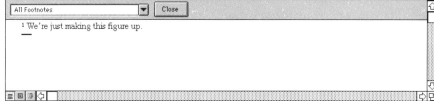

Here are some footnoting tips:

- To delete a footnote, highlight the footnote's number in your document and press the Delete key. Word magically renumbers any remaining footnotes for you. Wow.

- To view or edit footnotes, choose View⇨Footnotes.

- To quickly edit a footnote, double-click on the footnote number. The footnote text edit area opens.

Information on inserting feet and other graphics into your document can be found in Chapter 21, where I tell you almost all you'll ever care to know about graphics.

If you decide that some little fact would be better footnoted from another place in the text, you can cut (⌘-X), copy (⌘-C), and paste (⌘-V) footnotes even easier than normal text! Just block the number that denotes the footnote, move it to its new home, and — voilà — Word moves the rest. Better than U-Haul! (For step-by-step instructions on using Cut, Copy, and Paste key combinations, refer to "The Kindergarten Keys" section, in Chapter 3.)

Chapter 12

Using Tables and Columns

. . . .

In This Chapter

▶ Cobbling tables together

▶ Changing a table

▶ Doing the one-, two-, three-, four-column march

. . . .

*Y*ou can spice up your text with bold and italics and maybe even some large characters when your document doesn't run as long as you like. Paragraph formatting and page formatting add garlic to your document salad (just a touch — not enough to open your mouth, say "Hi," and watch flowers wilt, grown men cry, and women faint). What more can you do? Well, if you're really the daring type, you can pump up your document with fancy tables and formatting that's just one Cicero beneath the official realm of Desktop Publishing. Oh, we've come a long way from moveable type.

Cobbling Tables Together

A table is this thing with four legs on which you set things — but not your elbows when Grandma is watching. In Word, a *table* is bunch of stuff all lined up in neat little rows and columns. In the primitive days, you made tables happen by pressing the Tab key and your handy frustration tool. Face it: Making things align can be maddening. Even in a word processor. Even if you think that you know what you're doing.

Coming to your rescue, of course, is Word. "It's Table Man, Ma, and he's here to save us!" Word has an able Table command, which lets you create a prisonlike grid of rows and columns. Into each cubbyhole, or *cell,* you can type information or store society's miscreants, and everything is aligned nice and neat and suitable for framing. The printed result looks very impressive, and if you do things right, your table will be sturdy enough to eat off.

Creating a table (the traditional, boring way)

To create a table in your document, follow these steps:

1. **Place the toothpick cursor where you want the table.**

   The table is created and inserted into your text (like pasting in a block—a *cell block*). You fill in the table *after* you create it.

2. **Choose Table➪Insert Table.**

   Yes, Word has its own Table menu. How handy. Choosing the Insert Table command opens the Insert Table dialog box, shown in Figure 12-1.

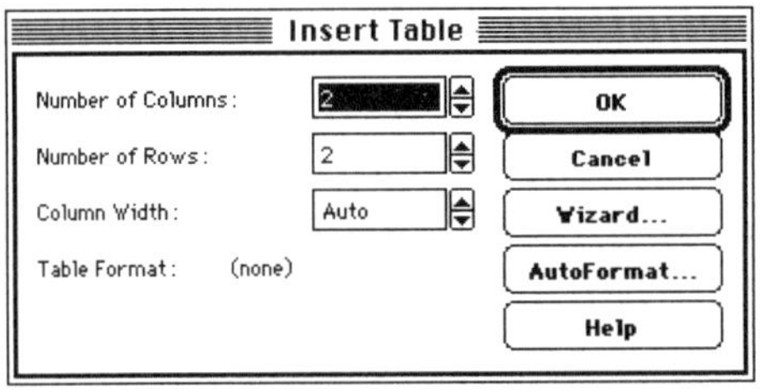

Figure 12-1:
The Insert
Table dialog
box.

```
═════════════ Insert Table ═══════════
Number of Columns:    [2    ]⏶⏷   (   OK   )
Number of Rows:       [2    ]⏶⏷   ( Cancel )
Column Width:         [Auto ]⏶⏷   ( Wizard... )
Table Format:   (none)           ( AutoFormat... )
                                 (  Help  )
```

3. **Enter the number of columns desired.**

   For example, enter **3**.

4. **Press Tab.**

   The cursor moves to the next box down.

5. **Enter the number of rows desired.**

   For example, enter **5**.

   Three columns? Five rows? Who really can predict the future? Accuracy isn't a big issue at this stage; you can change your table after it's created if you goof up (which I do all the time).

6. **Click OK to leave the Insert Table mini-dialog boxlet.**

   Welcome to prison! After you tell Word how many rows and columns to make, it builds you a table and shows it to you on-screen (see Figure 12-2). A Word table looks like a spreadsheet and smells like a spreadsheet, and if I weren't afraid of electrocuting myself, I'd tell you whether it tastes like a spreadsheet.

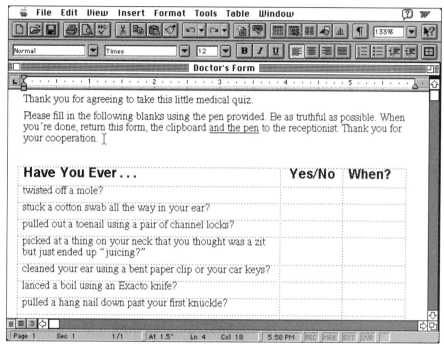

 File   Edit   View   Insert   Format   Tools   Table   Window

▣ Doctor's Form

Thank you for agreeing to take this little medical quiz.

Please fill in the following blanks using the pen provided. Be as truthful as possible. When you're done, return this form, the clipboard <u>and the pen</u> to the receptionist. Thank you for your cooperation.]

Have You Ever . . .	Yes/No	When?
twisted off a mole?		
stuck a cotton swab all the way in your ear?		
pulled out a toenail using a pair of channel locks?		
picked at a thing on your neck that you thought was a zit but just ended up "juicing?"		
cleaned your ear using a bent paper clip or your car keys?		
lanced a boil using an Exacto knife?		
pulled a hang nail down past your first knuckle?		

Figure 12-2:
A table is
born.

7. Fill in the table.

Use crayons to mark your screen or, better still, see the section, "Putting stuff in the table," later in this chapter.

If you can't see your table, choose Table⇨Gridlines to display the cell borders.

Incidentally, the grid you see around your table doesn't print. If you want to have lines in your table, see Chapter 20 for information on adding borders to your text.

You also can build a table from the Standard toolbar. For more information, see the very next section. (I advise making a table as described in the preceding numbered list until you feel comfortable with your table-creation skills.)

Dogs certainly are the highest form of life on this planet. The other day, I was watching my dog, and he had the most serious look on his face. He didn't even blink. Then, after I observed him for about a minute longer, he opened his mouth and a bee flew out. Dogs must know something we don't.

Use a table in your document whenever you have information that has to be organized in rows and columns. This feature works much better than using the Tab key because adjusting the table's rows and columns is easier than fussing with tab stops.

Be sure that at least one line of text, or a blank line if the table starts off a new section, is in front of any table. This technique gives you a place to put the cursor if you ever want to add stuff before the table.

You can always add or delete columns and rows to your table after you create it. See the section "Changing a Table," later in this chapter.

The table may have an ugly lined border around it and between the cells. You can change this feature, as covered in the section "Changing a Table."

For some Cheater McGee tips on making tables, see Chapter 15, "Templates and Wizards."

Alas, Word does not have a handy Chair command. (Rumor has it, however, that the Microsoft engineers are working on barstools.)

Creating a table (the unconventional, but easier, way)

Here's an easier way to create a table in your document, providing that you've already suffered through the steps listed in the preceding section and are ready for a more mousey alternative:

1. **Place the toothpick cursor where you want your table.**

   This action marks the spot where the table's prisonlike skeleton will appear.

 2. **Click the Table button, on the Standard toolbar.**

   A grid drops down, looking a lot like the maze of questions that daunts "Jeopardy" players but looking a lot more like Figure 12-3. By manipulating this grid, you can graphically set your table's dimensions with the mouse.

3. **Set the table's size.**

   Drag down and to the right to create a table with a given number of rows and columns. The precise values appear at the bottom of the grid.

4. **Release the mouse.**

   Your well-proportioned table is inserted into the document.

Figure 12-3:
You don't
need to use
the
keyboard to
create a
table in
Word.

Refer to the previous sections for any tips worth noting.

Putting stuff in a table

An empty table sits in your document. But before you break out the MinWax and clean it up, why not set the table?

A table is divided into rows and columns. Where a row and column meet is called a *cell* — just like they have in prison but without the TV and metal toilet.

Your job is to fill in the various cells with text, graphics, or whatever. Here are some pointers:

- ✔ Press Tab to move from cell to cell. Pressing Return just makes a new paragraph in the same cell. (Each cell is like its own little document.)

- ✔ Pressing Shift-Tab moves you backward between the cells.

- ✔ If you press Tab when in the last (bottom-right) cell, a new row of cells is added.

- ✔ You can press the cursor keys to move from cell to cell as well (how swell). But if there is text in the cell, pressing the cursor-control keys makes the toothpick cursor dawdle through the words. After all, you can still use the cursor-control keys to edit text in the cells. (It's best to press Tab to move from cell to cell.)

- ✔ Text-formatting commands also work in the cells. You can boldface, italicize, underline, center, left-align, and so on. Refer to Chapters 9 and 10 for the details. The formatting affects the text in only one cell at a time — or in the cells that you collectively mark as a block (see Chapter 6 for blocking instructions).

✔ You can apply styles to text in a table. See Chapter 14 for the details.

✔ To format a row or column all at once, you have to select it first.

✔ To utterly remove the table from your document, highlight the whole thing as a block and then choose Table⭢Delete Rows. The table is blown to smithereens.

✔ To erase a cell's contents in a table, block it and press the Delete or Del key.

Changing a Table

Suppose that you create a card table but really need a dining room table—or one of those long dual-time-zone tables that rich people eat at. Or, because you are participating in a back-to-nature movement, no table at all; you have decided to simply squat on your haunches around the fire. (A granola friend once told me that this method was really great for your lower back. After about five minutes, I lost all feeling in my legs.) Anyway, whatever table you create can be changed or adjusted.

Adding and deleting rows and columns

To add rows to your table, follow these steps:

1. Stick the toothpick cursor in the row below the spot where you want the new row.

2. Choose Table⭢Insert Rows.

Thud! The government of the People's Democratic Republic of Word is proud to add a brand-new story to the existing workers' apartment complex.

3. Repeat Steps 1 and 2 to add as many rows as you want.

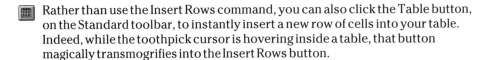 Rather than use the Insert Rows command, you can also click the Table button, on the Standard toolbar, to instantly insert a new row of cells into your table. Indeed, while the toothpick cursor is hovering inside a table, that button magically transmogrifies into the Insert Rows button.

To delete rows from your table, follow these steps:

1. Highlight the row that you want to delete.

To do so, move the cursor into the row and choose Table⭢Select Row.

2. Choose Table⭢Delete Rows.

3. Repeat Steps 1 and 2 to blast away as many rows as you want.

You also can select rows by moving the mouse into the left margin until its cursor changes its shape, to a nor'easterly arrow. Point the arrow at the row you want to select and click the mouse. You can select multiple rows by dragging the mouse up or down.

To add columns to your table, follow these steps:

1. **Stick the toothpick cursor in the column to the right of the spot where you want the new column.**

2. **Choose Table⇨Select Column.**

3. **Choose Table⇨Insert Columns.**

4. **Repeat Step 3 to add as many columns as you want.**

After adding new columns, you doubtless need to adjust the width of the table's columns. See the following section, "Adjusting the column width," for the details.

To delete columns from your table, follow these steps:

1. **Highlight the column that you want to delete.**

   Move the toothpick cursor to that column and pluck out Table⇨Select Column.

2. **Choose Table⇨Delete Columns.**

3. **Repeat Steps 1 and 2 to blast away as many columns as you want.**

Here are some things to keep in mind about rows and columns:

✔ You also can select columns by moving the mouse cursor above the column until it changes shape, to a down-pointing arrow. Point the arrow at the column and click. You can select multiple columns by dragging the mouse across them.

✔ New rows are inserted above the *current* row, which is the highlighted row or the one that the toothpick cursor is in.

✔ New columns are inserted to the left of the current column.

Adjusting the column width

Columns, like my waistline, tend to get fatter and, unlike my waistline, thinner, too. Fortunately, changing the width of a column in Word is a heck of a lot easier than going on a diet.

To adjust the width of a column, follow these steps:

1. Put the toothpick cursor anywhere in the table.

Anywhere.

2. Choose Table⇨Cell Height and Width.

This action opens the cute Cell Height and Width dialog box, shown in Figure 12-4.

Figure 12-4:
The Cell Height and Width dialog box.

Cell Height and Width

| Row | Column |

Width of Column 3 : `0.97"`

Space Between Columns : `0.15"`

OK

Cancel

AutoFit

Previous Column | Next Column | Help

3. Click on the Column tab.

Or press ⌘-C. This step brings forth the Column panel.

4. Enter the new width measurement for the column.

If you want a thinner column, enter a smaller number than the one already in the box. Larger numbers make columns wider, but keep in mind that a fat table — a gross concept unto itself — will probably not all fit on the page. Column width is measured in inches.

5. If you want to change the preceding or following column as well, press the Previous Column or Next Column button.

6. Click OK when you're done.

If you want to make several, or all, of the columns the same width, select them before you open the Cell Height and Width dialog box. Any changes you make apply to all the selected columns.

It's easier to change the width of columns by using the mouse — lots easier because you can see what is going on (like being thin enough to see your feet, I am told). Place the mouse cursor on the border between columns, and it changes its shape, into something that looks like a railroad track with arrows pointing east and west. Hold down the mouse button and drag the column border to give the column a new look.

If you look up at the ruler when the toothpick cursor is in the table, you see that each column is given its own miniruler. You can adjust the column width by using the mouse and the tiny washboard dojobbie. When you hover the mouse over the washboard, it changes to a left-right pointing arrow. Drag the washboard left or right to change the size of a column.

Doing the One-, Two-, Three-, Four-Column March

Columns — especially those you can see on-screen — are one of those features that all the magazines, gurus, and other pseudopundits demanded for word processors. Do we need them? No. Can Word do them? Yes. Do you want to mess with this? Sure, why not? It's something to do while the electric chair recharges.

Before I divulge my Word column secrets, here's a healthy bit of advice: The best way to make columns is to use a desktop publishing package, such as PageMaker, QuarkXPress, or any of the other fine products geared to such tasks. Those programs are designed for playing with text and making columns (although figuring out the instructions is like playing an eternal chess match with someone who wears a size-12 hat). In Word, columns remain more of a curiosity; they're not anything you or I want to spend more than 15 minutes on.

To start columns in your document, follow these next steps. If your text has already been written, Word puts it all in column format. Otherwise, any new text you create is placed in columns automagically.

1. **Move the toothpick cursor to where you want the columns to start.**

2. **Choose Format➪Columns.**

   The Columns dialog box opens, as shown in Figure 12-5.

3. **Enter the number of columns that you want.**

   Or click one of the illustrated, ready-to-wear buttons. (Two columns is sufficient enough to impress anyone. More columns make your text skinnier and may make your prose harder to read.)

4. **If you want a pretty line between the columns, click the Line Between box.**

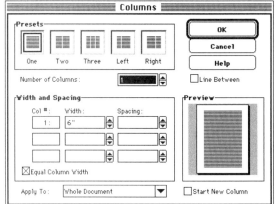

Figure 12-5:
The
Columns
dialog box.

5. **Open the Apply To drop-down list and choose to apply the columns to the Whole Document, to Selected Text, or just from now on (This Point Forward).**

6. **Choose OK.**

    OK!

Word shows you your columns right there on-screen. That's at least $15 of the purchase price right there!

 You also can use the Columns tool: Click the tool, and a baby box of columns appears. Click and drag the mouse to indicate how many text columns you want. When you release the mouse button, the columns appear.

The space between columns is called the *gutter*. Unless you have a bunch of columns or a lot of space to fill, it is best to leave this setting at .5" — half an inch. This amount of white space is pleasing to the eye without being overly much of a good thing.

Editing text in columns is a pain. The cursor seems to hop all over the place and takes an eternity to move from one column to another. I'm just complaining here because I'm bored and fresh out of rainy-day Popsicle-stick projects.

Using the mouse to poke the cursor to a new spot on a column seems to work nicely.

 To get rid of columns, go back and change the number of columns to one. (Or press the Undo shortcut, ⌘-Z.) Neat, huh?

The three-column text format works nicely on landscape paper. This method is how most brochures are created. Refer to Chapter 11 for information on Landscape orientation.

All the text and paragraph formatting mentioned in this part of the book also apply to text and paragraphs in columns. The only difference is that your column margins — not the page margins — now mark the left and right sides of your text for paragraph formatting.

Chapter 13
The Joys of AutoText

. . . .

In This Chapter

▶ The Tao of AutoText

▶ Creating an AutoText entry

▶ Using AutoText entries

▶ Editing AutoText entries

▶ Deleting AutoText entries

. . . .

*H*obart X. Zlotnik loves his name but hates to type it. It's not his fault. Grandma Boswell's maiden name was Xavier. And the guy who laid out the keys on a typewriter, he was mad at the world (and the wretch typed with only two fingers anyway, so what did he care?). So poor Hobart, no matter how careful he is or how hard he tries, inevitably fumbles over those frustrating X and Z keys.

How would you like to be Hobart? (It's OK — he's good-looking and makes tons of money.) Worse, how would you like to type that name a gazillion times over your life? Wouldn't it be easier to type, say, **Ho**, and have the rest of that massive moniker magically appear, thanks to your computer? You bet it would! And wouldn't it be nice if you could type **bye**, for example, and have Word automatically toss in your signature block at the end of a letter? Yup.

Well, someone type **Ha** for *Hallelujah*: It's all possible in Word, thanks to the miraculous (meaning that it's miraculous Microsoft included something to make life *easier*) AutoText command.

The Tao of AutoText (Required Reading If You Haven't a Clue)

AutoText is a shortcut. You need give Word only a teensy-tiny hint of what you want and it automatically types some text. It's like blowing up a balloon without the huffing and puffing. You type **balloon**, tap Word's AutoText magic wand, and the word *balloon* is expanded into something like "a bag of stretchy stuff filled with hot air . . . ." Sorry, but Word doesn't know how to make balloon animals.

The idea behind AutoText is this: To make typing easier, Word lets you enter shortcuts, which are expanded automagically into longer text, thanks to AutoText. It's incredibly handy when you have to type the same thing again and again and again and again.

Here are some tips for using AutoText:

✔ You must create an AutoText *entry* before you can use the AutoText command. The entry is usually text that you've typed in your document. That text is assigned a shortcut. The details are outlined in the following section.

✔ AutoText entries become part of the document template. See Chapter 15 for more information on document templates.

✔ AutoText can store more than text. You can use AutoText to automatically bring pictures and all sorts of graphic mayhem into a document with a flick of your wrist.

Creating an AutoText Entry

To create an AutoText entry, follow these steps:

1. **Type some text you want to use as an AutoText entry.**

   For example, type your name.

2. **Mark the text as a block.**

   Refer to Chapter 6 for the full details on marking a block of text. Keep in mind that all the text you mark is included in the AutoText entry.

3. **Choose Edit⇨AutoText.**

Or you can click the handy AutoText button, on the Standard toolbar. Either way, the AutoText dialog box opens, as shown in Figure 13-1. You can see the text you selected (at least some of it) in the bottom part of the dialog box.

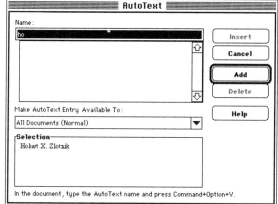

Figure 13-1:
The
AutoText
dialog box.

4. Give the AutoText entry a name.

Type the shortcut name, which can be very short, in the Name box. For example, after our friend Hobart highlighted his full name in the document, he typed the letters _ho_ in the Name box.

5. Click the Add button.

You're done. The AutoText entry is now ready to be used (see the following section).

 The shortcut name you type can be in upper- or lowercase. I usually keep everything in lowercase.

 When you're done working on your document, Word asks whether you want to save the document and template changes; answer Yes to keep any AutoText entry you just created.

Using AutoText Entries

To put an AutoText entry in a document, follow these steps:

1. Put the toothpick cursor where you want the AutoText entry to go.

2. Type the shortcut name.

Hobart would type the letters *ho*. That's all — no space or period. Suppose that your AutoText entry for your name, address, and city is called *me*. You type **me** and then . . . .

3. Press ⌘-Option-V

I suppose that's *V* as in the ⌘-V Paste key combination. Anyway, the AutoText entry is slapped into the document, replacing the shortcut name. So *ho* turns into Hobart's full, obnoxious name.

This list offers some tips for making AutoText entries:

✔ A mousey alternative to pressing ⌘-Option-V (in Step 3) is to click the AutoText button, on the Standard toolbar.

✔ You also can choose and insert the AutoText entry by opening the AutoText dialog box (choose Edit⇨AutoText), highlighting your bit of text, and clicking the Insert button.

✔ If the toothpick cursor is off by a little bit, Word complains that it doesn't recognize the AutoText entry. If you're sure that you've done everything right, choose Edit⇨AutoText and look up your AutoText entry to verify.

Editing AutoText Entries

Changing the contents or appearance of an AutoText entry isn't difficult. You open the AutoText dialog box (choose Edit⇨AutoText), zero in on the desired entry, change it, and save the changed entry with the same name.

Suppose that you create an AutoText entry (such as *me*) that reproduces your name and address. And though you hate messing with Word, one day you succumb to the idea of moving. As a result, you must update your *me* entry to reflect your new location. Here's how it's done:

1. Put the toothpick cursor where you want the AutoText entry to go.

You need to go through the motions here to make the operation run a bit smoother. Yes, this is a shortcut not sanctioned in the manual. (But then again, that's why you're reading this book.)

2. Type the shortcut name.

Do this just as though you were inserting the entry.

3. Press ⌘-Option-V or click the AutoText button thing.

The AutoText entry is inserted into the document at the place where the toothpick cursor is, replacing the shortcut name.

4. Edit.

Make the necessary changes to the AutoText entry just pasted into your document (type your new address, for example).

5. Mark as a block on-screen the text you want included as the AutoText entry.

6. Choose Edit⇨AutoText.

7. Click the existing AutoText name.

In other words, resave the edited AutoText entry by using the original name.

8. Click the Add button.

A dialog box opens, asking whether you want to redefine the AutoText entry.

9. Click Yes.

You're done. The entry has been edited in an underhanded but perfectly legal manner. The net effect here is that the original entry is changed, but the shortcut name is kept the same (to protect the guilty).

Deleting AutoText Entries

Nothing stays the same forever. Hobart flew to Brazil and was captured by a tribe of Amazons. He married their leader, Oota, and was forced to change his last name. And his first name. And he could never use a computer again. Guess it's OK to remove his shortcut from AutoText.

To delete an AutoText entry, follow these steps:

1. Choose Edit⇨AutoText.

The AutoText dialog box opens, listing all glossary entries.

2. Click on the name of the AutoText entry you want to delete.

Bye ho!

3. Click the Delete button.

Zap. The AutoText entry's name is history.

4. Click Close.

Actually, I hear that Hobart is quite happy now.

Chapter 14
Formatting with Style

. . . .

. . . .

*W*ant to stand out from the crowd? Then do what I do: eat massive quantities of garlic. When you're word processing, however, garlic won't help much (unless you buy garlic paper — refer to a funky former-hippie neighborhood in your town for a shop that carries the stuff). Instead, you can stand alone by using Word's Style command.

No matter how pretty your undies are, style — in Word anyway — is not what you wear or even how you wear it. A *style* is a series of formatting instructions — bold, centered, sideways — that are named and stored for future use. Suppose that you have a series of paragraphs that you want indented in bold tiny type. And you want a box drawn around each paragraph. Oh, and your boss wants an extra line placed at the end of each paragraph. You can create a style that slaps on *all* of these formats with a *single* keystroke. Styles may be advanced stuff, but they certainly can come in handy.

Using the Style Command

Styles bring together character and paragraph formatting under one roof — or in one Word dialog box. This one roof is found in the Format menu: the Style command. When you choose Format⇨Style, you see the Style dialog box, shown in Figure 14-1.

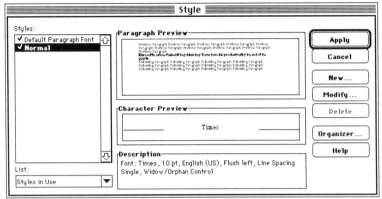

Figure 14-1:
The Style
dialog box.

Three items are worth noting in the Style dialog box: Styles, Description, and the preview boxes:

The Styles scrolling list displays easy-to-remember names assigned to each style. Word always starts with the Normal style — plain boring text. You can scroll through the Styles list to select a new style for your document or just to see what's available.

The Description area, near the bottom center of the dialog box, holds the technical mumbo-jumbo description of the style highlighted in the Styles list. For example, the Description area may list tab stops or mention fonts and such. No need to rest your weary eyes here for long.

The two preview boxes show how style affects paragraph and character formatting.

✔ You can use Word without ever messing with styles. Only if you want to get truly fancy should you ever bother with this stuff. (Refer to the section on AutoFormat in Chapter 15 if you're truly lazy and really don't care.)

✔ Styles are combinations of character and paragraph and other formatting, all saved under an easy-to-remember name.

✔ The idea behind a style is to save time: with styles, you don't have to keep selecting character and paragraph formatting while you're working on your document. For example, the style for this bulleted list is saved under the name Bullet. I format this file's main text under the style name Body. That way I can write without having to constantly mess with the Font dialog box. I just say "Gimme the Body style" and Word willfully obeys.

✔ The Normal style is Word's standard style, the one that always appears when you open a new document. Yeah, it's pretty plain and ugly, but you can add your own styles to make your text fairly fancy.

✔ The Styles list actually shows two types of styles. Styles listed in bold type contain both font and paragraph formatting. Styles in skinny type only affect character formatting. Refer to the section "Creating a character-only style" for the details.

✔ To apply a style to your document, select the style name from the Styles list in the Style dialog box.

✔ An easier way to select a style is to grab its name from the first drop-down box on the Formatting toolbar (the *ribbon*) — the box that typically says *Normal.* That drop-down list contains all the styles associated with your current document (those that you created yourself or that came prepackaged with Word).

✔ When you choose a new style, it is applied to any block marked on-screen or the paragraph that currently contains the toothpick cursor.

✔ For more information on character formatting, refer to Chapter 9.

✔ Refer to Chapter 10 for the details on paragraph formatting.

✔ The standard styles Word provides for your new documents are Normal, Heading 1, Heading 2, Heading 3, and the Default Paragraph Font style. The Normal style is Times text at 10 points (kinda small), with no other fancy features. The Heading styles are all blocky fonts, exemplifying the same lack of imagination that created the Normal style.

Creating a style

New styles are easy to create. Just follow these loosely outlined steps:

1. Type a paragraph of text.

A single line will do. Just remember to press Return when you finish typing to tell Word that you consider the text a paragraph.

2. Mark your paragraph as a block.

3. Select the character formatting that you want for your style.

The character formatting will be applied to the block. Select a font and font size.

Page wildly through Chapter 9 for more information on character formatting, but here's an important piece of advice: Stick to fonts and sizes — avoid bold, italics, or underline unless you want it applied to all your text. (Styles are broad things; for the most part, only individual words are given bold, italic, underline, and similar character formats.)

4. Select the paragraph formatting for your style.

With the block still highlighted, format the paragraph. Indent it, center it, or whatever. (For more information, refer to Chapter 10.)

5. Press ⌘-Shift-S.

This key combination activates the Style command. Actually, it highlights the Style drop-down box on the ribbon — the one that usually says Normal.

6. Type in a name for your style.

A descriptive one-word title usually does nicely. For example, if you create an indented paragraph that you want to use when listing things, you may name the style List. Or if you create a special musical style, name it Liszt.

7. Press Return.

The style is added to Word's repertoire of styles for your document.

✔ To use the style — to *apply* it to other paragraphs in your document — refer to the section "Using a style," later in this chapter.

✔ Give your style a name that describes the style's function. Names like Indented List or Table Body Text are great because it's easy to remember what they do. Names like Orville or Mr. Bean are somewhat less desirable.

✔ The styles that you create are only available to the document in which they're created. *Caveat:* If you create scads of styles that you love and want to use in several documents, then you need to create what's called a *template*. This procedure is covered in Chapter 15, in the section "Creating a Document Template to Store Your Styles."

✔ You also can create a style by using the Style dialog box, though this method requires more mental work than doing it the way I've already outlined: Choose Format⇔Style. Click on the New button, and the New Style dialog box opens. Click on the Format button to see a menu that allows you to play with the Font, Paragraph, Tabs, and much more. Click OK after setting the formatting. Then click in the Name box in the New Style dialog box to give your style a name. Click OK and then the Close button to return to your document.

Creating a character-only style

Some styles listed in the Styles list are in bold and some are in skinny type. The skinny ones are character-only styles: they affect only the character and not the paragraph formatting. So if you have a centered block of text and only want to change the font to big, ugly text, you can do so by selecting the Big Ugly character-only style, leaving the paragraph formatting alone.

To create a character-only style, follow these steps:

1. Choose Format⇔Style.

The Style dialog box appears (see Figure 14-1).

2. Click the New button.

The New Style dialog box appears. This dialog box allows you to create a new style — familiar turf if you've already done it.

3. In the Name box, type in a name for the style.

Be clever. If, for example, the character style applies small caps in a stocky font, name it Stubby.

4. In the Style Type drop-down list, select Character.

This selection gears everything in the New Style dialog box to accept only character- and font-related formatting stuff.

5. Click the Format button to select the font formats that you want.

Only two options are available: Font and Language. Forget Language. Choosing Font brings up the Font dialog box, where you can set various character attributes — similar to what I cover in Chapter 9.

6. Click OK when you're done defining the character style.

7. Click the Close button in the Style dialog box.

You're done.

✔ Character style names appear in skinny text in the Styles list.

✔ The special character-only styles don't affect any paragraph formatting. Selecting a character style only changes the font, style, size, bold, underlining, and so on.

✔ Also refer to the "Stealing Character Formatting" section, later in this chapter, for a shortcut method of applying font formats.

Giving a style a shortcut key combination

Styles let you quickly format a paragraph of text. Style shortcut key combinations make formatting even faster because pressing Control-B to get at the Body style is often faster than messing with the Style drop-down list or Style dialog box — especially when you have a gob of styles to mess with.

To give your style a shortcut key combo, follow these steps:

1. Choose Format⇨Style.

This command opens the Style dialog box.

2. Select a style for which you want a shortcut key.

Highlight that style in the Styles list by clicking on it.

3. Click the Modify button.

The Modify Style dialog box appears.

4. Click the Shortcut Key button.

A cryptic Customize dialog box appears. Don't waste any time trying to explore here. Just move on to Step 5.

5. **Press your shortcut key combination.**

   It's best to use ⌘-Shift-letter or Control-Shift-letter or ⌘-Option-letter key combinations, where *letter* is a letter key on the keyboard. For example, press Control-B or even ⌘-Option-B for your Body style shortcut key.

   You'll notice that the key combination appears in the Press New Shortcut Key box just as you press it. If you make a mistake, press the Delete key to erase.

6. **Check to see that the combination isn't already in use.**

   For example, Word uses ⌘-B as the bold character formatting shortcut key combination. This key combination appears under the heading Currently Assigned To, which is under the Press New Shortcut Key box. Keep an eye on that box! If something else uses the shortcut key, press the Delete key and go back to Step 5.

   If the key isn't used by anything, you'll see [unassigned] displayed under the Currently Assigned To heading.

7. **Click the Assign button.**

8. **Click the Close button.**

   The Customize dialog box sulks away.

9. **Click the OK button.**

   The Modify Style dialog box huffs off.

10. **Click the Close button in the Style dialog box.**

    Congratulations, you now have a usable shortcut key combination for your style.

I assign ⌘-Option-letter key combinations for my style shortcuts. When I write a magazine article, I use ⌘-Option-B for the Body style, ⌘-Option-T for "type-this-in-stuff" style, and ⌘-Option-C for figure caption style. The notion here is to make the shortcut keys kinda match the style name.

Information on using a style — *applying* the style, if you work for Microsoft tech support — is covered in the next section.

Using a style

As Microsoft aptly points out, you don't *use* a style as much as you *apply* it. The character and paragraph formatting carefully stored inside the style is applied to text on-screen, text in a block, or text that you're about to write. Using a style is easy:

1. **Know what you're applying the style to.**

   If it's a paragraph already on-screen, just stick the toothpick cursor somewhere in that paragraph. Otherwise, the style will be applied to any new text you type.

2. **Select a style from the ribbon.**

   Click on the down-arrow button beside the first drop-down box. Drag down the list to select your style. You also can type the style name directly into the box if you can spell.

   ✔ Applying a style is a paragraph-level thing. You can't apply a style to just a single word in a paragraph; the style takes over the whole paragraph.

   ✔ You also can apply a style by using a shortcut key combination, provided that you've created one for that style. Refer to the long, boring instructions in the preceding section for the details.

   ✔ To apply a style to your entire document, choose Edit⎮Select All. Then choose the style you want for *everything*.

   ✔ Herds of styles can be corralled in things called *Style Galleries*. Refer to Chapter 15 for more information.

   ✔ Refer to the section "Creating a new style," earlier in this chapter, for information on creating your own special styles for a document.

   ✔ Sometimes you can develop a style so sophisticated that it won't show on your monitor. If you exceed the capabilities of your printer or graphics card, you may see some strange stuff. Don't get excited, it's not the '60s all over again.

Uh, the Reapply Style dialog box means what?

As you're goofing with styles, you may stumble upon the Reapply Style dialog box, which tries in its own awkward way to explain the following: "Excuse me, but you selected some text and a style, but they don't match. Should I pretend that the style should match the text from here on, or should I reformat the text to match the style?" An interesting question.

The way Word puts it is Redefine the style using the selection as an example. Highlighting this option and clicking OK means that the style you already created will match the selected text. You probably don't want to select this option. (Of course, if that's what you want, click OK.)

The other option is Return the formatting of the section to the Style. Equally confusing, this option means that Word will format your highlighted text to match the style you selected. You probably want to choose this option; it keeps your style intact.

As a final word, be thankful for Word's Undo command. No matter what you select in the Reapply Style dialog box, the Undo command returns your text to the way it was before.

Changing a style

Styles change. Bell bottoms were once the rage, but now, well, now they mostly define West Greenwich Village from the East. Times — the bane of the Normal style — is a wonderful font . . . if you're into bow ties and think merengue is a type of pie or a salted tequila drink or an ex-Nazi who lived in Brazil. Still, Times is a workhorse that is used by everyone for almost everything. Maybe you want to put it out to pasture and use a different font in your Normal style. If so, you can change it.

Here are the instructions for changing a style — any style, not just the Normal style. In fact, I don't recommend that you play around with the Normal style.

1. **Choose Format⇨Style.**

    The Style dialog box opens.

2. **Select a style to change from the Styles list.**

3. **Click the Modify button.**

    The Modify Style box erupts on-screen.

4. **Click Format.**

    A list of formatting options drops down (see Figure 14-2). Font, Paragraph, Tabs, Border, Physique, Rx. It's all there..

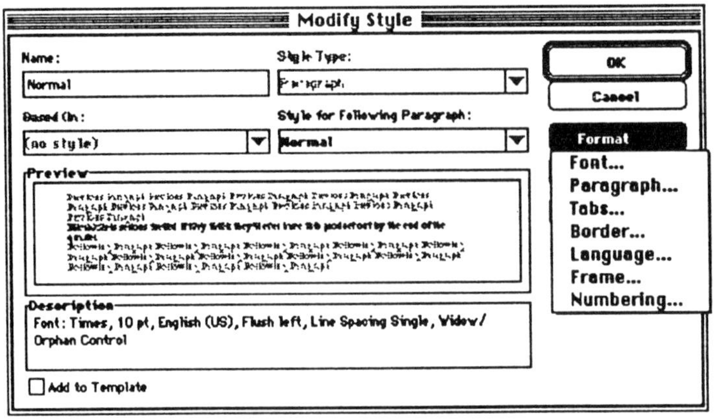

Figure 14-2:
The Modify Style dialog box, with its Format button hanging open.

5. **Choose the part of the style that you want to change.**

    For example, select Font to open the Font dialog box, where you can change the font, size, and so on (see Chapter 9). The other options allow you to change other formatting aspects.

6. **Choose OK.**

   Choosing OK closes whichever dialog box you were in. If, for example, you had opened the Font dialog box, clicking on its OK button closes that box and returns you to the Style dialog box.

7. **Repeat Steps 4, 5, and 6 as necessary.**

8. **Click OK in the Modify Style box when you're done.**

9. **Click Close in the Style dialog box to get back to your document.**

   ✔ Changing styles is advanced stuff — not recommended for the timid. It's entirely possible to use Word without bothering with styles at all, which is the way most people use the program.

   ✔ Changing a style changes all the paragraphs in your document that have that style. This is a great way to change a font throughout a document without having to select everything and then manually pick out a new font.

   ✔ Don't like it? Click on the Undo button (or press ⌘-Z) to make it all go away and return to your original headache.

Stealing Character Formatting

To heck with styles! Suppose that you create a neat character formatting and want to copy it to other text in your document. For example:

The look appeals to you and you imagine that it would be effective elsewhere. (I suggest that you read this book quickly, before the men in the white coats come calling.) To copy the character's format only — which sorta fits in with all this style nonsense — heed the following:

1. **Jab the toothpick cursor amid the text that has the character formatting you want to copy.**

   No need to select anything as a block here.

 2. **Click on the Format Painter button, on the Standard toolbar.**

    The cursor changes to a plus-I-beam pointer, depicted at left.

3. **Hunt for the text that you want to change.**

   Refer to Chapter 2 for information on Word's navigation keys.

4. **Highlight the text that you want to change.**

   Drag the mouse over the text that you want to change. You must use the mouse here.

5. Release the mouse button.

Voilà. The text is changed.

- ✔ Painting the character format in this manner only works once. To repaint with the same format, repeat the preceding steps. Or if you want to paint lots of text with the same character formatting, follow the steps as outlined. In Step 2, however, double-click the Format Painter button. That way, the format painter cursor stays active, ready to paint lots of text. Then after Step 5, you can continue changing text (repeat Steps 3, 4, and 5 as often as you like). Press Esc to cancel your Dutch Boy frenzy.

- ✔ If you tire of the mouse, you can use the ⌘-Shift-C key combination to copy the character format to another location in your document. Simply place the cursor amid any text that has the desired formatting. Then highlight the text in your document that you want to change and press ⌘–Shift-V.

- ✔ You can sorta kinda remember ⌘–Shift-C to copy character formatting and ⌘–Shift-V to paste because ⌘–C and ⌘–V are the Copy and Paste shortcut keys. Sorta kinda.

Part III
Working with Documents

"OOO-KAY, LET'S SEE. IF WE CAN ALL REMAIN CALM AND STOP ACTING CRAZY, I'M SURE I'LL EVENTUALLY REMEMBER WHAT NAME I FILED THE ANTIDOTE UNDER."

In this part...

"**M**y document" just sounds so much more important than "that thing I did with my word processor." It implies a crisp, masterful touch. No, you say, this isn't another dreary report; it's a document. This isn't just a letter complaining to the local cable affiliate; it's a document. It isn't a note to Billy's teacher explaining his, "rash;" it's a document. It sounds so professional. Never mind that you had to tie your fingers in knots and print several hundred copies before you got it just so — it's a document!

This part of the book explores the essence of Word: making documents. This includes printing documents, working with documents on disk, and the ugly, sordid story of mail merge, which is right up there next to paying taxes in mental agony and grief.

Chapter 15

Templates and Wizards

• •

• •

*T*emplates and Wizards both enable you to create attractive documents. And neither requires a black belt in typesetting.

Templates, the more old-fashioned approach, are collections of styles and other items that make writing documents easier. Word's templates work sorta like the huge STOP templates used by the Department of Transportation. The workers just spray paint over the template and a huge STOP appears on the roadway. Magic? Nah. If you want sleight of hand . . .

Check out Word's *Wizards* — they're along the lines of what used to be called *artificial intelligence* in computing circles. (It turns out that artificial intelligence is nothing more than a computer doing its job by helping you do your job.) In Word, Wizards can help you set up and write sample documents, sometimes even filling in the words for you. Wizards are ideal for lazy-minded typists who want to dazzle while expending a minimum of effort.

Creating a Template to Store Your Styles

Styles are collections of paragraph and font attributes stored under one convenient name. Chapter 14 has all the details on how styles are created and used.

Oftentimes, you'll want to store a bunch of your styles so that you can use them over and over. To do so, you create a template, a special type of document in which you can store all your styles.

You create a template like you do any new document. Start by creating a new document in Word:

1. **Choose File⇨New.**

   You must select the New command from the File menu; clicking on the New button (on the Standard toolbar) doesn't do the job.

   The New dialog box opens.

2. **Find the New area.**

   You see two radio buttons: Document and Template.

3. **Choose the Template button.**

4. **Click OK.**

   You see what looks like a new document on-screen. Don't be fooled. It's really a template thing. (The title bar of the new document indicates that you are working on a template.)

5. **Create the styles for your new template.**

   Create a number of styles that you want to save or use for particular documents (see Chapter 14 for instructions on creating styles). For example, this book has a template that has styles for the main text, section headings, numbered lists, figure captions, and a bunch of other stuff.

6. **Save the template to disk.**

   Choose File⇨Save As. The Save As dialog box appears. Type in a name and click OK. Then you can close the template document and you're done.

   ✔ Word's templates should be saved to a special template directory on your hard drive. Normally, this will be your Microsoft Word 6.0 folder. It's OK to save them someplace else but, eh, why bother?

   ✔ To use a template when you create a new document, refer to the "Using a template" section, later in this chapter.

   ✔ Templates are a very special type of document, so special that they even have their own file type; they're not normal documents.

   ✔ Be clever with your template names. I send out all my letters by using the *Letter* template; faxes start with the *FAX* template. These template names are accurate, brief, and describe the types of documents that they represent. Do the same and your Word guru will smile in a delightful manner.

   ✔ Word actually comes with a slew of templates ready for the taking. Refer to "Using a template," later in this chapter.

Creating a template complete with text

Templates need not contain only styles. They also can store text, especially text that you may use over and over again in certain types of documents. For example, a common type of Word template may contain a letterhead, appropriate for your correspondence. Another example is my FAX template: the first part of the template (the To, From, and Re lines) are already typed in, which saves me valuable energy that I need to do any business.

To create a template complete with text, follow these steps:

1. **Do everything outlined in Steps 1 through 5 of the preceding section.**

   Gee, a direction like that saves the author a lot of typing.

2. **Before you save your template to disk, type in some text that you want to be part of the template.**

   Anything you type will be saved along with the styles. You can, for example, create letterhead that, provided you read various other chapters in this book, looks like the one shown in Figure 15-1.

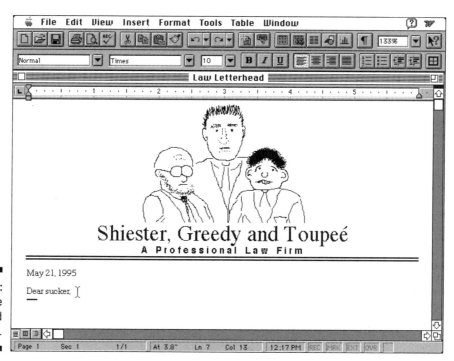

Figure 15-1:
A sample
letterhead
template.

3. **Save the template to disk, as outlined in Step 6 of the preceding section.**

    Give the template a clever name, something like *Letter* or *Letterhead*.

    ✔ If you want, you can store lots of text in a template. However, the idea here is to be brief. A specific template isn't as useful as a general one.

    ✔ You also can stuff graphics into a template. Refer to Chapter 22 for information on using graphics in your documents.

    ✔ Please refer to Chapter 19 for information on Mail Merge — although a concept distant from templates, the two can be easily confused.

Using a template

Oh, this is really dumb. To use a template, follow these steps:

1. **Choose File⇨New.**

    The New dialog box opens. (You choose File⇨New to start any new document in Word.)

Sticking the current date into a template

Any text that you type into a template becomes a permanent part of that template. This situation isn't good news for those of us who want to add the date to a template, as today's date may differ from the date when you print any letter based on that template. Fortunately, there is a solution. Though the procedure is a bit cumbersome, the following steps enable you to set an updating date field into your template:

1. Position the toothpick cursor where you want the date.

2. Choose Insert⇨Field. The Field dialog box appears.

3. From the Categories area, select Date and Time.

4. From the Field Names area, select Date.

5. Click the Options button. The Field Options dialog box appears. (Make sure that the General Switches panel is forward; click on that tab if it's not.)

6. Select a date format from the Date-Time list. The letters d, M, and y stand for day, month, and year.

7. Click the Add to Field button.

8. Click the OK button. The Field Options dialog box zooms outta sight.

9. Click the OK button in the Field dialog box.

Your template now has a date field in it, which is not the same thing as normal text. Instead, a *date field* is like a miniblock of text that always displays the current date. (You must highlight the block — select it — to delete it.)

2. Under the Template list, select the template that you want.

Creating a letterhead? Then pick out Letterhead from the list. The Normal template is Word's own boring normal template (which should be renamed *Yawn*).

3. Click OK.

Word *attaches* the template to your document, ready for use. You can take advantage of any styles stuffed into the template and view, use, or edit any text saved in the template.

✔ Special templates are given the surname Wizard. Refer to the section "Chickening Out and Using a Wizard," later in this chapter for more information.

✔ Opening a document with a template does not change the template; your new document is merely "using" the template's styles and any text it already has. To change a template, refer to the next section.

✔ Golly, don't templates make Word kind of easy? Only if the entire template-and-style fiasco hasn't already induced brainlock.

A template, a template, my kingdom for a template

Do you see any templates other than Normal in the New dialog box? If not, you need to tell Word where to locate them. This only needs to be done once, so follow these steps without paying careful attention:

1. Select Tools⇨Options. The Options dialog box comes atcha.

2. Click on the File Locations tab to bring the File Locations panel up front. (The tab is to the right.)

3. Click on User Templates to highlight it in the list of File Types.

4. Click the Modify button. An Open-type dialog box appears.

5. Find the Templates folder that's inside the Microsoft Word folder.

6. Switch to the Templates folder (double-click it so that its name appears above the file list box).

7. Press Return.

8. Click the Close button in the Options dialog box.

Now when you select File⇨New, you'll see a whole gaggle of templates you can have fun with. At least until someone comes for your head.

Changing a template

Changing or editing a template is identical to changing or editing a normal document. The only difference: you open a template rather than a document. Yes, Word deals with this task quite easily.

1. **Open the template.**

   Choose File⇨Open. In the Open dialog box, select Document Templates from the List Files of Type drop-down box. This option directs Word to list only templates in the Open dialog box file window.

2. **Open the template that you want to edit.**

   Double-click on its filename.

3. **Make your changes.**

   You edit the template just as you would any other document. Bear in mind that you're editing a template and not a "real" document.

4. **Save the modified template.**

   Choose File⇨Save.

   Or choose File⇨Save As to assign the modified template a new name and maintain the original template.

5. **Close the template document.**

   Choose File⇨Close.

✔ Changes that you make to a template do not affect those documents already created with that template. The changes only affect any new documents that you create.

✔ The Normal template is a special beast. Changing the Normal template affects all other templates. The moral to this story is, all together now, "Leave the Normal template alone."

Chickening Out and Using a Wizard

If all this template nonsense has you in a tizzy, sit down and have a cup of tea. And while you're relaxing, prepare to let Word do all your formatting work. This is possible, with desirable results, thanks to the wonderful Wizards of Word.

A Wizard enables you to create a near-perfect document automatically. All you need to do is choose various options and make adjustments from a handy and informative dialog box. Word does the rest.

To use a Word Wizard, follow these steps:

1. Choose File⇨New.

This command opens the New dialog box.

2. Select a Wizard from the Template list.

A number of Wizards come prepackaged with Word. At the top of the Template list, you may see the Agenda Wizard and Award Wizard. Elsewhere in the list, you may find the Fax Wizard, Letter Wizard, Memo Wizard, Lizard Wizard, and maybe the Wizard of Oz.

3. Click OK.

Word hums and churns for a few minutes. It's thinking — no doubt a painful process.

4. You're enlightened: a Wizard dialog box appears.

A sample Wizard dialog box is shown in Figure 15-2. Most of the Wizard dialog boxes look the same; you should pay attention to three areas: the preview window, which gives you an idea of what your document may look like; the list of options and descriptions; and four buttons.

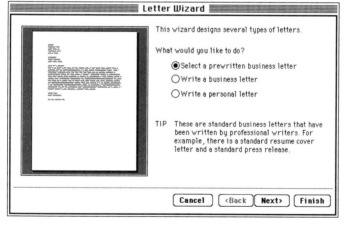

Figure 15-2:
The Letter
Wizard
dialog box
helps you
create the
perfect
epistle.

Generally speaking, you should repeat the following two steps as often as required to create your document.

5. Choose an option from the right side of the Wizard dialog box.

Indeed, choose them all, one at a time. Examine the preview window to see how the option affects your document; see which one you like the best.

Some options may require you to do a bit of typing, such as entering your name and hat size, maybe a return address, and so on.

Some of the options may ask you to enter measurements. Don't fuss over this part of the process; just guess! The preview window will show how your document will look based on your guesses.

If you're dissatisfied with an option, click the Back button and start again with a new option.

6. Click the Next button

This button moves you along to the next stage, giving you more options to choose from. At this point, you continue with Step 5 and select more options.

Eventually, you see `Those are all the answers the wizard needs to create your` `whatever`. A checkered flag appears (watch for it on the left of the Wizard dialog box), informing you that you're done (or that you've just won The Greatest Spectacle in Racing, the Indianapolis 500, without leaving your driveway).

Notice that the Next button is dimmed. Word is ready to slap together your document.

7. Click the Finish button.

The Wizard prepares your document and presents it to you, primed for editing and fine-tuning.

✔ Even though a Wizard created your document, you still must save it to disk when you're done. In fact, most Wizards may start you on your way. After that point, you work with the document just like any other in Word. Don't forget to save! save! save!

✔ Don't forget to look at the preview window. If you don't like what you see, you can click either the Back button (to rethink your strategy) or the Cancel button (to blow this gig and go back to watching TV and eating salty snack foods).

✔ The preview window shows *greeked* text, which is typesetter talk for very tiny text. This window gives you an idea of how your document will look.

✔ Some Wizards even fill in text for you. These are super-cheating Wizards. The Stephen King Wizard, for example, writes his books for him in under a day.

✔ Always read the information on the right side of the Wizard dialog box. I normally wouldn't mark this item with a tip icon, but too many people don't read stuff that the computer tells them, and the text in the Wizard dialog boxes is actually kinda informative.

✔ There. I've managed to finish this entire section with only one silly reference to *The Wizard of Oz*.

Using AutoFormat

Word's AutoFormat command has absolutely nothing to do with character or paragraph formatting. No, what it really does is clean up your document, remove excess spaces, add spaces where needed, and other minor housekeeping chores. In other words, it removes the slop most of us add to our documents without thinking.

Before AutoFormat can do its job, you need to create the document's text. Write! Write! Write! Write your letter, memo, chapter, poem, whatever. Then follow these steps:

1. Before you AutoFormat it, save your document to disk.

This step is most important. Remember, saving is something you should be doing all the time. Refer to Chapter 1 for the details on saving.

2. Save your document to disk.

Just in case you skipped Step 1.

3. Choose Format↭AutoFormat.

The AutoFormat dialog box appears, as shown in Figure 15-3.

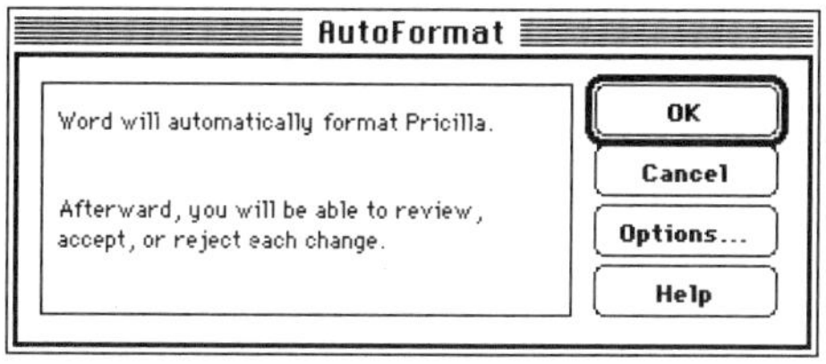

Figure 15-3:
AutoFormat
is about to
prepare the
document
Pricilla.

AutoFormat
Word will automatically format Pricilla.
Afterward, you will be able to review, accept, or reject each change.

OK
Cancel
Options...
Help

4. Click OK.

Ook! Eep! Ack!

5. Formatting completed.

The final formatting dialog box appears, as shown in Figure 15-4. Word has carefully massaged and adjusted your document. You may find new headings, bulleted lists, and other amazing, whiz-bang things automatically done to your text. If you like, you can click the Review Changes button to see exactly what was done. Otherwise . . .

Figure 15-4:
The final
formatting
dialog box.

6. Click the Accept button.

The changes that AutoFormat made to your document are slapped in place.

✔ If your text is kinda boring, it won't appear as though AutoFormat did anything. Don't despair. AutoFormat is good at creating headings and bulleted lists, but it can't read your mind.

✔ The AutoFormat tool has nothing to do with character or paragraph formatting.

✔ If you're interested in formatting your document automatically, refer to the section on Wizards earlier in this chapter.

Chapter 16

More Than a File — a Document

A *document* is what you see on-screen in Word. It's the text you create and edit, the formatting you apply, and the end result that's printed. But a document also is a thing you must deal with. It's a sheet of paper in a window on-screen — a bold new concept, eh? Further, a document is stored as a file on disk for later retrieval, editing, or printing.

This chapter is where you get reintroduced to the way Mr. Macintosh does things when it comes to files on disk. None of this is overly hard. It's just a little . . . different. And it can be fun because, unlike some *other* computers in the world, you can get really clever with the way you name your documents when you save them to disk.

Working on Several Documents Simultaneously

This is handy: Word lets you work on as many as nine documents at once. Nine! That's as many people as were in the Brady Bunch if you count Alice, the indentured servant.

This is so handy, I'm gonna repeat myself: Depending on how much memory your computer has, you can open up to nine documents without having to close any of them. You don't have to save one to disk — banishing Jan to her room, as it were — and start over.

In Word, each document is stored in its own window on-screen. Normally, that window uses most of the screen, so that document is all you see. To see other documents, access the Window menu; from there, you can choose the document you want to see by clicking on its filename.

In the Window menu, Word politely reveals which files are open. Figure 16-1 shows what the Window menu looks like when a bunch of documents are open.

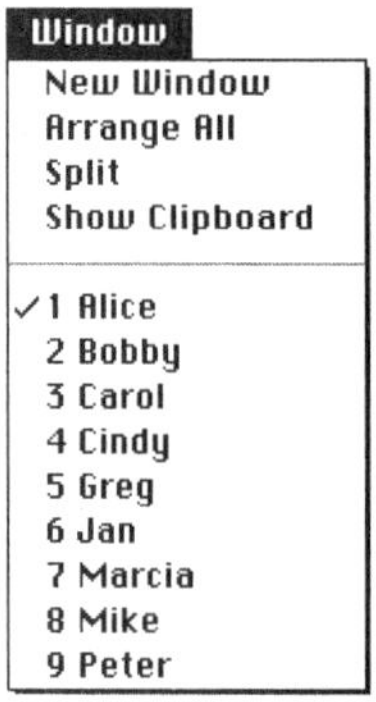

Window
New Window
Arrange All
Split
Show Clipboard
✓ 1 Alice
2 Bobby
3 Carol
4 Cindy
5 Greg
6 Jan
7 Marcia
8 Mike
9 Peter

Figure 16-1: Use the Window menu to track open documents.

✔ To switch from one document to another, click on its name from the Window menu. The names are alphabetized for your convenience.

✔ If you press Option-Shift-F6, you are taken to the "next" window; Option-F6 takes you to the "preceding" window. If you only have two windows open at a time, Option-F6 makes for a keen shortcut to skip-to-my-lou between 'em.

✔ The goings-on in one document are independent of any other: printing, spell-checking, and formatting affect only the *current* document, or the document with the highlighted title bar.

✔ You can copy a block from one document to the other. Just mark the block in the first document, copy it (⌘-C), open the second document, and paste the copied block in (⌘-V). (Don't forget that you can use the Copy and Paste buttons.) Refer to Chapter 6 for detailed block-party action.

Seeing more than one document

You can arrange all of your documents on-screen by choosing Window⇨Arrange All. This command puts each document into its own mini-window.

✔ Although you can see more than one document at a time, you can work on only one at a time: the document with the highlighted title bar. To work another document, make it current by clicking on it or toggle to it by pressing Option-F6.

✔ After the windows have been arranged, you can manipulate their size and change their position by using the mouse .

✔ Clicking on a mini-window's Size button (upper-right corner) restores that document to its normal, full-screen view.

✔ The Window⇨Arrange All command works great for two or three documents — when you're comparing text, for example. Arranging more documents than three makes the viewing area so small that it's of little use.

Working on two or more parts of the same document

You can look at two or more different parts of the same document — yes, the *same* document — by choosing Window⇨New Window. This command creates another window on-screen, in which you'll find another copy of your document. Unlike having different documents open in separate windows, each copy of this document is connected to the other; any change that you make in one copy is immediately made in the other.

✔ This feature is useful for cutting and pasting text or graphics between sections of the same document, especially when you have a very long document.

✔ You can tell which copy of your document you're looking at by looking at the title bar; Word displays a colon and a number after the filename. For example, this document is Chapter 16:1 in one window and Chapter 16:2 in the second window.

- ✔ You can move back and forth between these windows by pressing Option-F6.

- ✔ You cannot close one window without closing both documents. The second window is merely a new look at the same document. So . . .

- ✔ If you want to get rid of one window, close it by clicking in its close box. Don't choose File➪Close.

- ✔ Another way to view two parts of the same document is by using the old split-screen trick. This feature is discussed . . . why, it's right here.

Using the old split-screen trick

Splitting the screen allows you to view two parts of your document in one window. No need to bother with extra windows here. In fact, I prefer to use Word with as little "junk" on-screen as possible. So when I need to view two parts of the same document, I just split the screen and then undo the rift when I'm done. You can accomplish the same splitting-screen feat by following these steps:

1. **Place the mouse cursor on the Little Black Area — located just above the up-arrow button on the vertical scroll bar, on the upper-right side of your document window.**

   Oh, bother. Just refer to Figure 16-2 to see what I'm talking about.

Figure 16-2: The Little Black Area you use to split a window.

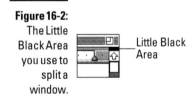

Little Black Area

When you find the sweet spot, the mouse pointer changes shape and looks like a pair of horizontal lines with arrows pointing up and down.

2. **Hold down the mouse button and drag the pointer down.**

   As you drag, a line drags with you and slices the document window. That line is where the screen will split.

3. **Release the mouse button.**

   Your screen looks something like Figure 16-3.

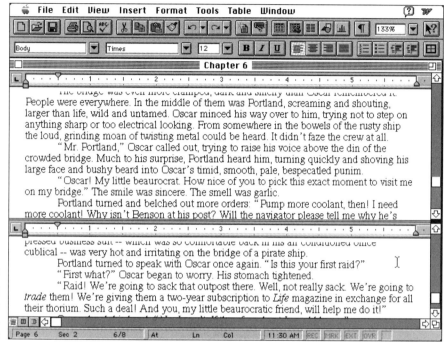

Figure 16-3:
Splitting the
screen.

- Each section of the screen can be manipulated separately and scrolled up or down. But the windows still represent the same document; any change that you make in one copy is immediately included in the other.

- This feature is useful for cutting and pasting text or graphics between sections of the same document.

- To undo a split screen, put the cursor on the Little Black Area and drag it back up to the ruler.

- You can also choose Window⇨Split to split your screen and Window⇨Remove Split to undo it.

Saving a Document to Disk

There's no need to save your document to disk only when you're done with it. In fact, saving should be done almost immediately — as soon as you have typed a few sentences or paragraphs. Save! Save! Save!

Saving a document to disk (the first time)

To save a document that hasn't already been saved to disk, follow the steps listed below. If you've already saved the file, move to the next section.

1. Summon the Save command.

Choose File⇨Save, press ⌘-S, press F12, or click the Save button. You see the Save dialog box, shown in Figure 16-4.

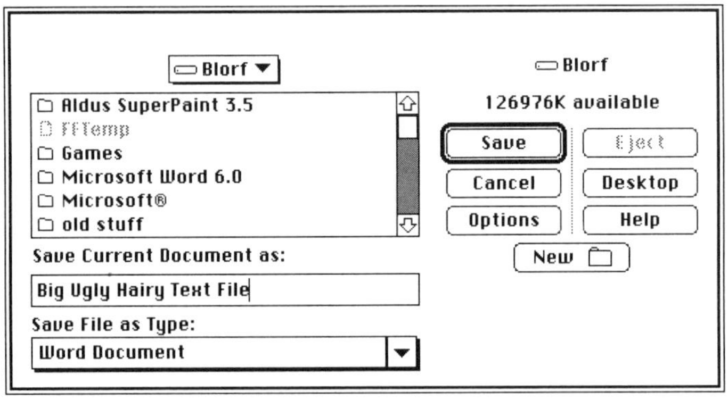

Figure 16-4:
The Save
dialog box.

2. Type a filename for your document.

You should be descriptive and to the point (thus ruling out most lawyers from effectively naming files).

3. Press Return or click the Save button.

4. If everything goes right, your disk drive churns for a few seconds and eventually your filename appears in the title bar.

Your file has been saved. If there is a problem, you'll likely see the error message

    Replace existing *Whatever*?

meaning a file on disk already owns the name you tried to give your document. Click Cancel, skip back up to Step 2, and type in another name. If you click Replace, your file will replace, or *overwrite*, the other file on disk, which is probably not what you want.

You can organize your files by storing them in special folders on your disk. This subject is covered in the Chapter 18 section "Finding a Place for Your Work." Technical mumbo jumbo on folders is hidden away in Chapter 24; see the sections "Organizing Your Files" and "Creating New Folders."

Saving a document to disk (after that)

Why save your file again and again and again? Because it's smart and smart and smart! You should save your file to disk every so often — usually after you write something brilliant or something so complex that you don't want to retype it again. (If you haven't yet saved your document to disk, refer to the preceding section.)

Saving your document to disk a second time updates the file on disk. This is painless and quick:

1. **Choose File⇨Save, press the ⌘-S shortcut, or choose the Save button.**

   See the status bar change oh-so-quickly as the document is saved.

2. **Continue working.**

   I recommend going back and repeating Step 1 every so often as you continue to toss words down on the page.

✔ Save! Save! Save!

✔ Save your document to disk every three minutes or so, or immediately after you've written something clever.

✔ If you are working on a network, you should execute the Save command between each keystroke.

✔ If you already saved your file to disk, its name appears in the title bar. If there is no name there, refer to the preceding section for instructions.

Saving a document to disk and quitting

You're done for the day. Your fingers are sore, your eyes glaze over, "I don't want to type no more!" Everywhere you look, you see a mouse pointer. You blink and rub your eyes and stretch out your back. Ah, it's Miller time. But before you slap your beer commercial buddies on the back and ride into the sunset, you need to save your document and quit for the day:

1. **Quit.**

   Choose File⇨Quit or press ⌘-Q. You see a box that asks

   > Do you want to save changes to *Document Whatever*?

2. **Click Yes.**

   The document is saved and Word closes — quit, kaput.

   ✔ If a second Word document is open and changes have been made to it since it was last saved, you see the Do you want to save changes message again. Press Y to save that document.

   ✔ If you haven't yet given your document a name, you can do so after pressing *Y* to save it. Refer to the instructions for "Saving a document to disk (the first time)," earlier in this chapter.

   ✔ After you quit Word, it sends you back to the Finder. There you can start another program or choose Special⇨Shut Down and turn Mr. Mac off for the day.

   ✔ Always quit Word and shut down your Mac properly. Never turn off your computer or reset when Word is still on-screen. Only turn off the computer when it says it's OK to do so.

Saving and starting over with a clean slate

When you want to save a document, remove it from the screen, and start over with a clean slate, choose File⇨Close. This method keeps you in Word.

✔ The keyboard shortcut for File⇨Close is ⌘-W.

✔ You also can start afresh in Word and begin working on a new document by choosing File⇨New or by clicking on the New button, on the Standard toolbar.

✔ If you haven't yet saved your document to disk, refer to the section titled "Saving a document to disk (the first time)," earlier in this chapter. Always save your document right after you start writing something (and approximately every 2.3 seconds after that).

✔ There is no reason to quit Word and start it again just to begin working with a blank slate.

Retrieving a Document from Disk

When you first start Word, or after you close a document to start over with a clean slate, you may retrieve a previously saved document from disk into Word for editing.

To grab a file from disk — to *retrieve* it — follow these steps:

1. Summon the Open command.

Choose File⇨Open, press ⌘-O, or click on the Open button (on the Standard toolbar). You see the Open dialog box, as shown in Figure 16-5.

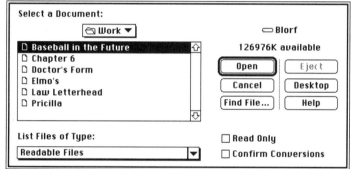

Figure 16-5:
The Open
dialog box.

2. Pluck the document you want.

Use the gizmos in the dialog box to browse through various disks and folders on your Macintosh. If you're not adept at such things, read through Chapter 24, "Contending with Mr. Macintosh."

3. When you find the document you want, click on its name.

Click.

4. Press Return.

Word finds the document and loads it on-screen for editing.

5. Go!

✔ If you load a file written by another word processor, you may see the Convert File dialog box. It's asking whether it's OK to convert it to Word-speak. Click on the OK button. Refer to Chapter 17 for more information on alien word-processor documents.

Loading One Document into Another Document

There are times when you want to load one document into another. When you do, follow these steps:

1. **Position the toothpick cursor where you want the other document's text to appear.**

2. **Choose Insert⇨File.**

3. **Find the file in the Insert File dialog box (which looks just like an Open dialog box).**

   Refer to the preceding section for more information on opening a file.

4. **Highlight the file and press Return (or just double-click on its name).**

   The document appears right where the toothpick cursor is.

   ✔ If you aren't really sure where you put the file that you want to include, you can select the Find File command to look for it. Refer to Chapter 18 for additional details on Find File.

   ✔ The resulting combined document still has the same name as the first document.

   ✔ You can retrieve any number of documents into your document. There is no limit, although you should avoid the huge hulking cow document if possible.

   ✔ These steps allow you to grab a block of text saved into one document and stick it into another document. This process is often called *boilerplating*, where a commonly used piece of text is slapped into several documents. It's the way sleazy romance novels are written.

Doing It All Simultaneously

You open. You save. You close. If you're a busy person (and you wouldn't take time to read this parenthetic clause if you were), it's nice to know that Word can handle these amazing tasks for a bunch of files all at once.

Opening a group of files all at once is covered in Chapter 18. Saving and closing groups of documents is covered next.

Saving a gang of documents simultaneously

With Word, you can work on a multitude of documents at once. To save them all, you could switch to each window and incant the Save command. Or you could be spiffy and choose File⇨Save All, saving all your work in one swift stroke. There is no prompting, no wait and see. Everything is just saved to disk as fast as your Mac can handle it.

- ✔ If a file has not yet been saved, you'll be prompted to give it a name. Refer to the section "Saving a document to disk (the first time)," earlier in this chapter, for more information.

- ✔ I use the Save All command any time I have to get up and leave my computer — even for a short moment, but especially when the phone rings.

Closing a gang of documents simultaneously

There's a Save All command, but why isn't there a Close All command? The answer is that, lo, a Close All command exists, but it involves some conjuring. When you want to close all your documents at once — tantamount to shutting up the entire Brady Bunch (bliss, indeed) — heed the following steps:

1. **Press and hold down the Shift key. Either one. Doesn't matter.**

2. **Choose File⇨Close All.**

   Normally, this item would read Close. But because you pressed the Shift key before accessing the File menu, it magically turned into Close All. Nifty.

- ✔ This trick only works with the mouse, not with the keyboard.

- ✔ Word still asks whether you want to save any unsaved documents before it closes them.

Chapter 17

Other Documents—Alien and ASCII

. . . .

In This Chapter

▶ Loading an MS-DOS text file

▶ Saving an MS-DOS text file

▶ Loading documents created by alien word processors

▶ Saving documents in alien formats

. . . .

*W*ord is not the only word processor in the world. (Too bad.) Other folks use other word processors, and occasionally you may have to tangle with the files that they create. You may also need to give someone a file in ASCII format. These are the moments when you must deal with non-Word documents, or what I call *alien* file formats.

Loading an MS-DOS Text File

Yes, it happens. An MS-DOS text file is a special, nondocument file that you can load into Word for editing. It's a nondocument file because it contains no formatting—no bold, underline, centering, headers, or footers. It's just plain old text, boring and dull like DOS.

To open an MS-DOS text file, follow these steps:

1. Do the Open command.

 Choose File➪Open or press ⌘-O, the Open shortcut. Or click the Open button. The Open dialog box appears.

2. Locate the DOS text file.

Use the controls in the dialog box to hunt down the file that you want on
your hard drive. (Please see the tip at the end of this section for information on making this task a bit easier.)

3. Choose Open.

Click the Open button or press Return. The DOS text file appears on-
screen, ready for editing just like any Word document — though the
formatting will be really cruddy.

✔ DOS text files are also called *ASCII* files. ASCII is a technospeak acronym
that loosely translates to English as "an MS-DOS text file." You pronounce
it *ask-EE*.

✔ ASCII files are primarily used to shuttle information between two computers that distrust each other. For example, someone who uses a strange
MS-DOS word processor can save his files in ASCII to a floppy disk; then
you can use the Mac File Exchange utility to read that disk. After you copy
the file to Mr. Macintosh, you can use Word to see the file. Strange.
Convoluted. But it happens.

✔ Yes, the Apple File Exchange program is not covered in this book. For
details, refer to *Macs For Dummies, Second Edition* from IDG Books Worldwide, written by my New York pal, David Pogue.

✔ A good way to locate MS-DOS text or ASCII files specifically is to force
Word to display only those types of files in the Open dialog box. To do so,
find the List Files of Type drop-down thingy at the bottom of the dialog
box. Select Text Files. This option allows you to view only text files (DOS
and ASCII) on your hard drive, not just Word documents. If you're totally
messed up, you can use the Find File command, which is covered in
Chapter 18.

✔ Information on opening Word document files lurks in Chapter 16.

✔ The only difficult thing about dealing with a text file is when you're
required to save the file back to disk in the DOS text format — on other
words, not as a Word document. You're in luck, though: I outline the steps
in the following section. This stuff doesn't come up when you're dealing
with other Mac users, but you may need to know how to do it when
sharing files with DOS people.

Saving an MS-DOS Text File

Because some applications can read files in an MS-DOS text format only, you need to train Word how to save them that way. Otherwise, Word assumes that you're saving a Word document to disk and junks up the text file with lots of curious Word stuff. (DOS folk hate that.) Because this procedure is about saving an MS-DOS text file, also known as saving a file in ASCII format, you have to be more careful.

To save an MS-DOS text file that you just loaded and edited, you need only save it back to disk. Choose File⇨Save, press ⌘-S, or click on the Save button (on the Standard toolbar). Word remembers, "Hey, this is an MS-DOS text file," and saves it that way. Miraculous.

To save a new document in the DOS text or ASCII format, follow these steps:

1. **Conjure the Save As command.**

   You must use the Save As command, not the Save command. Choose File⇨Save As or press F12.

2. **The typical Save As dialog box appears.**

   Normally, you enter a filename and Word saves the file as a document on disk. But you want to save the file as an MS-DOS text file, so you must change the *format* — see the Save File as Type box.

3. **Click on the down-arrow button beside the Save File as Type box and drag down to choose the Text Only format.**

   You can also choose the MS-DOS Text format.

4. **Give the file a name.**

   This is the tricky part for MS-DOS files. Click in the Save Current Document As box and type a name for the file. When you're saving a file for use on a Mac, you can type in any old name. But when you're saving a file for MS-DOS people, you need to follow these restrictive and archaic rules: The name can consist of one to eight letters. Only use letters, and type ALL CAPS, no spaces. That will please the DOS wieners.

5. **Choose Save.**

   Press Return or click Save to save the file to disk.

   If the file already exists, you'll be asked whether you want to replace it; press Y to replace it. This is one of the rare circumstances when it's OK to press Y to replace the file.

✔ Text files that you save for MS-DOS users must have a restrictive filename! Type from one to eight letters, ALL CAPS, no spaces. This is really lame but, hey, that's DOS.

✔ By the way, the same filename restrictions also apply to Windows. So if your DOS friends proclaim "But I have Windows!" slap then around. Windows and DOS are the same turkey.

✔ You can save a document as an MS-DOS text file *and* a Word document file. First, save the file to disk as a Word document with a very Macintosh name. Then save the file to disk as an MS-DOS text file, using a restrictive DOS name. You end up with a text file, which is what DOS wants, and a Word file, which contains secret codes and prints out really purty.

Understanding the ASCII thing

Word saves its documents to disk in its own special file format. That format includes your text — the basic characters that you type — plus information about formatting, graphics, and anything else you toss into the document. These elements are all saved to disk so that the next time you use Word, you get your formatting back for editing, printing, or whatever.

Every word processor has its own different document file format. So your Word documents are considered alien to other word processors, which use their own non-Word format. It's been this way since the dawn of computing, so to keep the confusion low, a common text format was developed. It's called the *plain text* or *ASCII* format.

ASCII is an acronym for something I won't mention because there will be no test on this material. Besides, you'd probably forget what the acronym stands for two minutes from now. What's more important is knowing how to pronounce it: *ask-EE*. It's not "ask-two." It's *ask-EE*.

An ASCII file contains only text — no formatting (not even bold or italics), graphics, or anything. Just text. This format is also called the *plain text* format or the *MS-DOS text* format. Whatever you call it, an ASCII file contains only text.

Because ASCII files aren't littered with word processing codes, any word processor can read the text. In a way, ASCII files are the Esperanto of document files. Any word processor can read an ASCII file and display its contents. The text will look ugly, but it's better than nothing. Also, to maintain compatibility, Word can save your files in ASCII format, as described in the section "Saving an MS-DOS Text File."

Loading Documents Created by Alien Word Processors

Suppose that crazy Earl gives you a disk full of his favorite limericks. Of course, Earl is crazy, so crazy that he actually uses WordPerfect for the Macintosh. Without thinking about it, Earl has handed you a disk full of WordPerfect documents.

First, don't press the panic button. Although one of Earl's WordPerfect files may seem as alien as a MS-DOS text file to you, it shouldn't matter one iota. Word can safely read Earl's limericks. To retrieve the files, just follow these steps:

1. **Poke out the Open command.**

    Choose File⇨Open or click on the Open button, on the Standard toolbar.

2. **Select All Files from the List Files of Type drop-down.**

   Normally, you see Readable Files there. Whatever. Sometimes, Word just can't figure out what Earl has done, so picking All Files helps Word find the whacko WordPerfect stuff.

3. **Use the controls in the dialog box to find the alien word processor document.**

4. **Open the document.**

   Click the Open button. If you're lucky, Word will recognize the file format at once and convert it for you — just as it did for the MS-DOS files mentioned earlier in this chapter. If you're not-as-lucky, you see the Convert File dialog box, shown in Figure 17-1.

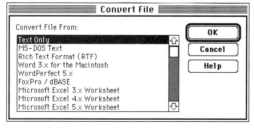

Figure 17-1:
The Convert File dialog box.

5. **Select the appropriate file format from the list. For a WordPerfect file, you'd select the WordPerfect option(s) that are listed.**

6. **The file opens and you can edit, print, ridicule it. And so on.**

✔ Nothing's perfect. The alien document you open into Word may require some minor fixing, adjusting fonts, and whatnot. This kind of task is at most a minor bother; at least you don't have to retype anything.

✔ After the file is in Word, you can save it to disk in the Word format. Just use the Save command as you normally do. Word asks whether the old file should be overridden with Word formatting. If so, answer Yes.

✔ Occasionally, Word finds something so utterly bizarre that it won't recognize it its existence. When this situation occurs, you can try to open the document, but it's probably better to ask the person who created the document to save it in ASCII format.

✔ Another common document format is RTF, the Rich Text Format. This format is better than ASCII because it keeps track of bold, italics, underlines, and other formatting. If you plan to share files often with other weirdo word processors, try to get everyone to settle on a common format, such as RTF. Better still, get everyone to settle on Word.

Saving Documents in Alien Formats

Now comes the time for you to give Earl your collection of leper jokes. Alas, they are all saved to disk in Word format. You could be lax like Earl and just hand him a diskette full of Word documents. But then he would call you up and complain or ramble on and on about some new word processor conversion program he found. Because you don't have time for that, just do Earl a favor and save the file in his own word processor's format.

This task is simple: follow the steps outlined in the preceding section, "Saving an MS-DOS Text File." In Step 3, however, select the proper alien word processor format from the list. (For Earl, that is WordPerfect.) This process saves the file in the alien format.

✔ Users on Venus prefer WordPerfect for the Mac.

✔ Users on Mars prefer MacWrite. But, hey, they've always been behind the times.

Chapter 18

Managing Files

· ·

· ·

*T*he more you work in Word, the more documents you create. And because you always save those documents, you make more files. And sooner or later, your hard drive gets full of stuff. In a way, your hard drive is like your closet. It's full of stuff. Unless you have a handy closet organizer — like the one I bought on TV for three low, low payments of $29.95 — things tend to get messy. This chapter dwells on documents as files and the handy File Finder/Manager Thing that Word uses to help you organize your hard drive.

Finding Files in Word

It's really hard to lose a file so thoroughly that Word can't find it, even if you have an absolutely horrid memory. I often find it difficult to remember which document contains the stuff that I want and also where the heck I put that file anyway. Of course, I also often find strange things next to the milk in the refrigerator. Cereal Fairies is what I think. In any case, Word's Find File command, in the File menu, can be a real time-saver here.

To locate documents, the Find File feature uses almost any information that you can remember — or guess at — about a document. You can, for example, find all documents that contain a reference to Hobart X. Zlotnik or all documents written in the month of May by a certain person wearing a red fez. (I'm kidding about the red fez part.)

To search for documents by using the Find File command, follow these mesmerizing steps:

1. Summon the Find File command.

Choose File⇨Find File. You also can click any button labeled *Find File*; these buttons are located in various dialog boxes, including the Open dialog box. After you choose the Find File command, the Search dialog box opens, as shown in Figure 18-1.

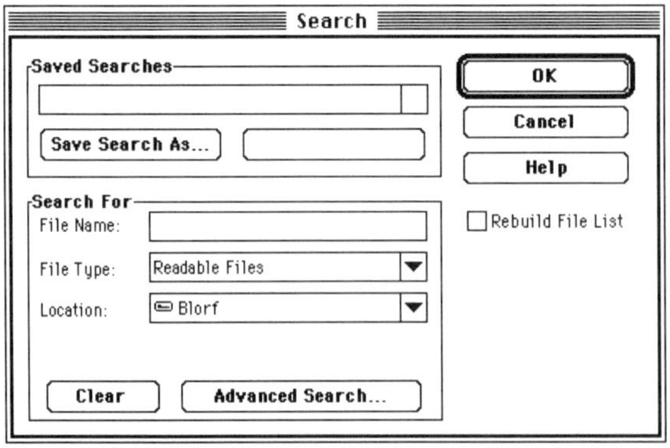

Figure 18-1:
The Search
dialog box.

If you see the Find File dialog box instead (see Figure 18-2), click the Search button.

2. Fill in the filename.

If you know the name, enter it in the File Name box. For example, type **Hobart X. Zlotnic** to look for that file.

3. Choose a file type.

If you know that you want a Word document, for example, then click on the down arrow by the File Type box and select Word Documents from the list. This step tells the Find File command to look for only Word documents.

4. Select a disk drive to scan.

Click on the down arrow by the Location box and select a drive.

5. Click OK.

Word sits and hums while it searches your hard drive. This task takes a while, depending on how slow your hard drive is and how far away you live from a gravity well.

6. The official Find File dialog box appears.

The Find File dialog box should look something similar to Figure 18-2. If not, click on the View drop-down list and select File Info.

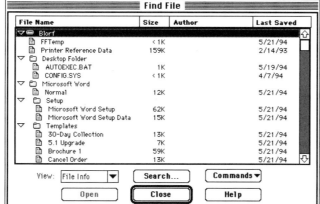

File Name	Size	Author	Last Saved
▽ 🖥 Blorf			⇧
🖹 FFTemp	< 1K		5/21/94
🖹 Printer Reference Data	159K		2/14/93
▽ 🗁 Desktop Folder			
🖹 AUTOEXEC.BAT	1K		5/19/94
🖹 CONFIG.SYS	< 1K		4/7/94
▽ 🗁 Microsoft Word			
🖹 Normal	12K		5/21/94
▽ 🗁 Setup			
🖹 Microsoft Word Setup	62K		5/21/94
🖹 Microsoft Word Setup Data	15K		5/21/94
▽ 🗁 Templates			
🖹 30-Day Collection	13K		5/21/94
🖹 5.1 Upgrade	7K		5/21/94
🖹 Brochure 1	59K		5/21/94
🖹 Cancel Order	13K		5/21/94 ⇩

View: [File Info ▼]   [Search...]   [Commands ▼]

[Open]   [Close]   [Help]

Figure 18-2: The Find File dialog box.

The Find File dialog box displays all the files that match the criteria you specified in the Search dialog box. If you don't enter a filename in Step 2, for example, the Find File dialog box lists all Word documents on a given hard drive.

Your job now is to find the file that you were looking for by scrolling through the list and then highlighting the file. Helpful instructions on doing this appear in the checklist that ends this section.

After you find your file, you can peek at its contents, open it, print it, or do a number of other amazing things with it, each of which is discussed in the sections that follow.

7. When you're done browsing the Find File dialog box, click the Close button.

The Find File dialog box goes away, and you're returned to your document.

✔ Disk drives, folders, and files appear in the Find File dialog box in bold text with various folder icons by them.

✔ When you find the file that you want, highlight it and click the Open button to open it into Word. An open folder (where you can see its files) has a down-triangle by it; a closed folder is preceded by a right-pointing triangle.

REMEMBER

  ✔ Don't forget that you can search other drives for your files as well. To do so, repeat the preceding steps but enter a different drive letter in Step 3.

  ✔ Clicking the Commands button drops down a menu of various things that you can do with a highlighted file in the list. You can print the file, delete it, rename it, and so on. These subjects are discussed later in this chapter.

Finding text in files

You can use the Find File command to locate text in your Word documents; as a result, it's a great feature for document fishing (those times when you've forgotten a document's name but don't want to wade through a bunch of documents individually to scan for text). Instead, do the following (and next time, remember that drinking and hard driving don't mix):

1. Open the Find File dialog box.

Choose File⇨Find File. Blup! The Find File dialog box appears.

2. Choose the Search button.

You only need to do this step if the Search dialog box doesn't come up when you first select the Find File command.

3. Fill in the information for your file hunting as per Steps 2, 3, and 4 in the preceding section, "Finding Files in Word."

You still need to tell Word where to look for your files.

4. Click the Advanced Search button.

Ooo! Scary stuff! Advanced search. But it's not too technical. The Advanced Search dialog box is shown in Figure 18-3.

Figure 18-3: The Advanced Search dialog box.

```
═══════════════ Advanced Search ═══════════════
┌──────────────────────────────────────────────┐
│   Location    │   Summary   │   Timestamp     │
│ Title:   [                                  ] │
│ Author:  [                                  ] │
│ Keywords:[                                  ] │
│ Subject: [                                  ] │
│ Options: [Create New List        ▼]  ☐Match Case│
│ ┌Containing Text──────────────────────────┐  │
│ │ [                                      ] │  │
│ │ ☐Use Pattern Matching    [ Special   ▼] │  │
│ └──────────────────────────────────────────┘ │
│   [    OK    ]   [  Cancel  ]   [  Help  ]    │
└──────────────────────────────────────────────┘
```

5. **Click on the Summary tab if the Summary panel isn't up front.**

   You can ignore many of the cracks and crevices in the Advanced Search dialog box. For finding text in a Word document, you need only worry about the Containing Text area, near the bottom.

6. **Type the text that you want Word to find in the Containing Text box.**

   For example, suppose that you've written a cheerful little poem for a friend who just had a baby. Alas, you've forgotten the filename; fortunately, you remember that you included the word *spittle* in the poem (it easily rhymes with *little*). Type *spittle* into the Containing Text box.

7. **Click OK.**

   The Search dialog box reappears. Don't fret: Word hasn't forgotten what you told it.

8. **Click OK in the Search dialog box.**

   Word looks for the documents on disk that contain your text. With any luck, the next screen that you see — the Find File dialog box — will list the exact file that you want.

> ✔ If Word finds no matching files, the Find File list will be empty, and the dreadful text No matching files found will appear. Weep bitterly and curse the computer. Or try again, searching for a word that you're *certain* is in your file.
>
> ✔ Don't forget that you can search other drives for matching files. To do so, repeat the preceding steps but enter a different drive letter.
>
> ✔ If Word finds the file, highlight it and click the Open button to load it into Word.
>
> ✔ If Word finds more than one matching file, highlight them all and open everything into Word. Refer to the upcoming section "Working with groups of files" for more information.

Looking at documents on disk

Wouldn't it be nice if you could peer into a document before you loaded it, like looking at a sneak preview of the year's blockbuster film without plunking down ten bucks? Well, nuke up some popcorn, because you can peek at a Word document by using the Find File command and dialog box. Follow these steps:

1. **Find a file by heeding Steps 1 through 6 in the section "Finding Files in Word," earlier in this chapter.**

2. **Select Preview from the View drop-down list.**

The View list is located in the lower-left corner of the Find File dialog box. Click on its down arrow to see some choices for viewing files, including Preview.

3. **A special preview window opens in the Find File dialog box.**

Everything works the same, but you can use the preview window to see what a file looks like (in teensy-tiny type) before you mess with it.

- ✔ Use the scroll bar on the preview window to peruse the file.
- ✔ Click the Close button in the Find File dialog box when you're finished.

Working with Groups of Files

The Find File dialog box enables you to work with files individually or in groups. To work with a group of files, you must select them by using the mouse (a typical Mac action):

1. **Press ⌘ and click on an item that you want.**

The item is highlighted and thus selected.

2. **Repeat Step 1 for each additional item that you want in your group.**

Et cetera and so on.

With the preceding steps, you highlight, or select, several files at once. You can then use the commands in the Find File dialog box's Commands drop-down menu to manipulate the files as a group.

- ✔ When the preview window is active, it only displays the contents of the last file in the group. See the preceding section, "Looking at documents on disk," for details on Find File's preview mode.
- ✔ The commands detailed in the following sections also apply to files selected in a group.

Opening files

The Find File dialog box is great for finding files, peering into their contents, and then snatching up the files that you (with luck) found. You open files by taking the following steps:

1. **Select the file(s) that you want to open from the Find File dialog box.**

2. **Click the Open button.**

Word places each file into its own document window.

3. **Work away!**

✔ There is a limit on the number of files Word can work with at once. No, I don't know what it is — but you will! You'll see some odd error message about not enough memory or heap space or something even more bizarre. Don't panic. Close a few windows — maybe even quit Word — and start over.

✔ Refer to Chapter 16 for details on saving and closing all your files at once. Wow. Doing it all at once. I'm sure that such a concept was promised in a computer brochure somewhere.

Printing files

You can print a single file without opening it, thanks to the Find File dialog box. Better still, you can print a whole gang of files all at once. To do so, obey the following steps:

1. Select the file(s) that you want to print from the Find File dialog box.

2. Click the Commands button.

A drop-down menu of commands appears.

3. Select the Print command.

The Print dialog box appears.

4. Click OK to print your document(s).

✔ Make sure that your printer is on and ready to print before you click the OK button in the Print dialog box.

✔ Chapter 8 has more information on printing. Refer to Chapter 8 for information on the Print dialog box, as well.

Copying files

You can use the Find File dialog box to copy files to and fro in your system. Here's how it works:

1. Select the file(s) that you want to copy from the Find File dialog box.

2. Click the Commands button.

Like bread out of a toaster, a list of commands pops up on-screen.

3. Choose the Copy command.

You see the Copy dialog box, shown in Figure 18-4.

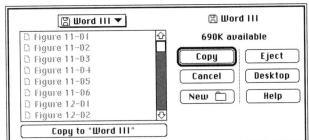

Figure 18-4:
The Copy
dialog box.

4. **Find a spot to copy the files to.**

   Negotiate around your disk system by using the dialog box's controls to find a disk drive or folder for the files. If you're copying to a floppy disk, stick it in the disk drive now and its name will magically appear in the Copy dialog box.

5. **Choose the Copy command.**

   Click the Copy button or press Return. The file(s) will be copied.

   If a file with the same name already exists at the desired destination, Word asks whether you want to replace it. My advice is to press N for No unless you're absolutely certain that you're not overwriting something important. Then try the Copy command again, but use a different destination or another disk.

Deleting files

You can use the Find File command to flick unworthy files from your hard drive. Before you begin your acts of utter destruction and lay the files to rest, heed one warning: *Don't delete anything that you need!* Instead, delete older copies of files, backups, or just plain old junk (junk files happen).

When you're ready to destroy, follow these steps:

1. **Select the file(s) to blow away from the Find File dialog box.**

   If you're feeling despotic, hold down ⌘ and click on more than one filename to mark them for demolition.

2. **Click the Commands button.**

   A menu of commands drops down.

3. Choose the Destroy command.

OK, it's really the Delete command. A message box asks whether you really want to delete the file (if you marked a group of files for slaughter, a dialog box with the appropriate roll call appears).

4. Choose Yes.

The file is no more. Or if you were needlessly greedy, the files have been vanquished. Gone! Gone! Gone! Purge dem files!

Oops! Deleting a file this way is *not* the same as putting it in the trash can. You cannot quickly recover the file after it's been deleted. Because of this, I don't recommend deleting files from Word. Use the Finder for your wanton acts of destruction.

Chapter 19
Mail Merge for the Mental

· ·

In This Chapter

▶ Understanding mail merge

▶ Using the Mail Merge command

▶ Preparing the main document

▶ Preparing the data source

▶ Adding data to the data source

▶ Inserting the fields

▶ Merge mania!

· ·

*M*ail merge. Ugh. What it is: a method of producing several custom documents without individually editing each one. We're talking form letters here—form letters so sneaky that you can't really tell they're form letters.

Face it, mail merge is not fun. For some reason, with every incarnation of Word, it gets more difficult and baffling. The boys and girls at Microsoft have always cheerfully "improved" mail merge, primarily by adding a hoary hoard of new and ugly terms. I wanted to pass on this topic, but the publisher insisted that would be shirking my civic duty. After all, chiropractic bills have skyrocketed and a record number of hernias have been reported as more and more users have hurled their User's Guide through the window. This chapter contains only the basic, need-to-know steps for mail merging.

Understanding Mail Merge

There are three ways to handle a mail merge:

✔ Read this chapter and then go out for a drink.

✔ Skip this chapter and head straight to the booze.

✔ Hire a professional to do it for you while you're in detox.

I outline the first part of the first approach here. The second approach you can attempt on your own. The third approach shouldn't be necessary. (If you've been through mail merge before, skip to the section "Using the Mail Merge Command.")

Mail merge is the process of taking a single form letter, stirring in a list of names and other information, and then merging both to create several customized documents.

The file that contains the names and other information is the *data source*. The file that contains the form letter is the *main document*. No, I didn't make this up. These are the terms Word uses. Get used to 'em.

You start by typing the main document, creating it as you would any other document, complete with formatting and other mumbo jumbo. But leave blank those spots where you usually put the address, salutation, or anything else that you want to change from letter to letter. In a bit, you will add some fill-in-the-blanks special codes, called *fields* (another term I didn't make up).

The data source is a file (kind of) that contains the names, addresses, and other information. You create this document by using a special method that resembles compiling information in a database program.

Each name, address, and piece of other information in the data source is a *record*. Word creates a custom letter by using the main file as a skeleton and then filling in the meat — records from the secondary file (the data source). I know — totally gross. But I can think of nothing else that describes it as well.

Because no one commits this routine to memory (and for good reason), the following sections outline how to create a mail merge document by using main and data files. Cross your fingers, count the rosary, and check the kids. We're goin'-a mail-mergin'.

Using the Mail Merge Command

Start your mail merging mania by choosing Tools⇨Mail Merge, which opens the Mail Merge Helper dialog box (see Figure 19-1). Don't let the title fool you.

You mail merge in three steps, as shown in the Mail Merge Helper dialog box. After you create the main document and the data source, you merge.

- Don't let the Spartan nature of the Mail Merge Helper dialog box fool you. Other buttons and gadgets appear as you wade further offshore. Beware of the undertow. Truly, it's frightening.
- The data source (Step 2) is really the second document: the names, addresses, and other information. I know, it's a horrible name, but it's supposed to make you feel more comfortable.
- Yeah, there really are more than three steps to this whole operation. Lots more.
- Take a deep breath and continue reading.

Preparing the main document

The main document is the fill-in-the-blanks document. To create it, follow these steps:

1. **Click on the Create button in the Mail Merge Helper dialog box.**

   A drop-down list drops, well, down.

2. **Select Form Letters.**

   Another, annoying dialog box appears. Ignore it and . . .

3. Click the New Main Document button.

This option lets you create a new document — your form letter.

4. Click the Edit button, which just appeared out of thin air next to the Create button.

See? I told you that the dialog box would get crowded. It gets worse.

The Edit button contains a drop-down list with one item, Form Letter: Document#.

5. Select the Form Letter: Document# item.

The Mail Merge Helper dialog box disappears, and you see a new document window, where you can edit your form letter document.

✔ Remember to save your main document while you're working on it. It's saved just like any other document on disk. Refer to Chapter 16 if you need to brush up.

✔ I stick in placeholders (in ALL CAPS) for the replaceable, fill-in-the-blanks stuff so that I can find the items more easily later (see Figure 19-2).

✔ The new toolbar you see on-screen (see Figure 19-2) is the Mail Merge toolbar. Don't bother messing with it; none of its buttons work at this point. It's an exercise in frustration if you try. Makes you wonder why it's there now, doesn't it?

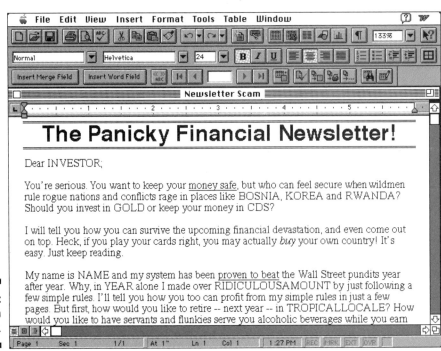

Figure 19-2:
A main
document.

Preparing the data source

A data source is not a traditional Word document. A database table of sorts, it includes information stored in fields and records. Each *field* contains a tidbit of text that will fill in a blank in the main document. A *record* is a collection of fields — one form letter. Don't sweat the details or the jargon. Word handles the details. I'll ease you through the jargon.

To start a data source, follow these steps:

1. **Choose Tools⇨Mail Merge.**

   The Mail Merge Helper dialog box reappears. It may look a little different. If so, don't bother checking against Figure 19-1; the thing has transformed again. You may see a new button plus some new information. As usual, ignore the details — in other words, don't look down. Listen only to me; I'll talk you in off the ledge.

2. **Click the Get Data button.**

   A drop-down list appears.

3. **Choose Create Data Source.**

   The Create Data Source dialog box appears, full of mirth and merriment (see Figure 19-3). This is the place where you create the fields — the fill-in-the-blanks items.

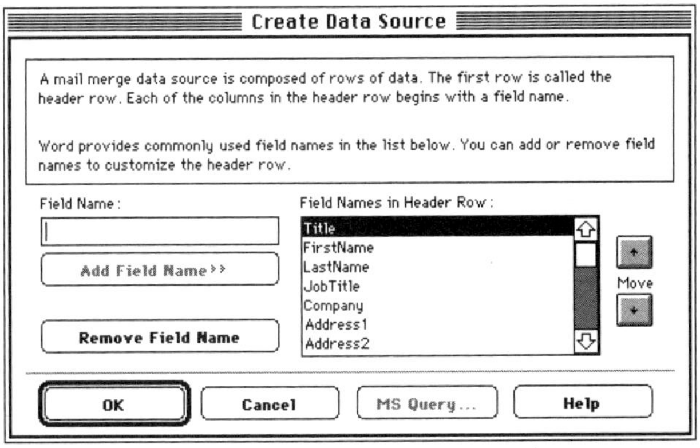

Figure 19-3:
The Create
Data Source
dialog box.

Ever helpful, Word has already dreamt up a whole parade of field names. Your first duty is to erase them all.

4. **Keep clicking the Remove Field Name button until all the names Word had concocted in the Field Names in Header Row list are gone, gone, gone.**

I had to click 13 times. You may have to do it more if you click too fast.

You are disposing of the preset names so that you can come up with your own.

5. **Type a field name into the Field Name box.**

Here are some suggestions for making this step make sense:

- The field should be named to reflect the kind of information that it will contain. For example, a field named *firstname* should contain first names.

- No two fields can have the same name.

- A field name must begin with a letter.

- A field name can contain up to 20 letters, numbers, and underscore characters.

- You cannot use spaces or punctuation marks in field names.

- You can tell when you use a forbidden character because the Add Field Name button gets embarrassed (grayed).

- When entering addresses, always make separate fields for city, state, and ZIP code.

6. **After typing your field name, click the Add Field Name button.**

This command inserts the newly created field into the list shown in the Field Names in Header Record box.

7. **Repeat Steps 5 and 6 for each field that you want to include in your data source.**

In my example (see Figure 19-2), I needed fields for INVESTOR, NAME, RIDICULOUSAMOUNT, and TROPICALLOCALE, for example. In fact, I had to go through Steps 5 and 6 ten times!

8. **Click the OK button when you're done creating field names.**

A Save As dialog box appears. This is when you save your data source document to disk.

9. **Give your data source document a name.**

Be clever. I called my newsletter document *Newsletter Scam* and the data source document *Suckers*.

10. Click the Save button.

Another annoying dialog box appears after your data source has been saved to disk. Ignore everything — you're almost done with this stage — and . . .

11. Click the Edit Data Source button.

The Data Form dialog box appears (see Figure 19-4). Continue to the next section.

Adding data to the data source

Because you're obeying step-by-step instructions here, editing the fill-in-the-blanks information — which is technically called *adding data to the data source* — is done via the handy Data Form dialog box, shown in Figure 19-4. Follow these steps:

Figure 19-4:
The Data
Form dialog
box.

1. Fill in the blanks!

Each field in your document needs information. For a NAME field, for example, type in a name. Then type in other necessary information as displayed in the Data Form dialog box: street, ZIP code, phone number, hat size, and so on. Press Tab to move from box to box.

2. When you've filled in all the blanks, click the Add New button.

You don't have to click the Add New button after typing the last record. Instead, go right to Step 4.

3. Repeat Steps 1 and 2 for every person to whom you want to mail your form letter.

4. When you're done, click the OK button.

Clicking OK sends the Data Form dialog box away, saving all the information to disk.

- Data is pronounced *DAY-ta*.

- The names for the boxes in the Data Form dialog box are the field names that you created in the preceding section.

- Move from box to box by pressing Tab.

- You can press the Record buttons to scan and modify information that's already entered.

- If you need to reexamine or edit the data source, skip to the next section.

Editing the data source

If you need to look at your data source information, for recreation or for editing, follow these steps:

1. Choose Tools⇨Mail Merge.

The Mail Merge Helper dialog box from hell appears.

2. Under Data Source, click the Edit button.

A list with one item drops down.

3. Select the highlighted data item.

The Data Form dialog box appears. There you can peruse or edit your information as you see fit.

- Edit the text in the fields and click the OK button when you're done.

- Press the Delete button in the Data Form dialog box to remove a record.

- Use the Record buttons to scan the various records.

- Clicking on the View Data Source button also displays the Data Source dialog box. (If it doesn't, and I've seen it work about half the time, then follow the preceding steps to see the Data Source dialog box for sure.)

Inserting the fields

You need to place the fields — the blanks — into your main document. To do so, follow these steps:

1. Position the toothpick cursor where you want the field to be placed.

For example, you want a name field in your letter's greeting, so position the cursor between the *Dear* and the colon.

The fields created in the data source document do not have any punctuation in them. If you want a space, a comma, or anything else, you need to insert it in the main document.

2. **Click on the huge Insert Merge Field button, in the Mail Merge toolbar.**

    A list of your fields drops down.

3. **Select the field that you want to place in the document.**

    For example, after placing the cursor between *Dear* and the colon, select the firstname field with the mouse. This selection inserts the cryptic code <<firstname>> into the main document, which is what Word thinks of as a blank for fill-in-the-blanks stuff.

    - You can put more than one field on a line.

    - A tad bit of editing of the main document may be required after you insert the field. I typically have to add a space, comma, colon, or whatever after fields.

    - If you created fake fields by using ALL CAPS (as I did in Figure 19-2), then you need to delete them after inserting the real fields.

4. **Continue adding fields until the document is complete.**

    Repeat Steps 1, 2, and 3 as necessary to create all the blanks in your document.

✔ Don't worry if the formatting looks too funny with the <<Fields>> in your document. Things get formatted nicely when Word fills in the blanks — *after* merging.

✔ To delete an unwanted field, highlight it and press the Delete key. *Note:* You can't use the Delete key by itself! You must highlight a field marker and then delete it.

Merge mania!

After creating the main and data files, you're ready to merge away! First, ensure that both the main and data files have been saved to disk. This part of the process is very important! When you want to do the merge, follow these steps, which are, you will be glad to learn, a whole bunch simpler than anything else connected with merging:

1. **Choose Tools⇨Mail Merge.**

    Take a look at the Mail Merge Helper dialog box one last time.

2. Click the Merge button, near the bottom of the dialog box.

The Merge dialog box appears, in which you can dally later — after you have the whole process down pat.

3. Click the Merge button.

As if by magic, Word creates several documents merging your main document with the information in your data source. All the new documents appear, one after the other, in Word on-screen.

Congratulations, you just merged.

✔ Word merges the names and other information from the data source into the main document and creates lots of custom documents, all displayed in one Form Letters# window. That's what you see on-screen right now. Your options at this point are to review all the documents, save them, or print them. You made it!

✔ It's a good idea to view several merges before printing. Check for punctuation and spacing.

✔ The main document appears several times in the document you now see on-screen, with information from the data source plugged into each copy. All files are separated by section breaks or hard page breaks.

✔ If your merge isn't humongous, you should save your mail merge in this on-screen format.

✔ You can print right from the screen view of the merged files by selecting File⇨Print.

✔ Now you know how to get those uniquely crafted, custom documents out to the foolhardy who actually think that you took the time to compose a personal letter. Ha! Isn't mail merge great?

✔ Always examine the results of the merge. Some things may not fit properly, and some editing no doubt will be required.

Part IV
Working with Graphics

The 5th Wave   **By Rich Tennant**

"These kidnappers are clever, Lieutenant. Look at this ransom note, the way they got the text to wrap around the victim's photograph. And the fonts! They must be creating their own—must be over 35 typefaces here...."

In this part...

Word processing is words, so what's the subject of graphics doing here? After all, you struggle to write; now they want you to struggle to draw?

Fortunately, using graphics in a word processor isn't that painful, thanks especially to the Macintosh, which lives and breathes graphics — and that's the thrust behind this part of the book. Adding graphics in Word is more than just cutting and pasting pretty pictures, yet, if you're lucky, there's very little actual drawing involved. (So dash those images of stick figures lining your literary masterpieces.)

Many things in Word can help you create graphics — stuff you may never know unless you read this part. But it's all covered here in the cheery manner you expect. Be prepared to make your writing not only literary, but flowery as well.

Chapter 20
Making Purty Pictures

*T*hank goodness a picture isn't really worth a thousand words — otherwise we'd never get some artist types to shut up. And you know how much they love to talk. Go visit a coffee bistro sometime to find out. Makes you wonder if Michelangelo ever said, "How about this, your holiness: What if you and I just sit here and sip café mocha wambooli and discuss didacticism and moral fortitude of the first century?" Probably not, on second thought: Julius II would have strewn Mickey's entrails 'round the Sistine Chapel!

Graphics can tastefully accent your document, like a dash of basil. Of course, graphics can be obnoxious as well, like a spatula of chili pepper. Using Word, you can easily enhance your creative work by adding illustrations, simple drawings called *line art*, and even photos. On multimedia-equipped Macs — *multimedia* defined as "I paid through the nose for this computer" — you can add movies, or animation with sound (you can even record your own voice as a soundtrack). Cool, but tasteless. Fortunately, Word lets you throw purty pictures into your documents with a minimum of effort, as this chapter shows.

Adding a Graphic

You can add a graphic to a Word document in three ways:

  ✔ Paste it in wherever the toothpick cursor is.

  ✔ Put it in a table.

  ✔ Put it in a frame.

Each method has something going for it; each has something going against it, too:

✔ Pasting is the latter half of copy-and-paste. You start by finding an image. (Or you can create one in another application, one suited to graphics.) Then you *copy* the image. The Mac remembers it. Then you *paste* it into Word. This procedure works like copying and pasting text, and the same Kindergarten Keys, ⌘-C (Copy) and ⌘-V (Paste), apply to all your Mac programs.

✔ In the old days, the Macintosh came with a simple painting program, called MacPaint. It could be used to create interesting, albeit primitive, images for use in other programs, such as the old MacWrite and Word. Today, a ton of sophisticated graphics programs exist. Incidentally, the graphics you see in this book's figures were created with my old favorite, SuperPaint.

✔ Inserting an image into a table works just like pasting text at the toothpick cursor's position. The difference is that the image fits snugly into a cell in a table. Refer to Chapter 12 for more information on tables; your local hardware store has lots of books on making chairs and lawn furniture.

✔ Putting an image into a frame is nice because you can write text *around* the image. Otherwise, the image kinda sits by itself, all lonely without text to insulate it.

From whence cometh thy image?

Before you write anything, you should have a good idea of what you want to write about. (If you don't, and you just stare at the blank screen, then you have what it takes to be a *real* writer!) The same holds true with graphics. In fact, not only should you have a good idea of what you want to illustrate (actually, even a bad idea will do), you must be able to get your hands on the image so that you can paste it into your text. You can do a lot of things with Word, but you can't exactly draw with it. Not really.

Graphics — pictures — come from several places. You can create an image in a graphics program, buy a disk full of images or *clip art*, or you can use a device called a *scanner* to electronically convert pictures and other printed images into graphics files that you can store in the computer.

✔ Word can deal with many popular graphics file formats (they probably are listed in the manual somewhere), which appear on the List Files of Type drop-down lists in the various graphics-related dialog boxes. As long as your graphics can be saved in a *compatible* format, Word won't balk.

✔ You don't need a graphics file on disk to use it in a document. You can paste anything you can get onto the Clipboard directly into a Word document as a graphic. This means that you can create a graphic with a drawing program, copy it to the Clipboard, and then paste it into your Word document. This is the "do it on the fly" school of graphics creation.

✔ The most common graphics file formats are PICT, MacPaint, TIFF, and EPS. On the PC, there are also the PCX (PC Paintbrush), WPG (WordPerfect Graphic), and the Windows bitmap and Windows metafile formats. As shocking as it sounds, you may someday have to deal with those PC-formatted files. They're creepy. Table 20-1 discusses the formats in a brief manner. If you can save your graphics in any of these formats, you're in business, and Word is happy-bappy.

Table 20-1	Common Graphics Formats	
Format	**Pronunciation**	**File Type**
PICT	Picked	Picture file, a "draw" image, or such.
MacPaint	Mac-Pain-ta	Bitmap image.
TIFF	Tiff	Tagged Image Format file, used by most sophisticated drawing programs.
EPS	Ee-Pee-Ess	Encapsulated PostScript file.
GIF	Jiff (the peanuttier peanut butter)	Graphics Interchange Format, used primarily on CompuServe for "naked lady" images
WMF	Double-U-Em-Eff	Windows metafile, a common graphics file format
WPG	Double-U-Pee-Jee	WordPerfect Graphics file.
BMP	Bee-Em-Pee	Windows bitmap, used by Windows Paint and other programs

Slapping an image into a document

To stick an existing image into your text, follow these whimsical steps:

1. Position the toothpick cursor where you want your picture.

If there's any text already there, it will be shoved aside to make room for the graphic.

2. Choose Insert⇨Picture.

You see the Insert Picture dialog box, as shown in Figure 20-1.

```
┌─────────────────────────────────────────────────────────────┐
│ Select a Picture to Insert:                                   │
│         ☐ Work ▼          Preview           ⊖ Blorf           │
│  ☐ Letterman TIFF    ⬆                     ┌─────────┐        │
│  ☐ Newsletter Scam                          │ Eject   │        │
│  ☐ Plus-I-beam Pointer                      ├─────────┤        │
│  ☐ Pricilla                                 │ Desktop │        │
│  ☐ Shock Therapy                            ├─────────┤        │
│  ☐ Suckers                                  │ Insert  │        │
│  ☐ The Boys          ⬇                     ├─────────┤        │
│                                             │ Cancel  │        │
│  List Files of Type:      ⊠ Preview Picture ├─────────┤        │
│                           ☐ Link to File    │Find File…│       │
│  All Files          ▼    ⊠ Save Picture in Document ─────┤     │
│                                             │ Help    │        │
└─────────────────────────────────────────────────────────────┘
```

Figure 20-1:
The Insert
Picture
dialog box.

3. Make sure that an X is in the Preview Picture box.

If not, click on the box to put an X in the box. Only when an X is in this box can you see the pictures associated with the various cryptic filenames.

4. Navigate through the drives and directories until you find the image that you want.

5. Select the image.

Select All Graphics Files from the List Files of Type list box and highlight the filename.

6. Choose Insert!

Splat! The image is pasted into your document at the cursor.

✔ "Ugh! That wasn't the image I wanted." Hurry and choose Edit➪Undo, press ⌘-Z, or click on the Undo button and try again.

✔ You don't have to choose Insert➪Picture if you copy and paste an image. To do that, create the image in another application and copy it; then return to Word and paste.

✔ The image appears right where the toothpick cursor is. In fact, you can almost treat the image as if it were a character in your document.

✔ The section "Adjusting the Image" offers information on adjusting the image after you place it into your document.

✔ Some images are colorful on-screen. Unless you have a color printer, however, they'll only print in black, white, and — with a laser printer — shades of gray.

✔ A cool thing to stick at the end of a letter is your signature. To create your John Hancock, use a painting program or have it *scanned* with a desktop scanner. Save it as a file on disk and then follow the usual steps to insert it in your document.

✔ If you have faithfully followed the preceding steps, and that blasted graphic just won't show up on-screen, it's probably because the paragraph formatting got messed up. Put the cursor in the paragraph that has the graphic, open the Format⇨Paragraph dialog box, and change the Line Spacing to something other than Exactly.

✔ This method of inserting a graphic does not allow you to put multiple lines of text next to the image. See either the "Slapping it in a table" or "Frame the thing" section, later in this chapter, to learn how to do this.

✔ Word has an assortment of oddball characters that you can insert into your text, right along with the normal human characters. For example the ● or the ♥ are ever-popular with hippie-wanna-bes. Refer to Chapter 9 for more information on Word's oddball characters.

✔ Nothing slows down Word like a few images on-screen. Try pasting them in last.

✔ You can't erase over an image. To get rid of it, mark it as a block and press Delete.

Slapping it in a table

Tables are wonderful places for a graphic. You can put your image of, say, your favorite late-night talk show host in a cell and then place text in any cell before or after the graphic. This keeps everything neat without interfering much with the text before or after the table. Figure 20-2 shows what I mean.

Figure 20-2: Text and graphics mix nicely in a sneaky table.

To insert a graphic in a table, follow these steps.

1. Make the table.

Refer to Chapter 12, "Using Tables and Columns," to learn about tables. Keep in mind that it's OK to make a table with only one row. You can put the image in one column and text in the other.

2. Position the toothpick cursor in the cell where you want your picture.

Point and click.

3. Choose Insert⇨Picture.

Navigate through the drives and directories until you find the graphic you want.

4. Select the image and choose Insert.

Zap! The image is pasted into your table.

✔ If the image has already been saved to the Clipboard (you copied it from another program), then you just need to press ⌘-C, the Copy command, in Step 3 and you're done.

✔ You can "grab" the edges of a cell in a table to change the cell's size or position.

✔ To change the size of your image, see the section "Adjusting the Image," later in this chapter.

Frame the thing

The third, and most satisfying, way to put an image into a document is to put it in a frame. A frame is an area in your document where you can stick things — text and graphics, mostly. The frame then becomes a container that you can move around in your document. Text in a document flows around the frame without disturbing the frame's delicate contents.

To put a graphic into a frame, you must first make the frame. Obey these steps:

1. Switch to Page Layout view.

Choose View⇨Page Layout. This step is necessary. If you forget it, Word reminds you later.

2. Choose Insert⇨Frame.

The toothpick cursor changes into a little crosshair doodad. (Here is where you're reminded to switch into Page Layout view if you haven't already; click the Yes button if you're so reminded.)

3. **Put the little crosshair doodad where you want the upper-left corner of the frame to be.**

4. **Create the frame by dragging out a rectangle; drag down and to the right.**

   This action creates a rectangle on-screen. Your picture will appear inside that rectangle — OK, *frame*.

5. **Move the frame to where you want it.**

   You can move the frame around by pointing the mouse pointer at one edge of the frame. When the pointer changes into a four-headed arrow kabob, hold down the mouse button and drag the frame to a new location.

After the frame has been constructed, you can plop a graphic into it with these steps:

1. **Select the frame by moving the mouse to an edge of the frame until the pointer changes into a four-headed arrow kabob.**

2. **Click on the frame.**

   The frame becomes selected and is surrounded by a box with *handles* on it. There are eight handles, one for each of Elizabeth Taylor's husbands.

3. **Do Insert⇨Picture.**

   The Insert Picture dialog box graces your screen. Navigate through the drives and directories until you find the graphic you want.

4. **Select the image and choose Insert.**

   Plop! The image is pasted into the frame. Lovely.

   ✔ More information on Page Layout view can be uncovered in Chapter 23.

   ✔ You also can paste an image into a frame, provided that you just copied it to the Clipboard from a graphics program.

   ✔ If something goes wrong, nine times out of ten it is because the frame was not selected before you imported the image.

   ✔ The following section explains how to change the size of your image after you plop it in Word.

Adjusting the Image

To get an image into your text, follow the steps in the preceding section. After the image is there, you can adjust its size — but that's about it. Word won't let you redraw or edit the image. It's a word processor, after all.

Here are the basic "I want to tweak my graphics" steps:

1. Click on the image.

The graphic is enveloped in a box that has eight tiny *handles*. You use these handles to adjust the image's size (see Figure 20-3).

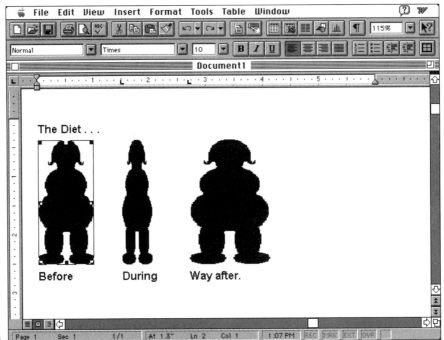

Figure 20-3: An image is altered in Word.

2. Grab an handle and drag it to change the image's size.

Generally speaking, grab one of the handles and drag toward or away from the image. Grab the top handle to make the image taller or shorter. Grab a side handle to make the image narrower or fatter. The corner handles change the image's length and width simultaneously.

3. Release the mouse button when you're done dragging.

Word resizes the image to your specifications.

✔ The graphic can be *scaled* (made larger or smaller without distortion) by holding down ⌘ while dragging one of the corner handles.

✔ The graphic can be *cropped*, or chopped off, by holding down the Shift key while dragging a handle.

✔ If you drag the image in a direction without pressing any key, the image stretches or squashes in that direction. This is how the three dieters were made in Figure 20-3. The first was an image I made in SuperPaint. The second is the same graphic but made thinner. The third is the same thing again but made fatter.

✔ Refer to Chapter 21 to learn how to work with graphics and Microsoft Draw.

Chapter 21

Word's Amazing Applets: Equation Editor, Graph, Picture, and WordArt

. . . .

In This Chapter

▶ The Great Word Applet Hunt

▶ Installing the applets

▶ Employing the Equation Editor

▶ Grappling with Microsoft Graph

▶ Poking around with Microsoft Picture

▶ Activating Microsoft WordArt

. . . .

*W*ord is not alone. Just as your Macintosh came with its own "suite" of little programs — such as Teach Text and others too lame to mention — Word comes with a host of li'l programs as well, but only four are worth the bother: the enigmatic Equation Editor, Microsoft Graph (for making charts and graphs), Microsoft Picture (a drawing program), and the interesting WordArt program. This can be really strange stuff and, unfortunately, most people ignore them as a result. However, everyone I've shown them to seems to enjoy them, so maybe you will, too. That would be a nice switch.

The Great Word Applet Hunt

My mom went on one of these a while back. She was hunting for something called Applets and Cotlets, a.k.a Turkish Delight. She dashed madly about, claiming that it could be found only in my neck of the woods (or Turkey, no doubt). Eventually, she found some and hoarded it for the trip back home. I tried some of the candies and found them to be, well, gross. So, fortunately, the Great Word Applet hunt has nothing to do with the Turkish Delight my mother loves so much.

The four best miniprograms, or *applets*, that come with Word are

- ✔ Equation Editor (or Microsoft Equation), used to create mathematical-looking equations

- ✔ Microsoft Graph, a graphics/statistical program

- ✔ Microsoft Picture, a drawing program (more exact than a painting program)

- ✔ WordArt, a fancy word/letter display program

They may or may not have been installed when you installed Word. To see whether you have these programs installed, follow these steps:

1. **Choose Insert⇨Object.**

   The Object dialog box appears, similar to the one in Figure 21-1. This box contains a list of objects or things you can stick into a Word document.

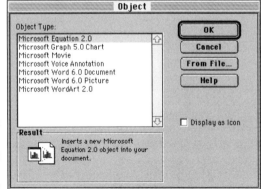

Figure 21-1: The Object dialog box.

2. **Scan the list of items.**

   You're looking for Microsoft Equation 2.0, Microsoft Graph 5.0 Chart, Microsoft Word 6.0 Picture, and Microsoft WordArt 2.0. If you can't find one or more, you need to install the applets, as described in the following section. If they're all there, then you're in business.

3. **Click Cancel to close the Object dialog box.**

   It's gone.

- Many other items are listed in the Object dialog box. These are the various things you can paste into a Word document. For example, if you have Excel, you may see an item representing an Excel Worksheet or Chart.

- The idea behind objects is that you don't have to go somewhere else, create something, copy it, and paste it back into Word. The Object dialog box lets you instantly create something and stick it into Word without the excess travel expenses.

- The applets are programs unique to Word, and you can't access them from other programs.

- Don't despair if the applets' version numbers don't match up with what you see on-screen. Later versions of Word will probably have higher numbers, but most of this stuff should work the same.

- Each applet has a specific function and produces a specific graphic object that you can insert into your Word document.

Installing the applets

The Word applets should have been installed when you first set up Word. However, they may not be where you need them for a number of reasons:

- You don't have enough space on your hard drive.

- You elected not to include them when you installed Word (probably because you didn't know what they were).

- Someone else set up Word and was a big ninny and wanted to cause you additional pain. We arm-chair psychologists call it *passive aggression*. Resist the urge to retaliate by putting all of his/her underwear in the freezer. Prove your emotional superiority.

The following steps tell you how to install the applets:

1. **Find your original Word diskettes.**

   These are the floppy disks that came with Word. They may still be in the box, or you may have stored them away in a disk caddy or fire safe somewhere. I keep my disks in the original box, which is buried under a mound of stuff in the back corner of my office.

2. **Locate the Microsoft Setup icon in the Finder.**

   Word put this icon on your hard drive when Word was first installed. It should be somewhere in the Microsoft Word 6.0 folder.

3. Double-click the Microsoft Setup icon.

This runs the Word setup program.

If you're running Word right now, a dialog box appears and asks you to close Word. Do so: Click the Exit Setup button, click on it again, and then click OK. Then quit Word. (Instructions for quitting Word are offered in Chapter 1 of this book.)

4. Click the Add/Remove button.

A huge, ugly dialog box appears. To the left, you see a list of Word's options. One of the items with a box by it reads Graph, Equation, and WordArt.

5. Click in the box by Graph, Equation, and WordArt.

This puts an X in the box, which indicates that you want to install it. (You may need to click twice to get the X in there.)

6. Click the Continue button.

7. Heed the instructions on-screen.

Read everything and answer the questions so that the applets are installed on your system. If you're faced with a choice, always press Return. This action selects the default item, which you most likely want.

You will be asked to insert one of Word's original distribution diskettes. Do so as instructed on-screen. This may happen several times. Don't try to make sense of why the setup program asks for some disks and not others. Heck, it may ask for them all in sequence. Just consider this amusing and laugh every so often during the process.

8. Eventually, the setup program ends.

Finally. Click the Restart button if the Mac needs to be restarted.

The Word applets are now installed, and you can enjoy using them.

✔ Oh, to heck with it all anyway! You may find that your Mac doesn't have enough memory to use the applets, even if you can summon the disk space. Oh, well.

✔ If you can't find the original Word distribution diskettes (or a copy you might have made), then you're out of luck. Sorry.

✔ If there wasn't enough room on your hard drive when you first installed Word, there may not be enough room now. If so, the setup program warns you of this problem. There's nothing you can do, aside from freeing up space on your hard drive. That's a technical subject, so you better force your Mac guru to help you.

✔ If you do try the underwear-in-the-freezer thing, lightly mist them with water first. And do the socks, too. And don't say anything. Let them just look in the freezer, like for ice cream or something.

The gestalt of the applets

The Word applets are like little programs that produce what are called *objects*. As far as you and I are concerned, the objects are graphics — things that you can paste into your documents. But Word thinks that the graphics are *objects*, or items of extreme importance around which Bill Gates hops and jumps like a little kid high on Cocoa Puffs.

What if, heaven forbid, you want to toss some formula — like the one in Figure 21-2 — at your readers. (By the way, it's rumored that this formula will appear on this year's tax form. Thanks, Mr. President.)

Figure 21-2:
Sample
Equation
Editor object
thing.

$$S_{xg} = \sqrt{\dfrac{\sum x_i^2 fi - \dfrac{(\sum xifi)2}{\sum fi}}{(\sum fi) - 1}}$$

In Word, the item in Figure 21-2 is an *equation object*, created with the Equation Editor. It's really nothing at all. Neither is the professional-looking and highly impressive graph in Figure 21-3, which was created with the Microsoft Graph applet by the same unskilled laborer who wrote this book.

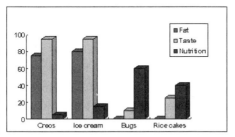

Figure 21-3:
Sample
Graph
object thing.

The steps to get to these impressive doodads are simple:

1. **Position the toothpick cursor where you want the object to appear.**

   The object is a graphic. In some cases, it can appear right in the middle of a sentence or at the start of a line. Other times, it should go where it can be dealt with more easily — on a line by itself or amid a table or in a frame.

2. **Choose Insert⇨Object.**

   The Object dialog box opens.

3. **Select the object that you want to insert.**

Suppose that you want to insert a formula for toxic waste in your kid's Sunday School newsletter. You click on the Microsoft Equation 2.0 object in the Object dialog box, highlighting it. (Following sections outline how to use all four of the applets.)

4. **Choose OK.**

This zooms you to the applet, where you can create the object or graphic for your document.

5. **Toil! Toil! Toil!**

Create that object or graphic! This can be really easy, so *toil* is misleading. (But you don't want anyone to assume that you're having fun here, right?) Just last night, I created a simple object for a document by using WordArt. It took maybe five minutes, although it was impressive enough to bill my client for three hours of work.

6. **Quit the applet.**

You are returned to Word and the graphic is inserted into your document.

✔ These things sure can slow down Word. Chugga-chugga.

✔ The advantage of inserting an object into a Word document — especially one created by a Word applet — is that the object is "hot-linked" back to the program that created it. To edit your object, all you need to do is double-click on it. Zoom! Word takes you back to the applet, where you can tweak the object.

✔ The Word applets are available only in Word. You cannot use them in any other application, at least nothing that I've found yet.

✔ After the object is placed into your document, it functions like a graphic. You can click on the object once and the telltale dotted outline box appears. You can use the mouse to change the graphic's size by dragging any of the outline's edges or corners. The image resizes itself accordingly.

✔ To maintain the art's original proportions, hold down ⌘ while dragging one of the corner handles.

✔ To crop the image (literally, to hack off excess white space around the graphic), hold down the Shift key while dragging the handles.

Employing the Equation Editor

Unless you are, like, an algebra instructor or woefully sadistic (let's be honest here, they are really one and the same), you will probably never need the Equation Editor applet. Yet I suppose that there may be some users who want to express mathematical mysticism in its glorious "how'd they do that?" format. And working with the Equation Editor is much better than trying to use the fractured and fragmented symbols from the keyboard to express your Greek math things.

Then there also may be to curious users. Nothing can be more fun than *pretending* that you know advanced quantum physics and dreaming up some Einsteinium-level-IQ equation to impress the in-laws in your Christmas letter.

Follow these steps:

1. **Move the toothpick cursor where you want your equation to be inserted.**

   Put that toothpick anywhere — even in the middle of a sentence.

2. **Choose Insert⇨Object.**

   The Object dialog box opens.

3. **Click on Microsoft Equation.**

   If you see more than one Microsoft Equation in the list, click on the one that has the highest number after it.

4. **Click OK.**

   This activates the Equation Editor applet, which appears on-screen (see Figure 21-4).

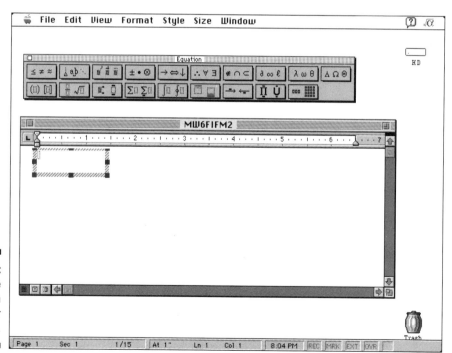

Figure 21-4:
The
Equation
Editor
on-screen.

4. **Make up an equation.**

Use the Equation Editor toolbar's buttons to get at various palettes of equations, doohickeys, and mathematical thingamabobs. This is how you select various items to go into your equation — to build the equation graphically.

At this point, you're on your own. The Equation Editor can build just about any equation, but it's up to you to know what you want in the equation. Remember that you select items from the palettes, fill in the dotted rectangles, and poke and change things with the mouse. Have fun!

5. **When you're done editing, click the mouse outside the equation box.**

That click plops you back into Word and you can see your glorious equation, there to baffle mankind or whomever you send your memos to.

✔ The equation you created appears in your document like a graphic.

✔ If you click on the equation, it becomes outlined like a graphic window frame. To resize the equation, drag one side of its frame to a new location. The equation changes shape accordingly.

✔ To edit the equation, double-click on it. The Equation Editor opens and you can edit the object.

✔ No, Word will not solve your equation. If you're interested in such things, a program called Mathmatica does that job. It's very expensive but well-suited to the pointy-heads among us.

Grappling with Microsoft Graph

Nothing can spin the dust off numbers better than a real cool graph. You don't even need to mess with a spreadsheet or futz with a chart program. Everything can be done neatly from within Word, thanks to the novel Microsoft Graph applet.

To insert a graph into your document, follow these steps:

1. **Move the toothpick cursor to the place you want the upper-left corner of the graph to go.**

Graphs are big square things. Word inserts the big square thing into your document, so move your cursor where you want the graph *before* you start.

2. **Choose Insert⇨Object.**

The Object dialog box appears.

3. Choose Microsoft Graph and click OK.

The Graph applet opens (see Figure 21-5). There are two windows, one for the graph and another for the data. The Datasheet window looks like a spreadsheet or table. The Graph window looks like a graph. Both windows contain phony data at this point, which you can replace. And you can select another type of graph (pie chart, line chart) if you like.

 If you click on the Graph tool, you can skip the object box and start at the Graph applet.

4. Replace the sample data with the information that you want displayed.

You can add and delete columns and rows in the same way that you do in any table. See Chapter 12 for info about tables. You need to click on the Datasheet window to activate it before you can input new values.

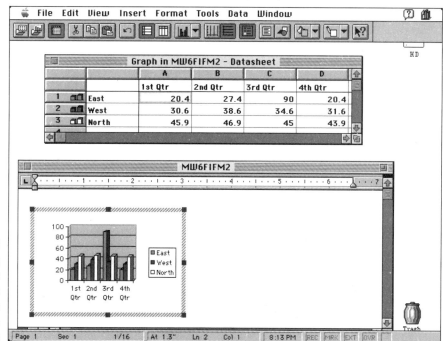

Figure 21-5:
The
Microsoft
Graph
applet.

5. Change the graphic, if you like.

Pressing the Chart Type button drops down a list of all the chart options. If you want a pie chart, for example, you can choose a pie chart (but only if you finished your broccoli).

6. Fiddle and play!

Click on the View Datasheet button to see the datasheet, where you can enter and change the values for your chart.

Any information you enter is immediately updated in the chart. This allows you to see your graph evolve. It can really be fun, but please don't let anyone watching you believe that you're having fun. That isn't fair.

7. You're done!

Click outside of the chart area in your document to return to Word.

Your document now has a beautiful graph, suitable for framing. (See Chapter 20 for information on framing a graphic.)

✔ You also can make a chart from data already in your document. Suppose that you have numbers sitting in a table. To make it into a Microsoft Graph thing, mark the entire table as a block and then follow all of the preceding steps for creating a new chart. Your data, instead of the "bogus" data, fills in the datasheet. Thoughtful, eh?

✔ If you make a chart from a table already in your document, you can use the first cell for the title of the chart. Any words that you put in this cell (the upper-leftmost) will be centered above the graph like a normal title.

✔ Many different flavors of charts are available; poke around in the Chart Type drop-down list to find the one that perfectly highlights your data.

✔ After the graph appears in your document, it can be treated like a graphic. If you click on the graphic-object, it will be outlined like a graphic window frame. You can use the mouse to resize the chart by dragging one side of its frame to a new location. The graph changes shape accordingly.

✔ To edit the graph, double-click on it; doing so reactivates the Microsoft Graph program and loads the graphic-object for editing.

Poking Around with Microsoft Picture

Microsoft Picture is a neat little applet that you can use in a bunch of way. Primarily, it's a draw program, which is different from a painting program, such as SuperPaint. Although you create pictures in a draw program, you create them with objects — circles, squares, and lines. Unlike a painting program, Picture lets you easily move or manipulate objects after they're created. You can align them, flip them, group them, and so on. As a result, Picture is ideal for technical illustrations, flow charts, and the like.

Obviously, there isn't enough space here to explain the entire Microsoft Picture application. So I encourage you to explore it on your own. Also, refer to the checklist at the end of this section for some suggestions on how best to use Picture if your exploration time is hindered by something looming and ominous.

To insert a Picture graphic-object thing into your document:

1. **Put the toothpick cursor where you want the graphic-object thing to appear.**

2. **Choose Insert⬥Object.**

   The Object dialog box opens.

3. **Choose Microsoft Word 6.0 Picture and click OK.**

   The Picture applet appears right inside your Word document, as shown in Figure 21-6. A floating palette and a Drawing toolbar appear.

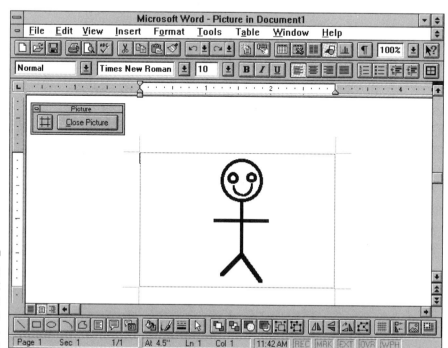

Figure 21-6:
Microsoft Picture explodes on-screen.

4. Do something wondrous.

You can create a graphic here, just as you would in any paint program. Dibble and dabble.

Drawing programs like this don't let you paint pixels on-screen as if you were drawing with an electronic crayon in MacPaint. Instead, you work with graphic objects — more like an erector set. When you create a box, for example, you can move the box or change its size *after* creating it. The box is an *object* on-screen, not a set of pixels or electronic crayon gunk. (I'm getting too philosophical here.)

5. When you're done, click the Close Picture button.

You see the graphic right there in your document. Stand back and be amazed.

✔ The buttons on the left end of the Drawing toolbar allow you to draw straight lines, boxes, and circles. The colors along the bottom of the screen allow you to choose the line colors and a fill pattern (the color for the graphic's "middle").

✔ You can put text into your drawing by clicking the Text Box button. Unlike a paint program, the text you create appears in its own box. It can be edited later just like you edit text in Word. Choose Format➪Font to change the text style.

✔ By choosing Insert➪Picture, you can import any graphic that shows up in the Insert Picture dialog box. Refer to Chapter 20 for more information on inserting pictures.

✔ When your drawing is in your document, it behaves like any other graphic. You can click on it once to "outline" it and then use the mouse to change its size. The graphic resizes itself to fit the outline accordingly.

✔ To edit the graphic in Picture again, double-click on it.

Activating Microsoft WordArt

Sadly, WordArt is neglected by most Word users. This is too bad because with WordArt you can quickly add a lot of dazzle to your documents. And it's a fun place to waste time.

Like the other applets, WordArt produces a graphic-object thing in your text. It's not text! For formatting text, you really need to follow the character formatting rules and regulations outlined in Chapter 9. WordArt is art.

To put WordArt into your document, follow these steps:

1. **Position the toothpick cursor in your document where you want the WordArt to appear.**

2. **Choose Insert⇨Object.**

   The Object dialog box opens.

3. **Select Microsoft WordArt and click OK.**

   The WordArt applet appears, as shown in Figure 21-7.

Figure 21-7: Microsoft WordArt looks like this, sorta.

4. **Type the text you want "artified" into the Enter Your Text Here box.**

   What you type won't appear in the Preview box until you click on the Update Preview button, though.

5. **Mess with it!**

   The Choose a Shape drop-down list contains various patterns for your text to flow in or around. Choose one! The second drop-down list contains fonts. Choose one! The next list sets text size. Buttons after that set text attributes. Mess with 'em to find out what they do. I encourage you to play here — especially if you're billing someone by the hour.

6. **When you're done, click OK to see the text in your document.**

   This action returns you to your document, and the WordArt object appears like a graphic in your document.

   ✔ Like with any other applet's graphic-object, double-click on the WordArt image to edit it.

   ✔ Refer to the section "The gestalt of the Word applets," earlier in this chapter, for more information on tweaking your WordArt.

   ✔ Refer to Chapter 22 for information on creating a drop cap in your document. This is a task that WordArt can handle, but the Drop Cap command does much better.

The 5th Wave

By Rich Tennant

"THERE YOU ARE SIR. ONE MACPAINT, A MACWRITE, A MAC-ACCOUNTANT, TWO MACSLOTS, A MACPHONE AND A MACDRAW. WOULD YOU LIKE FRIES WITH THAT?"

Chapter 22
Your Basic DTP Stuff

Some graphics-related things you can do in Word don't involve graphics at all. Rather, these items approach that fuzzy border between word processing and desktop publishing (DTP). Indeed, the stuff I describe in this chapter was reserved for desktop publishers only just a few years ago.

So what else is there besides graphics and text? Shading. Boxes. Fedoras (well, drop caps). And interesting ways to slap fancy titles and other things into your document. You see, I'm not really talking about graphics; it's just basic DTP stuff.

Dropping the Cap

A drop cap is where the first letter of a report, article, chapter, or story is larger (and, often, in a more interesting font) than the other characters (see Figure 22-1). The drop cap trick, which requires hours of painstaking work and adjustments in other word processors, is a snap in Word. Just use the handy Drop Cap command, nestled in the Format menu.

Figure 22-1:
A drop cap
starts this
intriguing
novel.

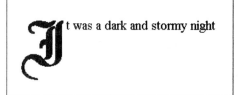

t was a dark and stormy night

Here's how to start your prose off right with a drop cap:

1. **Position the toothpick cursor at the start of your text.**

   Don't put it in the title. Don't put it just anywhere. Put the toothpick cursor to the left of the first character of the first paragraph. (It helps if this paragraph is flush left and not indented with a Tab or any of the tricky formatting discussed in Chapter 10.)

2. **Select the first character of the first word.**

   For example, the *O* in "Once upon a time."

3. **Choose Format⬐Drop Cap.**

   The Drop Cap dialog box appears, as depicted in Figure 22-2.

Figure 22-2:
The Drop
Cap dialog
box.

4. **Select a drop cap style.**

   The first one, None, isn't a drop cap at all. The second style is Dropped, and the third is In Margin. I prefer the Dropped style myself. Click on the box you prefer.

5. **Select a font.**

6. **Click OK.**

Word asks you to switch to Page Layout view to see the drop cap in action.

7. Click Yes.

The drop cap appears in your text, looking like you fussed all afternoon to get it right.

✔ The drop cap looks best in Page Layout view (choose View➪Page Layout), where it appears inside a little chain-link fence.

✔ If you switch back to Normal view (choose View➪Normal), the drop cap'd letter appears on the line above your text. Funky, but that's the way Word does it. Don't try to "fix" it; instead, return to Page Layout view (choose View➪Page Layout) to see the drop cap more properly.

✔ By the way, Chapter 23 details the Page Layout and Normal view commands.

✔ A drop cap is not a graphic or graphic-object thing (see Chapter 21). To fix it, you must follow the preceding steps again and make adjustments in the Drop Cap dialog box.

✔ Flourishy drop caps seem to work the best for pretentious stuff. Otherwise, choose a big, blocky font for your drop caps.

✔ You can undo a drop cap by clicking on its box in your text and then selecting Format➪Drop Cap. In the Drop Cap dialog box, double-click on None, and the drop cap vanishes.

Creating Cool Document Titles

Nothing dampens the fire of an exciting paper like a dreary, dull heading. Consider the plight of the hapless garden slug, which is essentially a crawling stomach, lubricated with a thin coating of slime and built-in fear of salt. But enough sandwich trivia for now. "Your Garden's Gastropod" is a good title — *gastropod* comes from the Latin words for stomach and foot, of course — but to make your slug paper stand out, you need more than just a title. You need a *creative* title.

Figure 22-3 shows various ways in Word that you can title your slug paper. It's possible to mix and match the styles to create the ideal title you want. The rest of the chapter details how to format text and paragraphs, as well as how to create special effects.

Example 1:

The Slug
Your Garden's Gastropod

Example 2:

Slimy, Sticky, Oozy
S L U G S
In Your Garden

Example 3:

Your Glistening Gastropod Gardening Newsletter

SLUG & SNAIL

Vol II, Issue 6   June 11, 1994

Figure 22-3:
Sample
document
titles.

Formatting text just so

When formatting text, you follow three basic steps:

1. **Select a font.**
2. **Select a type size.**
3. **Select character attributes.**

To select a font, follow these steps:

1. **Choose Format⇨Font.**

   The Font dialog box opens.

2. Scroll through the list of fonts and select one that catches your fancy.

If you know the name of the font you want, you can type it in the Font box. Otherwise, the list-o-fonts displays all the fonts known to Word. The best fonts to use for titles are the blocky, no-frills fonts, including Helvetica, Avant Garde, Optima, and Futura. One of those fonts is bound to be in the list. The Preview box, on the bottom right, helps you shop around, showing you through almost-virtual-reality what the font looks like.

3. Enter a size for the font in the Size box or choose a size from the list of available sizes.

To make your title big, select a large font size (14 points or more). I like a 24-pt title, which is nice and readable from across the hall (with my glasses on).

4. Select a style from the Font Style menu.

You may want to bold your title.

5. Choose some effects from the Effects area.

To select an attributes, click in its little check boxes. When an X appears in the box, that attribute is selected. Notice how the Sample text, at the bottom of the dialog box, reflects your changes. You may want to try small caps.

6. Click OK!

Click the OK button or press Return after you've made your selections.

7. Type your title.

✔ Don't worry about centering or shading yet. Character formats come first.

✔ More information on formatting characters is offered in Chapter 9.

✔ If you have a multiline title, you can use different type sizes and styles on each line. Avoid the temptation to change the font, however.

✔ In Figure 22-3, Example 1 is in bold, 14-pt Courier. This is painfully boring, but it's better than nothing.

✔ In Figure 22-3, the first line of Example 2 is in bold, 12-pt Helvetica. The second line is bold, 30-pt type, and all uppercase. The third line is bold, 18-pt type.

✔ In Figure 22-3, Example 3 uses the Helvetica font as well. The first line is bold, italic, 18-pt type. The second line is bold, 24-pt type in small caps. The third line is plain, old, normal 12-pt text. (Refer to the techy sidebar "Fancy — and not required — alignment information" to see how the date is shoved to the right side of the box.)

✔ To insert the date in your title, use Word's Date and Time command. Move the toothpick cursor to where you want the date and choose Insert⊅Date and Time. Highlight a date format in the list and then click OK.

✔ Don't go nuts.

✔ OK, go nuts if you want to.

Centering your title perfectly

After you write text, it's time to align things on-screen. You do this by formatting the paragraphs, which means centering or justifying the titles.

The typical title is centered. To center existing text, follow these steps:

1. **Mark the text you want to center as a block.**

   Refer to Chapter 6 for all the block-marking instructions you'll ever need to know.

Fancy—and not required—alignment information

In Figure 22-3, Example 3, at the bottom of the title, you see the volume number on the left side of the page and the date on the right. Both these items of text are on the same line. The trick is to use Word's alignment formatting to slam one against the left margin and the other against the right. Blithely follow these forbidden steps:

1. Press Return to start a new line of text. It's best to start with a blank line, so if you're already on a blank line, there's no need to press Return. I'm just being safe, that's all. You know, meticulous instructions are my trademark.

2. Type the text you want aligned along the left side of the page. Type away, la, la, la.

3. Don't press Return when you're done!

4. Instead, click on the Tab button on the ruler, until you see the right-align tab, which looks like a backwards L.

5. Click on the ruler about a quarter inch or so to the left of the right-margin triangle. (The right-margin triangle is on the right side of the ruler, between the white and gray parts. If you can't see it, click on the left-pointing arrow on the bottom horizontal scroll bar.) This action places the right-align tab-thingy right there and erases all the other tab stops on that line.

6. Press Tab. The cursor hops over to the right side of the page.

7. Type the text you want aligned along the right side of the page. Type away, la, la, la. Or insert the date, as discussed in the "Formatting text just so" section.

8. Press Return. You're done.

---

2. Choose the Center command to center the block on-screen.

 Click on the Center button, on the Formatting toolbar. You also can choose Format⇨Paragraph and select Centered as the alignment (and then choose OK). Or just press ⌘-E.

 ✔ No need to mark a line or paragraph. Just place the toothpick cursor somewhere in that line or paragraph and click the Center button.

✔ To center the page from top to bottom, refer to the section "Centering a page, top to bottom," in Chapter 11.

✔ Additional information on formatting a block of text is found in Chapter 10.

Using the Borders and Shading Command

You can make titles more interesting by putting a box around them, or maybe just some lines along the top and bottom, or some fancy shading. You can do this to any text in Word. If you want to set aside a paragraph of text from the rest of the page, for example, you can box it or shade it. Just choose Format⇨Borders and Shading.

Drawing a box around your text

If you're creating a title, you can draw a nice square box around it. Or you can draw a box around any paragraph (or group of paragraphs). To do so, follow these steps:

1. Mark the paragraph you want to box as a block.

Use the handy block-marking instructions in Chapter 6 to carry out this step. You can mark any text, such as a title you want to snazz up.

2. Choose Format⇨Borders and Shading.

The Paragraph Borders and Shading dialog box opens, as shown in Figure 22-4

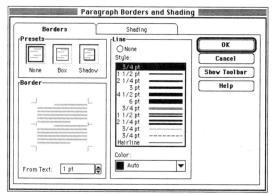

Figure 22-4: The Paragraph Borders and Shading dialog box.

3. **Make sure that the Borders tab is up front.**

   If not, click on the Borders tab.

4. **Look for the area labeled Presets (in the panel's upper-left corner).**

   This area contains three quick, easy-to-use, pop-n-fresh border styles.

5. **Double-click on the icon above Box.**

   Your title now has a box around it, similar to the one shown in Example 3 of Figure 22-3, but without shading. To get shading, refer to the following section.

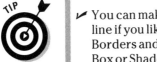

✔ Word draws lines only around full paragraphs of text — not bits and pieces.

✔ To put a border with a shadow around your text, double-click on the Shadow icon.

✔ You can make the border thinner or thicker, or use a double- or dashed-line if you like. Just select a line style from the Style list in the Paragraph Borders and Shading dialog box. Do this before you double-click on the Box or Shadow icon.

✔ To remove a border from your highlighted text, double-click on the None icon.

✔ You can also place a border around a graphic in your document. Refer to Chapter 20 for more information.

Putting less than a box around your text

In Figure 22-3, Example 2, the boxed title has lines only on the top and bottom. To make that happen with your title or any other text, follow Steps 1, 2, and 3 as outlined in the preceding section. And then do the following:

1. **Click on the Box icon to put a box around your text.**

   Yeah, this isn't how you want to end up, but it's how you must start. (Just click once — don't double-click here.)

2. **Select a line style from the Style area.**

   You can choose from several thicknesses of double- or single-line patterns. Click on the line style you want. Notice that the text in the Border preview box changes to match the line style you select.

3. **Now focus on the Border preview box.**

   The box tells Word where to put lines around your text — top, bottom, left, right, middle, and so on.

4. Click on the left and right lines in the Border preview box.

This eliminates those lines.

5. Click OK when you finish making your box.

The box is now missing two sides, so it's really not much of a box at all. All your text may spill to the floor if you tip your paper the wrong way, so be careful.

Using the Border toolbar

Word is heavy on toolbars. One of them is the Border toolbar, which allows you to create borders in your document without messing with the Paragraph Borders and Shading dialog box.

 To activate the Border toolbar, click the Borders button, on the Formatting toolbar. A new toolbar appears, with drop-down lists and buttons for adding borders to highlighted text.

> ✔ The first drop-down list on the Borders toolbar sets the size of the border's lines.
>
> ✔ The buttons on the Borders toolbar tell Word where to stick a border around your highlighted text: Top, Bottom, Left, Right, Inside, Outside, and None.
>
> ✔ The second drop-down list sets the shading for the boxed-in area. Refer to the next section for more information on shading text.
>
> ✔ To make the Border toolbar go away, click the Borders button a second time.

Shading your text

The neatest Border dialog box effect of them all is shading, such as the sample title in Example 3 of Figure 22-3. You can shade a title with or without a border around it. Use these steps:

1. Mark what you want shaded as a block.

Refer to Chapter 6 for efficient block-marking instructions. If you want the shaded area to cover more than the title line, highlight the lines before and after the title.

2. Choose Format⟹Borders and Shading.

The Paragraph Borders and Shading dialog box appears.

3. Make sure that the Shading panel is up front.

If not, click on the Shading tab to coax it forward, as in Figure 22-5. Lots of interesting things can happen here, but you should focus on the large Shading menu box.

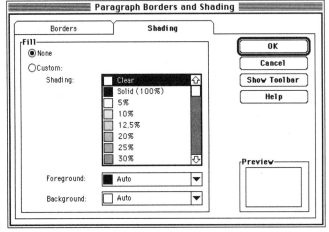

Figure 22-5:
The Shading tab in the Paragraph Borders and Shading dialog box.

4. Scroll through the Shading list to find the degree of shading you desire.

Shading patterns vary from 5% to 90% (percentages of black), including clear and solid. A value of 50% is equal parts black and white — that is, solid gray. The 90% value is almost solid black. Other patterns appear at the end of the list, but don't pay any attention to them. That just encourages them.

The best values to select for shading your text are 10%, 20%, or 30%. I prefer 20% because my laser printer prints a 20% shade that's dark enough to see but not too dark that it overpowers the title text.

5. Select your shading from the list.

6. Click OK.

Your text appears shaded on-screen! I think that this is definitely the coolest way to format the title of your in-depth slug report.

✔ Nope, just because you visited the Border dialog box doesn't mean you have to put a border around your text.

✔ If the shading stinks (and we're all allowed a little latitude for screwing up here), then you can remove it. Just follow the steps outlined in the preceding numbered list, but select the Clear pattern in Step 5.

✔ At the bottom of the list of shades are some shading patterns as well. Choose something to match the drapes.

✔ Shaded titles look best when they're at the top of your first page — not on a page by themselves.

Printing white on black

After shading, the next most fun thing to do is print white text on a black background. This is a very bold move and makes your words stand out prominently in your text — like being hit in the face with a cinder block. So don't use this technique casually.

> Oh, La-di-da

To produce white-on-black text, you must do two things. First, you must create a black background; second, you must create white-colored text. Here's how you create a black background:

1. **Mark your text as a block.**

   Chapter 6 has all the details. It's best to start with text already on-screen. At some point here, you will have black text on a black background, which you cannot see. If the text is already written, it will be easier to see when you're done.

2. **Choose Format⇨Borders and Shading.**

   The Paragraph Borders and Shading dialog box appears.

3. **Make sure that the Shading panel is forward.**

   If not, click on the Shading tab. The Shading card reshuffles itself to the top of the pile (refer to Figure 22-5).

4. **Click on the down arrow by the Background drop-down list.**

   You see a bunch of colors displayed in the drop-down list (which may actually pop up on-screen). The current color is probably Auto.

5. **Select Black from the list.**

   This sets the background color to black — one half of your white-on-black text.

6. **Click OK to exit the Shading dialog box.**

   Now you don't see anything on-screen because you have black text on a black background. (Actually, with the block highlighted, you will see what looks like a large white block floating over a black block. Don't freak!)

Yes, the text is really black on black, even if you see a white block on black right now. You must do these things deliberately in Word. Never make assumptions.

With the block of text still highlighted, you need to change the text color to white. To do so, you need to use the Font dialog box, as follows:

1. **Choose Format⇨Font.**

   The Font dialog box opens.

2. **Make sure that the Font panel is up front.**

   If not, click on the Font tab.

3. **Look for the Color drop-down list in the dialog box, just above dead-center.**

4. **Click on the down arrow by the Color drop-down list.**

   You see a bunch of colors displayed.

5. **Select White from the list.**

   This is the color you want; white text over the black background you already created.

6. **Click OK.**

   You can now deselect your block (click anywhere). The text appears on-screen and printed in white letters on a black background.

- ✔ Yes, although I said that you can't print in color in Chapter 8, you can print white text on a black background.

- ✔ I don't recommend reversing vast stretches of text. White text on a black background prints poorly on most computer printers. This stuff is best used for titles or to highlight small blocks of text.

- ✔ You cannot reverse out only a word or part of a paragraph. The black background can be applied to an entire paragraph only.

- ✔ When you select a block of white text on a black background, it appears on-screen "normally." That is, the reversed text appears inverted — or black on white — when you mark it as a block. This can really goof you up, so just try not to go mental when you highlight reversed text.

- ✔ You can use the white-on-black text sample you created to make a white-on-black style in Word: Highlight that text and then press ⌘-Shift-S. In the Style box, type **Reverse** or some other appropriate name. Press Return to add the style to your document. (Refer to Chapter 14 for more information on styles.)

Part V
Help Me, Mr. Wizard!

The 5th Wave   By Rich Tennant

In this part...

*W*ord is not the sole cause of your woes. When you use a computer, you must contend with several things: the computer, the Finder, a vast hoard of Inits and goofy programs that you've installed, your printer, phases of the moon . . . . It's like starring in a bad French farce with too many villains.

Fortunately, some humans — yes, humans — really like computers. When you're in dire straits, you can call on their expertise. Call them wizards; call them gurus; call them when you need help. And when you can't call on them, refer to the chapters in this part of the book to help you through your troubles.

Chapter 23
Face to Face with the Interface

*B*y now, you probably have noticed that approaching Word and the strange and unusual ways that it shows stuff on your screen is about as calming as having the waiter personally assure you that the food is supposed to taste that way and nothing is wrong — and meanwhile you hear a siren approaching and the cook rushes to the bathroom holding his mouth with one hand and his stomach with the other.

Don't you agree that there are too many buttons, icons, gizmos, and whatzits? Don't answer too quickly because there are even more than that — including some wild things that you've never seen and probably don't want to see. This chapter mulls over the lot, explains what's what on-screen, and tells you whether it's important and why.

Looking at Your Document

The way you look at your document is controlled by Word's View menu (see Figure 23-1). The View menu contains all sorts of options for controlling the display: the way your document appears, whether various goodies show up alongside your document, and how big the document looks (set by the Zoom command).

View	Insert	Format
• Normal		
Outline		
Page Layout		
Master Document		
Full Screen		
Toolbars...		
✓Ruler		
Header and Footer		
Footnotes		
Annotations		
Zoom...		

Figure 23-1:
The View
menu.

✔ The Normal command enables you to look at your document in Normal view — the view you probably want most of the time while you work in Word. The Normal view button, at the far-left end of the horizontal scroll bar, also switches you to this view.

✔ The Page Layout command directs Word to let you see your entire document, including the header and footer plus the graphics and other effects that may not look proper in the Normal view. Clicking on the Page Layout button on the horizontal scroll bar also activates this view.

✔ In Page Layout view, a vertical ruler appears along the left side of your document. You also see a misty gray region to the top and bottom of each page in your document. That void is made of the same stuff that they find in the Bermuda Triangle.

✔ Several Word commands automatically shift you into Page Layout view.

✔ The Outline command shifts Word into Outline mode, which is so horrid that it isn't even discussed in this book! The last of the three view buttons on the horizontal scroll bar switches you to Outline view.

✔ I touch upon the Master Document view in Chapter 28.

✔ The interesting Full Screen command lets you look at your document without being encumbered by menus, toolbars, or any other whatnot. This command is suited for the white-page purists among us. Click the only remaining button on-screen to return yourself to Normal mode.

✔ Other commands in the View menu are discussed elsewhere in this chapter.

✔ Yet another check mark item.

✔ Chapter 16 offers information on working with document windows, including splitting them, Windexing them, and so on.

"My toolbar (or ruler) vanished!"

Missing something? Notice that the sample screens in this book don't look a darn thing like what you see on-screen? Frustrated?

Everything on-screen is adjustable, so you can change the appearance of just about anything by using the View menu, shown in Figure 23-1.

- ✔ To retrieve the ruler, choose View⇨Ruler.

- ✔ To get other toolbars back — or to rid yourself of them — refer to the next section.

- ✔ Other funky things can happen to the display. Just keep reading.

- ✔ Word also has the capability to view multiple documents at a time. Refer to Chapter 16 for more information.

Summoning toolbars

You control toolbars in Word — and, whew, there are a lot of them — by choosing View⇨Toolbars, which displays the infamous Toolbars dialog box, depicted in Figure 23-2.

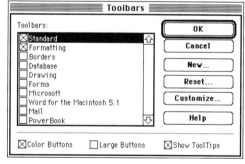

Figure 23-2:
The
Toolbars
dialog box.

To display a toolbar, click on its name so that an X appears in the box. Removing an X from the box makes the toolbar go away. Click the OK button to return to Word and enjoy (or be freed from) the toolbars.

- ✔ Some toolbars appear like the Standard and Formatting toolbars — as a strip of buttons across the screen. Other toolbars appear as *floating palettes*, or movable groups of buttons. You can make floating palettes vanish by clicking on their li'l close box (in the upper-left corner of their wee window).

✔ Some toolbars appear automatically when you're working on specific things in Word. For example, the Drawing toolbar appears when you're working with Microsoft Picture (see Chapter 21). A special Merge toolbar appears when you're merging documents (see Chapter 19).

✔ You can create your own, custom toolbars by clicking on the New button in the Toolbars dialog box. This topic is way too advanced to be covered in this book. Besides, Word junkies have probably already messed around with custom toolbars even before reading this little note.

✔ Having tons of toolbars sates the button gluttons but leaves little room on-screen for your all-important text. Typically, you only need the Standard and Formatting toolbars. Everything else is just for show.

Out, Damn Spots!

This·can·be·very·annoying.¶

What you see on-screen when your text looks like the preceding line are *nonprinting characters*. These symbols represent spaces (produced by the spacebar), end-of-paragraph marks (the Return key), and tabs (duh, the Tab key). They show up on-screen but — fortunately — not when printed. There are two ways to feel about these characters:

✔ The marks let you see things that would otherwise be invisible, such as rogue tabs and spaces and other stuff that can foul up your document.

✔ The marks look gross on-screen; who wants to edit a document that looks like it has chicken pox?

 ✔ You can turn off the specks from the Standard toolbar by clicking the Show/Hide button.

✔ A good way to clean up rogue spaces and such is to use the AutoFormat command. Refer to Chapter 15.

"There's a Line Down the Left Side of My Screen!"

That annoying line down the left side of your screen doesn't mean that your monitor is out of whack. Instead, you have discovered the *style area*, which shows you what style is applied to what paragraph. There's really no reason to have it visible. To turn off the style area, follow these steps:

1. **Choose Tools⇨Options.**

   The Options dialog box appears.

2. **Coax the shy View panel forward.**

   Click on the View tab.

3. **At the bottom-left corner of the dialog box, find the Style Area Width.**

4. **Type 0 (zero) into the box.**

   Or use your mouse and the spinner buttons to reset the value to zero.

   You've just set the width of the style area thing to zero inches, effectively making it nonexistent. Yeah!

5. **Click OK.**

   The style area is forever gone.

 Although the style area is annoying, it can really help you edit strange documents. If you're having trouble applying styles to your document, switch the style area back on: just follow the preceding steps again and enter a value of .5 or 1 for a half-inch or inch-wide style area.

"The Mouse Button Produces This Pop-Up Menu Thing!"

Don't look now, but your mouse has five buttons. One is on the mouse, of course. The other four are on the keyboard: Shift, Control, Option and ⌘.

Normally, you click the button on the mouse to select things, pull down menus, and poke on-screen buttons. But when you click the mouse while pressing one of the keyboard mouse buttons, you can do other wondrous things, most of which are laced throughout this tome.

When you click the mouse while pressing the Control key (known as *Control-click*), Word pops up a handy menu, full of shortcuts and other useful items. Figure 23-3 shows the pop-up menu that appears when you position the mouse over your text and Control-click. The top items in the menu are Cut, Copy, and Paste; the bottom items deal with text formatting.

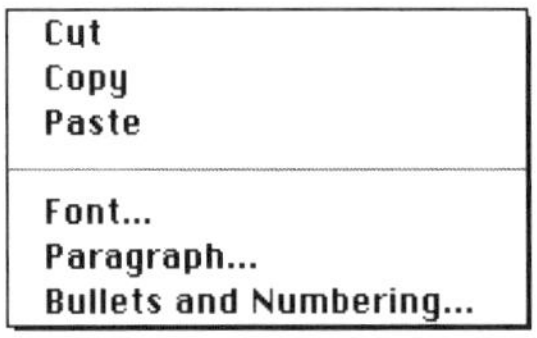

Figure 23-3:
Control-
clicking over
text.

| Cut |
| Copy |
| Paste |
| Font... |
| Paragraph... |
| Bullets and Numbering... |

Figure 23-3: Control-clicking over text.

Figure 23-4 shows what appears when you Control-click over one of the toolbars. This pop-up menu is essentially a mini-toolbar menu; from here, you can summon various toolbars.

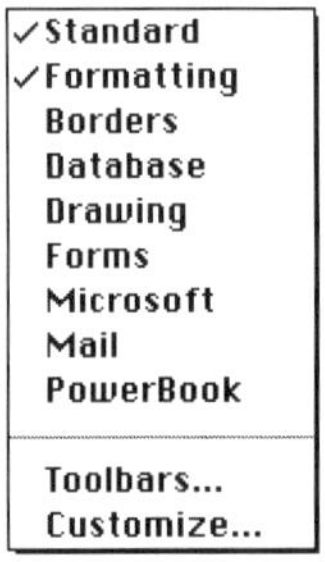

| ✓ Standard |
| ✓ Formatting |
| Borders |
| Database |
| Drawing |
| Forms |
| Microsoft |
| Mail |
| PowerBook |
| Toolbars... |
| Customize... |

Figure 23-4: Control-clicking over a toolbar.

✔ Additional items may appear in the menu when you Control-click in a picture box or graphic.

✔ For more information on Cut, Copy, and Paste, refer to Chapter 6.

✔ More information on the Font command can be read in Chapter 9; Chapter 10 covers paragraph formatting.

✔ Information on the various toolbars is covered earlier in this chapter. See the section "Summoning toolbars."

"There's a Line of Arrows, Numbers, and Whatnot On-Screen!"

If you see a row of arrows, numbers, and whatnot on-screen, you've simply discovered Outline view. This feature is a really neat gizmo designed especially by Microsoft for people who really, really love to outline stuff. Word's outlining function isn't covered in this book because it's kind of an advanced subject. If you stumble onto Outline view and see those weird arrows instead of a ruler, you can choose View⟹Normal to return to Normal view.

Zooming About

The Zoom command, at the bottom of the View menu, controls how big your document's text looks. No, it doesn't change the text size — that's done in the Font menu. Rather, the Zoom command controls how much of your text you can see at once. Follow these steps for a quick demonstration:

1. **Choose View⇨Zoom.**

   The Zoom dialog box appears, looking much like the one depicted in Figure 23-5.

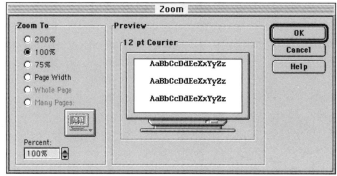

Figure 23-5:
The Zoom
dialog box.

2. **Select a Zoom size from the Zoom To area.**

   For example, 200% makes your text look real big — ideal for Grandpa. The Page Width option sets the zoom so that you see your entire document from left to right margins.

   You can set individual percent sizes by using the Percent box.

3. **Click OK to view your document at a new size on-screen.**

✔ You can only choose some of the options in the Zoom dialog box when you're in Page Layout view. Choose View⇨Page Layout and then select the Zoom command to play, er, experiment with those options.

✔ When zooming takes you too far out, your text will change to shaded blocks, called *greeking*. Although not keen for editing, zooming out that far gives you a good idea of how your document looks on the page.

✔ Click on the Zoom drop-down list, on the Standard toolbar, to quickly set a Zoom size.

✔ Unless your Mac has some type of funky sound program, you have to make the *zoooooom* noise yourself when you select the Zoom command.

Chapter 24
Contending with Mr. Macintosh

. . . .

In This Chapter

▶ Browsing for documents

▶ Diving out into the Finder

▶ Organizing your documents

▶ Viewing your work

▶ Formatting disks

▶ Backing up your files!

. . . .

*T*he Macintosh was to make computing easy for "the rest of us." And for the most part, it does. Using a Mac is effortless compared to working a DOS computer. Even Bill Gates admitted this when he "discovered" Windows and claimed it was the future. Ack, but I won't get into that.

Although the Macintosh is a marvelously simple computer to understand, some computerish things still creep into the scene. Also, if you're like me and write a lot, you'll need to keep your stuff organized — a major thrust of this chapter.

This chapter is seriously optional reading for the typical Word user! Peer into these pages only if you're stuck (or bored) and have nowhere else to turn.

Browsing for Documents

Word documents are stored as *files* on your Mac's hard disk. But they aren't just thrown on disk like a cancer-riddled smoker flicks a cigarette butt out the window of a pollution-belching '67 Impala. Cough, cough. Mr. Macintosh takes better care of you. And he doesn't irk Smokey the Bear.

You save documents to disk by using the Save or Save As command. Documents previously saved to disk are plucked back from disk by using the Open command. Either way, you're faced with a dialog box that looks a lot like Figure 24-1.

Figure 24-1:
A Save
dialog box.

Save dialog box contents:

Word 6 For Macs Figures ▼   ⚏ Laurie's HD

☐ Cheat Sheet Fig 1   104652K available
☐ Cheat Sheet Fig 2   [Save]   [Eject]
☐ Cheat Sheet Fig 3
☐ Figure 01-01   [Cancel] [Desktop]
☐ Figure 01-02   [Options] [Help]

Save Current Document as: [New 🗀]
`MW6FIFM2`

Save File as Type:
`Word Document` ▼

The scrollable list, on the left of the dialog box, shows you two things: documents already saved to disk and folders on your disk. The folders hold even more documents.

The idea here is to use the Open or Save dialog boxes to find your work or a place to save your work. You do so by manipulating the dialog box's doodads to find that one folder that's just the perfect storage place. Here are some hints:

✔ The name of the current folder appears above the list of files. In Figure 24-1, the current folder is named *Microsoft Word*.

✔ The current folder name is also a drop-down menu. You can click the mouse on it to move "up" to the next folder on your desktop.

✔ To access a folder displayed in the file list, double-click on it. That folder opens: its name appears atop the file list and any documents in the folder appear inside the file list.

✔ The drop-down list includes the Desktop, your disk drive(s), and folders in those disk drives.

✔ You can create a new folder by clicking the New button in the Save or Save As dialog box. However, I recommend saving this work for when you're in the Finder. Refer to the "Creating new folders" section, later in this chapter.

✔ OK, you don't really have to mess with folders at all. You can tell Word to automatically put your documents in one place and one place only. Choose Tools➪Options and click on the File Locations tab. Select Documents from the list of File Types and click Modify. Then choose where you want Word to always stick your files when you save. (I don't recommend this approach, however, if you work on lots of projects and are a stickler for organization. Instead, refer to the section "Organizing your documents.")

Diving Out into the Finder

Word is an application on your Macintosh. It creates files and then stores them on disk. To work with those files outside of Word, you must contend with the Finder, which is the Mac's operating *shell*. The Finder is where you start various applications, organize your files and their icons, and do all sorts of other fun stuff. Even if you're a full-time Word user, you should meet the Finder and learn to use its graphic funness to help keep your work organized.

The Finder is what you see when you quit Word, but you don't have to quit Word to use it. The Finder can be found by clicking on the Applications menu, on the far right side of the menu bar. In the list that appears, select Finder (see Figure 24-2). Word is caustically shoved aside, and the Finder jumps up front.

Figure 24-2:
The Finder hangs out in the Applications menu.

With the Finder out in front, you can manage files, create new folders, start other programs (as long as you have gobs of memory), and play games on your network.

To return to Word, go back to the Application menu and select Microsoft Word.

You also can switch between Word and Finder by clicking on one of the other's windows. If you accidentally click on a Finder window, you're switched there against your wishes; click on a Word window to hop right back.

Organizing your documents

I recommend that everyone save all their documents to disk; refer to Chapter 1 for the details. The problem with all this saving is that eventually you wind up with a gazillion Word documents strewn over your hard drive. Or worse, all those documents end up jammed into the Microsoft Word folder.

I recommend that everyone use folders to organize their various projects. You can even place folders within folders for varying levels of organization. This stuff can be fun, but it's not without its cryptic aspect.

For example, I have a general work folder titled, uh, *Work*. Inside it, I have folders for all my various projects, into which I save the proper Word documents. With everything in its place, I can always find a document quickly. Not only that, I can save graphics and other related project files in those same folders.

To create a Work folder, go out to the Finder and locate a place where you want to keep your folder. I recommend using the Microsoft Word window; you can keep all your Word documents in there if you like. Or you can put your new folder in your main Desktop window.

To create a folder, follow these steps:

1. **Move to the window where you want to create your folder.**

2. **Choose File⇨New Folder or press ⌘-N.**

   The new folder appears in the window. It's named *untitled folder* (it's ready for you to name it something better).

3. **Type a descriptive name for your folder.**

   I named mine *Work*. Another popular name is *Projects*. Be equally clever.

4. **Press Return.**

   The folder is named and ready to be opened.

You can open the folder and create more folders by following the preceding steps.

Viewing your work

Even the most creatively devised folder organization system can't defeat icon clutter. In the folder that I created for this book's samples and figures, I have almost 100 items. This doesn't mean that I'm not organized, it just means that a lot of icons are staring me in the face. To solve the problem, I selected View⇨by Small Icon. This command shows all my stuff in a way I can easily find things (see Figure 24-3).

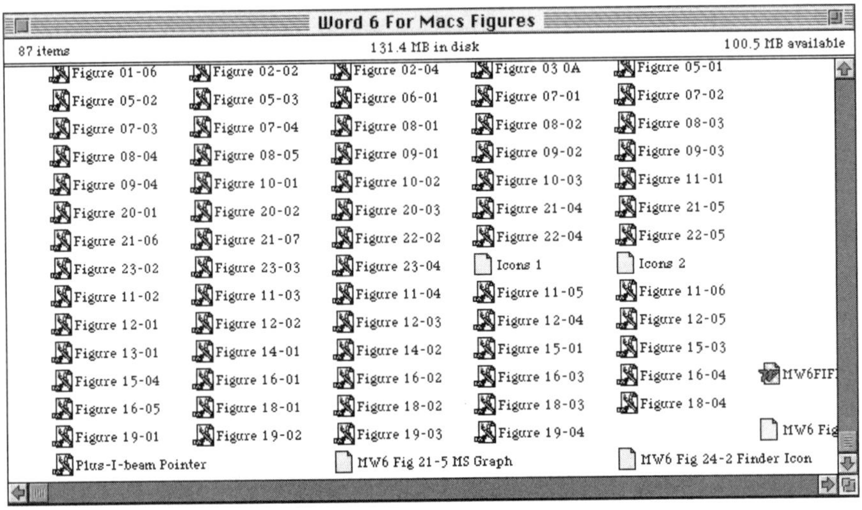

Figure 24-3: It's easy to see lots of stuff after choosing by Small Icon view.

Another popular, though entirely non-Macintosh, way of viewing files is to select View⇨by Name. In this view, everything is listed in alphabetic order by name; this view also includes a bunch of other statistics that would placate only a DOS user. Still, this view is nice for scanning long lists of files. If you're writing a novel and only care about your documents as chapter names, then by Name is an ideal view.

Formatting Disks

Formatting diskettes is something that we all have to do. Disks begin life "naked." Not even a birthday suit. They have nightmares about arriving at work in their underwear, and they give public speaking advice about picturing the audience wearing only black socks. All the disks in a new box are blank, like blank audio cassettes and videotapes. But you must *format* a computer disk before you can use it.

Formatting a disk is no problem when using a Mac. All by itself, it detects that the disk is unformatted and begs you to either *initialize* (format) it or eject it (spit it out: ptttooey!). This happens whether you're in Word or the Finder.

- ✔ I bring up the subject of formatting disks because it's closely tied to backing up your work, covered in the next section.

- ✔ If you need to use a DOS disk, then you must run the Apple File Exchange program that came with your Mac. Refer to IDG Books' *Macs For Dummies* for the details.

- ✔ Sometimes, you can buy formatted diskettes. They're a tad more expensive than the other diskettes, but they save you time and the hassle of having to format a disk while you're in the middle of doing something else.

Back Up Your Files!

Backing up your stuff is as important as saving a document to disk. But when you back up, you create duplicate documents on a second disk, usually a floppy disk. That way, should anything ever happen to your Mac or its hard drive, you can recover quickly by using the backup copy. If Earl comes over and sits by your computer and — because Earl has a big butt — accidentally knocks your computer off the table and breaks it, you won't feel so bad knowing that you have a safety copy of your files well-distanced from Earl.

Backing up is usually done by running a special backup program. This task is definitely something your guru needs to set up for you. Also, the guru needs to give you a list of instructions detailing how and when to back up.

The second way that you can back up is to use the Word Save As command in the File menu. When you need to save your files to a different place, a floppy is best. This method is a royal but worthwhile pain until your guru teaches you how to use a real backup program.

- ✔ You should back up your files every day. You can do this with the Find File command in Word: Choose File⇨Find File. Select the file(s) you want to copy in the Listed Files list (⌘-click on each one). Then select Copy from the Command button's pop-up list. Select the Desktop from the drop-down list at the top of the Copy dialog box, and then pick a floppy disk listed there. Copy the files to that disk.

- ✔ Every day you should back up every document that you worked on that day. You can check the file's date by using the Find File command as described in the preceding check mark. Select File Info from the View menu and highlight those files with the day's date. Copy them all off to a floppy disk for safe keeping.

- ✔ Backing up works a lot better if you have a "real" backup program.

- ✔ If you accidentally delete a file, one of the only ways to really undelete it is to restore it from a backup copy. If you just copied the document to disk, then insert the disk and use the Find File dialog box to copy the document back to your hard drive. If you're using a sophisticated backup program, you'll need to properly *restore* the document.

Chapter 25
The Printer Is Your Friend

*1*s the printer your friend? Perhaps. Unfortunately, friend or foe, the printer is just as stupid as the computer, which means that you must beat it with a stick a few times to get it to behave. If you don't, you usually wind up hitting yourself on the head with the same stick (I know, it feels so good when you stop). But before you start waving your Tonya Harding-autographed baton, give your printer (and your skull) a second chance and leaf through this chapter.

Feeding It

The way the paper feeds into your printer depends on which printer you have. Some printers eat paper one page at a time. Other printers may suck up continuous sheets of *fan-fold* paper directly from the box (the "spaghetti" approach). And laser printers delicately lift one sheet of paper at a time from their paper tray and then weld the image to the page by using dusty toner and infernolike temperatures. Printing can be quite dramatic.

No matter how your printer eats paper, make sure that you have a lot of it on hand. The end result of a word processor's labors is the printed document. So buy a box or two of paper at a time. I'm serious: You'll save money and trips to the store in the long run. I also suggest that you look for a huge paper store or supplier and buy your printer paper from them rather than an office supply or computer store. The prices will be better.

✔ Try to get 20 lb. paper. The 18 lb. paper is too thin. I like the thicker 25 lb. paper, which holds up very well, but it's more expensive. Paper that's too thick, such as card stock, may not go through your printer.

✔ Colored papers and fancy stuff are OK.

✔ Do not print on erasable bond paper! This paper is awful. Besides, erasing a computer printout makes as much sense as using that old pink eraser to wipe away a word on-screen.

✔ Avoid fancy, "dusted" paper in a laser printer. Some expensive papers are coated with a powder. This powder comes off in a laser printer and gums up the works.

✔ Only buy the two-part or three-part fan-fold papers if you need them. These contain carbon paper and are commonly used for printing invoices and orders. By the way, the old "green-bar" paper is lousy for correspondence. It has nerd written all over it.

✔ If you need to print labels in your laser printer, get special laser printer labels. I recommend the Avery labels.

✔ Laser printers can print on clear transparencies — but only those specially designed for use in a laser printer. Anything other than this kind melts inside your printer, and then you have to clean out the gunk. If you plan to print transparencies, it's cheaper to print on a piece of paper and then have the image photocopied onto transparency film, anyway.

✔ Always buy double-ply toilet tissue. It's comfier.

Unjamming It

"Dan, why can't the paper always go through the printer like it's supposed to?" Finally, after years of pondering, I know how to ease your mind. Next time you're in San Francisco, go visit this little psychic in The Haight. She'll do a chart for your printer that explains why it jams on some days and not on others.

If you have a dot-matrix printer and the paper jams, click the Cancel button in the "now printing" dialog box. Then turn the printer off. Rewind the knob to reverse-feed the paper back out of the printer. Don't pull on the paper because it will tear, and then you'll have to take apart the printer to get the paper out. (If dismantling the printer becomes necessary, call someone else for help.)

For laser printers, you need to pop open the lid, find the errant piece of paper, remove it, and then slam the lid down shut. Watch out for various hot things inside your printer; be careful of what you touch. There's no need to cancel printing here because laser printers have more brain cells than their dot-matrix cousins. However, you may need to reprint the page that got jammed in the printer. Refer to the Chapter 8 section "Printing a Specific Page."

If the jam was caused by using thick paper, retrying the operation probably won't help. Use thinner paper.

Stopping That Incessant Double-Spacing!

Nothing is quite as disenchanting as a printer that constantly double-spaces documents. This problem is terribly annoying, but it's easily solved — if you kept the manual that came with your printer.

Somewhere on your printer is a tiny switch that controls whether your printer double-spaces or single-spaces. If your printer is double-spacing a single-spaced document, you need to find that switch and turn it off.

- ✔ You won't get this double-spacing nonsense with Apple printers, only PC printers.

- ✔ Sometimes the little switches are on the back or side of your printer; sometimes they're actually inside your printer.

- ✔ Turn your printer off and unplug it before you flip the switch. Cutting the power is especially important if the switch is inside the printer; that way, you prevent people from trying to print while your fingers are in the way of the printer's buzz-saw-like gears.

- ✔ The switch may be referred to as "LF after CR" or "Line feed after carriage return" or "Add LF" or "Stop double-spacing!" or something along those lines.

Changing Ribbons and Toner

Always have a good ribbon or toner cartridge in your printer. Always! Most printers use ribbons; laser printers use toner cartridges. Never skimp on this aspect of printing lest the Printer Pixies will come to you while you're sleeping and smear ink on your fingers.

- ✔ Keep a supply of two or three extra ribbons or toner cartridges. The extra supplies will hold you in case you need a new one over a working weekend.

- ✔ When the ribbon gets old and faded, replace it. Some places may offer reinking services for your ribbon. This service works if the ribbon fabric can hold the new ink. If your ribbon is threadbare, you need to buy a new one.

✔ You can revitalize an old ribbon by carefully opening its cartridge and spraying some WD-40 on it. Reassemble the cartridge and put the ribbon on some paper towels. Let it sit for a day before reusing it. This action gives the ribbon some extra life, but it can only be done once (and this tip works only with ribbons — not toner cartridges!).

✔ Ink printers use ink cartridges. Replace the ink cartridges when they run low on ink, just as you would replace a ribbon or toner cartridge.

✔ When a laser printer's toner cartridge gets low, you see a flashing "toner" light or the message "Toner low" displayed on the printer's control panel. You can take the toner out and rock it a bit. Shaken, not stirred, the cartridge may last about a week longer. When you see the message again, replace the toner immediately.

✔ There are services that offer toner "recharging." For a nominal fee, they take your old toner cartridges and refill them with new toner. You can then use the toner cartridge again and squeeze some more money out of it. Nothing is wrong with this service, and I recommend it as a good cost-saving measure. But never recharge a toner cartridge more than once, nor should you do business with anyone who says it's OK.

Chapter 26
Help Me! I'm Stuck!

· ·

In This Chapter

▶ "Double-clicking my document won't start Word!"

▶ "I can't start Word!"

▶ "Where did my document go?"

▶ "What do you mean, the application unexpectedly quit?"

▶ "Where am I now?"

▶ "It's not printing!"

· ·

"**T**here I was, minding my own business, when all of a sudden — for no apparent reason — Word *fill-in-the-blankety-blank*. Where is my baseball bat?"

It happens all too often. And it happens to everyone. "It worked just great when I did this yesterday. Why doesn't it work today?" Who knows? Retrace your steps. Check the grounds for signs of gypsies. But in the end, turn to this chapter for some quick solutions.

"Double-Clicking My Document Won't Start Word!"

Horror of horrors! This happens to everyone, at least once in their Mac lifetime. You double-click on a Word document icon and you get the nefarious `Application not found` error box. When that happens, take these steps:

1. **Jump-start your heart.**

2. **Double-check — I'm serious — that it's a Word document you're trying to open.**

   It could be something else, something funky, you know.

3. **Start Word and try to load the document by choosing File⇨Open.**

If that works, or even if it doesn't, it's time to *rebuild the Desktop*. To do that, heed these steps:

1. **Go to the Finder.**

   Quit all your open applications, such as Word, before you do this.

2. **Choose Special⇨Restart.**

   The computer restarts.

3. **Quickly, press and hold the Option and ⌘ keys. Keep holding them.**

4. **Keep holding both those keys.**

   The Mac goes through its start-up routine.

5. **Eventually you see the "rebuild the Desktop" box.**

6. **Click OK.**

This process takes a few minutes, but it restores all your Word icons. That way, any non-Word files masquerading as Word files will be unveiled. For some reason, rebuilding the Desktop also makes sounds crisper, colors brighter, and smells sweeter.

"I Can't Start Word!"

Click-click. And then ...

```
There is not enough memory to open Word.
```

If you were able to run Word in the past, this ominous-sounding message just means that the Mac is doing too much right now. Consider closing other applications that are open. Word is a memory hog; if you're used to running two things at once, give up the idea right now.

✔ If your system is burdened with fonts and Inits, you may want to consider unloading a few of them. I mean, having Ronald Reagan's eyeballs follow the cursor around impresses a few PC folk, but it sucks down memory that Word needs.

✔ Also see *Macs For Dummies* for more detailed information on solving "out of memory" problems.

"What Do You Mean, the Application Unexpectedly Quit?"

Error 3 errors are jewels: they mean that Word has unexpectedly quit. (If you look up *error 3* in any official Mac documentation, you find out that "the application unexpectedly quit." So much for being user-friendly.)

To cure these errors, rebuild the Desktop (refer to the preceding section). This should work most of the time.

✔ Consider that you may already be running Word. Click on the Application menu (the far-right icon-thing on the menu bar) and look for Microsoft Word in the list. If it's there, select it from the menu, and you'll be back in Word.

✔ Word does not self-destruct. If you used your computer and Word yesterday, it's still there today. It may be hidden or out of reach, however. Under no circumstances should you reinstall Word unless your guru directs you to do so.

✔ If you can't find the Word icon, it may be hidden. Or some joker may have dragged it to another window — or even to the Desktop. To find it, press ⌘-F to bring up the Find dialog box in the Finder. Type in **Word** and press Return. The Finder locates the first icon/folder with *Word* in the name. If that's not Word, press ⌘-G to have the Finder hunt again. Keep pressing ⌘-G until you locate the familiar Microsoft Word icon. Then drag it back into the folder you know and love best.

✔ If all else fails, check your wallet for missing credit cards and then call the airlines. Remember, even in the summer months, Word can find great skiing bargains south of the equator.

"Where Did My Document Go?"

Ever get the sensation that the computer is making faces at you when you turn away? Sometimes, when you look back, the computer won't even have your document still on-screen. In the rush to hide its sneering grin, the Mac may even put up DOS on-screen.

The first thing that you should try is pressing a key, any key. Gremlins like to install things like screen savers on unsuspecting computers. These thingamajigs turn your file into flying toasters, star fields, alien landscapes, or — worst of all — nothing. Pressing a key or moving the mouse usually brings everything back in order.

✔ If you see the Finder, you should try looking for Microsoft Word in the Applications menu, the far-right icon-thing on the menu bar. Drop-down that menu and pluck Microsoft Word from its contents to return to Word.

✔ Try moving the cursor up or down a few pages. You may simply be seeing a blank page that's in your document. Fiddling with the cursor-control keys should get you reoriented.

✔ Look in the Window menu to see whether you accidentally switched windows.

✔ As a last resort, press ⌘-Z — just in case you deleted everything.

"Where Am I Now?"

If the keys appear to be too close together, or your fingers suddenly swell, you may find yourself accidentally pressing the wrong cursor-control keys and, lo, you're somewhere else in your document. But where?

Rather than use your brain (thinking hurts too much), press Shift-F5, the Go Back command. Pressing this key combo moves you to the preceding cursor position and resets your document as you remember it. (Refer to Chapter 2 for more information.)

"It's Not Printing!"

Golly, the printer can be a dopey device. You tell Word to print, and the printer just sits there — deaf as a post! "Doe, dee, doe," it says. "Aren't you glad you paid twice as much money for a laser printer? Yuk! Yuk! Yuk!"

Believe it or not, the printer is not being stupid. Now stop banging your head on the table — it's not you either. Someone's connections are probably just loose. Check the printer's first. Make sure that the printer is on. Make sure that it is on-line. Check that it has paper to print on. Then confirm that the printer cable is still connected. Only after these steps should you phone the local computer store about free pickup of loony-bin merchandise. (It does happen.)

✔ A large picture or drawing in your document makes the computer and printer think harder before it starts to print. Have patience.

✔ Do not try printing again: If you keep pressing the Print command, each print order just stacks up. Then if (when, I mean) you do finally get the printer to respond, it will spend the next 72 hours printing out 85 copies of your report on the mating habits of Monarch butterflies. We really don't want that, do we?

✔ Don't try pressing harder on the keys. When the printer doesn't work, it doesn't work. Fixing this problem requires more attention than telepathy.

✔ Refer to Chapter 8 for additional information about printing.

✔ Make sure that the computer and printer are off — and unplugged — before you plug in a printer cable.

✔ The printer probably needs to be connected to the computer before the two are simultaneously turned on so that they can *recognize* each other.

Part VI
The Part of Tens

The 5th Wave — By Rich Tennant

"YEAH, I'VE FINISHED REVIEWING THE MONITOR, KEYBOARD, CPU AND PRINTER, AND I'M JUST FINISHING UP MY REVIEW OF THE MOUSE RIGHT NOW."

In this part...

Don't you just love trivia? (Most intelligent folk do.) And what's the best type of trivia? Lists! For example, "Ten tasty snacks you can make with Cheez Whiz and Spam," or "Ten clever things to say when you barge into an occupied stall," or "Ten nonaquatic things you may find floating in your swimming pool." This book deals with Word, so this part of the book is devoted to interesting lists about Word.

Most of the chapters in this section contain ten items. Some chapters contain more, some less. After all, if I was as thorough as I could be in Chapter 30, "Ten Features You Don't Use but Paid for Anyway," this book would be as fat as those other books on Word.

Chapter 27
The Ten Commandments of Word

In This Chapter

▶ Thou shalt not use extra spaces

▶ Thou shalt not press Return at the end of each line

▶ Thou shalt not neglect thy keyboard

▶ Thou shalt not reset or turn off thy Macintosh until thee quittest Word

▶ Thou shalt not manually number thy pages

▶ Thou shalt not use the Return key to start a new page

▶ Thou shalt not quit without saving first

▶ Thou shalt not clicketh OK too quickly

▶ Thou shalt not forget to turn on thy printer

▶ Thou shalt not forget to back up thy work

*J*ust imagine Bill Gates as Moses: his spindly frame draped magnificently with those ancient Hebrew robes, he towers over the word-processing masses. And the tablets . . . OK, so someone else is helping him hold the tablets. But anyway, upon the tablets are written The Ten Commandments of Word. Nay, isn't that the fire of the Lord in his heart — or just indigestion from too many tacos at the commissary? And, lo, it came to pass that the tablets were transcribed. And over the course of time, the lordly wisdom found on these tablets tiptoed its way into this book.

Ahem! It's very hard for me to write stiffly, like the characters in a Cecil B. DeMille movie. Let me put it simply: This chapter contains a bunch of dos and don'ts for working in Word. Most of these items are covered previously in this book, especially way back in Part I (the contents of which has probably spilled out your left ear by now — so listen closely to the recap).

I: Thou Shalt Not Use Extra Spaces

Generally speaking, you should never find more than one space anywhere in a Word document. Yeah, I know, most of us former touch typists insert two spaces at the end of a sentence. In a word processor, that's unnecessary, so wean yourself from the habit. Any time you're tempted to use more than one space in a row in your document, you should probably be using the Tab key instead. Use the spacebar to separate words and to end a sentence. Use the Tab key to align lists of information. And use the Table command (see Chapter 12) to organize information into rows and columns.

II: Thou Shalt Not Press Return at the End of Each Line

Word automatically wraps your text down to the next line as you approach the right margin. There is no need to press Return, except when you need to start a new paragraph. (Of course, if your paragraph is only a line long, it's OK to press Return.)

III: Thou Shalt Not Neglect Thy Keyboard

Word is Mac, and Mac is mousey. You can get a lot done with the mouse, but some things are faster with the keyboard. For example, I routinely switch documents by pressing ⌘-F6. And stabbing the ⌘-S key combo to quickly save a document or ⌘-P to print works better than fumbling for the mouse. You don't have to learn all the keyboard commands, but knowing the few I outline in this book will help a lot.

IV: Thou Shalt Not Reset or Turn Off Thy Macintosh Until Thee Quittest Word

Always exit properly from Word. Don't ever turn off your computer until it says that it's OK to do so. Usually, this is done by selecting the Shut Down command from the Finder's Special menu. Then and only then is it OK to turn off Mr. Macintosh. Believeth me, if ye don't heed mine instructions, ye are asking for mucho trouble. Yea, verily.

V: Thou Shalt Not Manually Number Thy Pages

Word has an automatic page numbering command. Refer to the Chapter 11 section "Where to Stick the Page Number."

VI: Thou Shalt Not Use the Return Key to Start a New Page

Sure, you could press the Return key a couple dozen times to create a new page. But that's not the proper way, and you'll mess up your new page if you go back to the preceding page and re-edit text. Besides, it's quicker to press ⌘-Enter, which inserts a hard page break into your document. Refer to the Chapter 11 section "Starting a New Page — a Hard Page Break" for the details.

VII: Thou Shalt Not Quit without Saving First

Save your document to disk before you quit. ⌘-S is the key combo to remember.

VIII: Thou Shalt Not Clicketh OK Too Quickly

Word asks many Yes/No/OK-type questions. If you press OK without thinking (or press Return accidentally), you could delete text, delete files, or perform a baaaad Replace operation without knowing it. Always read your screen before you press OK.

IX: Thou Shalt Not Forget to Turn on Thy Printer

The biggest printing problem anyone has: Telling Word to print something when the printer isn't on. Verify that your printer is on, healthy, and ready to print before you tell Word to print something.

X: Thou Shalt Not Forget to Back Up Thy Work

Keeping emergency copies of your important documents is vital. Computers are shaky houses of cards that can collapse at any sneeze or hiccup. Always make a safety copy of your files at the end of the day or as you work. Refer to the Chapter 24 section "Back Up Your Files."

Chapter 28

Ten Cool Tricks

*D*etermining what's a "cool trick" (and what's not) is purely subjective. I'm sure that people who formerly numbered their pages manually think Word's Page Numbers command is a cool trick. I think that AutoCorrect is a great trick — one which may become an on-the-fly spell-checker someday. And don't forget the handy Undo and Redo commands. Now if the boys and girls in the Word labs could only come up with a handy tool that lets you take back something you said aloud, we'd all truly be blessed.

This chapter explains some of the neater Word tricks — mostly obscure stuff that I may not have mentioned elsewhere in this book. Some are simple and straightforward; some take a little longer for the human brain to grasp.

Printing Labels

Labels are those gummy things that you can peel and stick to envelopes. Because my handwriting is so darn lousy, I print labels with my return address on them and stick those on my bills and whatnot I send out. I do it as a favor to the U.S. Postal Service.

To print labels, you choose the same command as when you want to print envelopes. Same command, different panel. Before you mess with this, I recommend that you go out and buy some Avery sticky labels for your computer. I use Avery laser labels in my laser printer. Stock number 5160 is ideal for return address and mailing labels.

Here are the instructions — way too terse for the main part of this book — for printing labels in Word:

1. **Choose Tools⇨Envelopes and Labels.**

2. **Make sure that the Labels panel is in front.**

3. **Click the Options button.**

4. **Select Avery Standard from the Label Products list.**

5. **Select 5160 (or whatever product number you're using) from the Product Number list.**

6. **Click OK.**

7. **Type what you want printed on the label in the Address box.**

8. **Make sure that the printer is on, ready to print, and loaded with the proper label sheet.**

9. **Click the Print button.**

If you're disgusted with the font the labels print in (and I'm disgusted), click the New Document button rather than the Print button in Step 9. When the labels appear in a document window, you can change their font and so forth by using the Font and Paragraph dialog boxes. Refer to Chapters 9 and 10 for the details. (The New Document button essentially sticks your labels in a giant table; see Chapter 12 for more information on tables.)

Bullets and Numbering

Often, you need to drive home several points, and nothing brings stuff home like putting bullets in your text. No, these aren't the lead-propelled things used to kill tourists and innocent bystanders. Bullets are typographic dingbats, like this:

- Bang!
- Bang!
- Bang!

To apply bullets to your text, highlight the paragraphs you want to shoot and choose Format⇨Bullets and Numbering. There's no need to dawdle in the dialog box; just click OK and your highlighted text will be all shot up, nice and neat. (You also can click on the Bulleted List button, on the Formatting toolbar.)

 You also can apply numbers to your paragraphs. To do so, when you see the Bullets and Numbering dialog box, click on the Numbered tab to bring that panel forward and then click OK. (Or click on the Numbered List button, on the Formatting toolbar.)

Revision Marks

Rumor has it Abe Lincoln really struggled over that Gettysburg address. Draft after draft after draft. Time and time again, Mary Todd would hear him utter, "Stupid pen." Then brilliance hit him, and he composed the speech most of us memorized in grade school. Ever wonder how he did it? Well, had he written in Word, you could use the Revisions command to check out how his initial drafts compared with the final one. You would see what words were changed and what phrases were added. You would see, right there on-screen, the various *revisions* old Abe made.

Less noble documents can suffer the same fate. Want to see what changes your `malevolent` **smart** editor made to your masterpiece? Run Word's Revisions command and you'll find out.

The Revisions command requires that you compare one document with another. Changes are noted on-screen in the second document: Blue text indicates changes, with new text underlined and deleted text crossed out. Unchanged text remains the same. And the areas where text was changed are flagged by a line on the left side of the document. Figure 28-1 shows what Abe may have seen on his screen.

Figure 28-1:
Revision marks show how versions of your text compare.

Eighty-seven Fourscore and seven years ago, our dads and grandads fathers brought forth upon this land continent a new nation.

To work the Revisions command, start with the most recent version of your document on-screen. Select Tools⇨Revisions. In the Revisions dialog box, click the Compare Versions button and then select an earlier version of your document on disk.

Don't bother trying to edit away the colored text on your screen: those are revision marks and not text formatting. From the Revisions dialog box, you can click on the Reject All button to do away with the revisions or click Accept All to keep the changes. Click the Close button to make the Revisions dialog box revise itself outta here.

Draft View

Word demands a lot of its owner. If you have a file that has a lot of graphics or a lot of different fonts, a slower computer can take forever to display a page of text. You can avoid this delay by switching on the ugly Draft view for your document:

1. **Choose Tools⇨Options.**

2. **Locate the View panel and bring it forward.**

3. **Put an X in the Draft Font box, in the upper-left corner of the panel.**

4. **Click OK.**

There is a problem here, however. Because no graphics appear and because you can't see the different fonts, you may as well be using a PC. Yech! Buy more memory; buy a better machine; sell your dog; anything but that!

Repeat the preceding steps to remove the X and rid yourself of Draft view. (But keep in mind that it does pep things up on slower computers.)

Draft view works only from Normal view. This option is not available from Page Layout view.

Select All

There are times when you want to block the whole shooting match, when you want to select the entire document, when you want to highlight everything from top to bottom and left to right and beginning to end. When you want to do so, click the mouse three times in your document's left margin. Click. Click. Click.

Zowie! There it is.

Oh, and you also can press F8 five times. Zap. Zap. Zap. Zap. Zap. Zowie! There you go again.

Oh, and choosing Edit⇨Select All does the same thing. Press ⌘-A. Zowie!

Inserting the Date

Word's date command is named Date and Time and hangs under the Insert menu. Selecting this command displays a dialog box full of date and time formats, one of which you're bound to favor.

Sorting

Sorting is one of Word's better tricks. When you learn it, you go looking for places to use it.

Of course, you can sort text—alphabetically or numerically—and paragraphs. You also can sort rows and columns in tables.

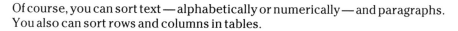

Always save your document before sorting.

Sorting is not difficult: all you have to do is save your document before sorting, highlight the stuff you want to sort, save *again*, and then choose Table⇨Sort Text. Then mess around in the dialog box and decide how you want the information that you selected in the file you saved to be sorted— though clicking OK usually sorts in alphabetic order.

Why all this concern with safety? Well, sorting takes a bunch of memory, and the machine could hang, or crash.

Automatic Saves

When the Auto Save feature is active, your document is periodically saved to disk. This isn't the same as pressing ⌘-S to save your document. Instead, Word makes a secret backup copy every so often. In the event of a crash, you can recover your work from the backup copy—even if you never saved the document to disk.

To turn on Auto Save, choose Tools⇨Options. Select the Save tab to bring that panel up front. Click on the Automatic Save Every box to put an X in that box if one isn't there already. Then enter the backup interval in the Minutes text box. For example, I type **10** to have Word back up my documents every ten minutes. If the power is unstable at your home or office, enter **5**, **3**, **2**, or even **1** minute as the backup interval. Press Return to, uh, return to your document.

With Auto Save, you won't recover all your document after a mishap, but you will get most of it back.

Fast Saves

Fast Saves is one of those ideas that sounds real good . . . until you use it. The idea is to avoid having to save everything every time. "Why not just save the changes? This will make things go oh-so-much-faster," the folks at Microsoft said. "Because," retorted this Word Dummy, "you can't give a Fast-Saved file to other people and expect them to be able to read it on their computers."

If Word only saves your changes to disk, what's someone else going to make of such a file? What if Tolstoy only changed a character's name in Chapter 43? He would have turned in a disk to his publisher with a Chapter 43 file that contained only the single word *Ludmilla*. That just doesn't work.

My advice is to disable Fast Saves. Choose Tools⇨Options. Then select Save panel by clicking on its tab. If the Allow Fast Saves box is checked, click on it. Make it empty. Click OK to return your document.

Cool Characters

You can use the Symbol command in the Insert menu to stick odd and wonderful characters into your document. Quite a few fonts have a few weird and wonderful characters in them. The Symbol font is full of neat stuff; the Wingdings font has all sorts of fun doodads; even the "normal" font, Times Roman, has several cool characters in it.

You can insert any of these funky characters into your document at your whim. Simply put the toothpick cursor where you want the symbol to appear, choose Insert⇨Symbol, point at the cool character you want inserted, and click your mouse. (Refer to Chapter 9 for more information.)

Chapter 29

Ten Weird Things You Probably Don't Know About

*W*elcome to the bizarre. No one could say that better than Rod Serling. If good old Rod were still with us, I'm certain he'd love using Word to help him concoct more wonderful and, yes, bizarre stories. He'd probably enjoy using the strange and macabre features discussed in this chapter. No, none of this is secret. None of it is cool. It's all weird, strange, not-really-necessary, and somewhat bizarre.

Paste Special

Paste is paste, right? Well, not according to the folks at Microsoft. You can't just paste anything anymore. I mean, it's so, well, *kindergarten*. Now, thanks to the Paste Special command, you can employ "enhanced" paste tactics. Choosing Edit⇨Paste Special brings up a Paste Special dialog box, which enables you to paste something into your document in several ways. Which paste methods are available depend on what you just cut or copied. You usually can paste in text as "Unformatted text," which I do all the time because I don't like copying stinky formatting between documents.

You also can experiment with "linking" items, which is the strange OLE stuff Microsoft is so big on. Worthy of playing with, provided you have other Microsoft-happy programs, but definitely too weird to go anywhere but in this chapter.

The Style Gallery

The Style Gallery is a fun place to play. Basically, it's a workshop where you can experiment, applying various Word styles to your document. To do so, choose Format⇨Style Gallery. A humongous Style Gallery dialog box appears, with a list of styles on the left and a preview of how they affect your document on the right. It's kind of fun to poke around with different styles and see how they tweak your work.

If what you see in the Style Gallery preview box doesn't impress you, consider clicking on the Example button. That way you'll see a preview of a sample document rather than your own text.

More style madness can be found lurking in Chapter 14.

The Language Command

The Language command, in the Tools menu, allows you to mark a block and tag it as something from another language, say Norwegian Bokmål. There's only one reason to do this: When Word is spell-checking and comes across a foreign word, it uses the appropriate language's dictionary instead of attempting to decipher the word as English.

A better purpose behind the Language command is to format some text as "no proofing." In other words, you tell Word not to spell-check that text. For example, suppose you're doing up a table of abbreviations and technical stuff and tire of Word assuming that all the stuff is misspelled. No problem, just mark the text as a block and set the Language to "no proofing." This step can truly save you a lot of time.

- ✔ Catalan is spoken in Catalonia. I wonder how many people use Word there?

- ✔ No, dude, there is no Surfer language. Bummer.

The Customize Command

The Customize command, in the Tools menu, is a cool place where you can not only waste mountains of time but also feel that you have ultimate control over Word's fate. This command tears at the heart of the very fabric that is Word. By using the various controls in the Customize dialog box, you can actually change the way Word looks — for the better, for good.

The three panels in the Customize dialog box let you change Word's toolbars, menus, and keyboards. Hey, this stuff is real, and it's not for the faint of heart. You can build a toolbar, add or remove menu items, and assign keyboard shortcuts. The whole program is up for grabs! I don't recommend messing with anything here — yet. Wait a few months. Get comfy with Word. Then slash away and make the program your own!

Using the Options Dialog Box

Choosing Tools⇨Options accesses the Options dialog box. In this dialog box, you get 12 — count 'em, 12 — panels that control how Word behaves. There are really no hints or secrets in the Options dialog box. In fact, you've probably visited this dialog box a few times already if you've chosen any Options buttons in the various Word dialog boxes. No big deal. Just weird.

Inserting Fields

A field looks like text in your document. It smells like text. And it prints like text. But it's not text. Rather, it's a special marker — a fill-in-the-blanks thing that Word knows to complete at some later time. For example, typing the date in your document just slaps some words on the page. But sticking a date *field* in your document means that field always displays the current date, no matter what the current date is.

You insert fields into your document by choosing Insert⇨Field. The Field dialog box displays a list of field categories and then individual types of fields. For example, the Date and Time category lists several types of date fields: the date the document was created, saved to disk, printed, the current date, and so on. An Options button lets you further customize the field.

In your document, fields appear like selected text but with a hazy gray background. Unlike real text, you must select and delete the entire field all at once. (Remember, fields are not text.)

It Floats! It Sticks! Making Your Toolbars Float

Word has various toolbars, including the Standard and Formatting toolbars you see on-screen right now. These can appear in two ways: as a bar stuck on-screen or as a floating palette. You can change them back and forth at your whim.

To make a stuck-down toolbar float, first take two scoops of ice cream.... Seriously, double-click the mouse on a "gray" area in the toolbar — not on a button or drop-down thing. The toolbar becomes a floating palette.

To make a floating palette toolbar a stuck-down toolbar, double-click on its title bar. Click-click.

You can also drag the stuck-down toolbars around the screen, moving them to the bottom or top. It's bizarre, which is why it's in this chapter.

Mousey Shortcuts

Here are some interesting things you can do with the mouse:

- ✔ Double-click *on* the ruler to see the Document Layout dialog box.
- ✔ Double-click *in* the ruler to see the Tabs dialog box.

- ✔ Click on the Help button (on the Standard toolbar) and then point at some text on-screen. A pop-up cartoon balloon appears, describing that text's formatting. (Press Esc to quit.)
- ✔ Press Control and click over your document to see a quick pop-up menu with several editing and formatting commands on it.
- ✔ Press Control and click over a toolbar to display the Toolbars menu.
- ✔ Double-click on the three-letter acronyms on the status bar to toggle those items on or off.
- ✔ Double-click elsewhere on the status bar to bring up the Go To dialog box.

Constructing a Master Document

How big should your document be? Technically speaking, Word can handle a document probably as big as you can write it. Practically speaking, you don't want things to get too big. Word starts acting weirder than normal with big documents.

But how big is big? Here's my advice: Keep your documents at chapter-size.

Each chapter in this book is a document unto itself. This chapter is called *Chapter 29* on disk. That's the way most writers work; a chapter is a document. The only drawback to this plan is that it makes printing everything a pain. And if you dare to take advantage of Word's indexing and table of contents commands (I don't), they just don't work with multiple documents unless . . .

The solution to the problem is to create what Word calls a Master Document, which is just another Word document. But a Master Document contains information about other documents and kinda links them all together. You still work with each chapter as its own document. But the whole shooting match can be printed, indexed, table-of-contents-ed, or otherwise manipulated through the Master Document.

Yes, it's a novel concept. Unfortunately, wrestling with it in Word is not fun.

To create a Master Document, start with a new document in Word (choose File⇨New). Then choose View⇨Master Document. This changes the display and adds the Outline/Master Document toolbar. The buttons on the far right of the toolbar are used to add documents to the Master Document. (Hover the mouse over a button to see its function balloon display.)

Alas, that's all the help I can give you here. Though it's a cool trick, working with a Master Document involves a full tutorial.

The Unbreakables

There are two weird keys on your keyboard: the spacebar and the hyphen. Both keys produce characters on-screen, but these are not "normal" characters.

The space. What is that? Space! Outer space? And the hyphen isn't really a character at all. It's used to split text — to hyphenate words. In fact, both the space and the hyphen will *break* your text between two lines. Of course, this is not a problem unless you don't want to break a line in two.

There are times when you want to be sure that a space was not interrupted by something as mundane as the end of a line. For example, suppose that you work for the firm of Bandini, Lambert, and Locke and, by golly, Mr. Locke doesn't like to be left on a line by himself. If so, insert a nonbreaking (*hard*) space between each name to make sure that they're always together.

To prevent the space character from breaking a line, press Option-spacebar.

The hyphen key, which also is the minus key, works to hyphenate a long word at the end of a line. But, sometimes, you may not want the hyphen to split a word. For example, you may not want a phone number split between two lines. Inserting a hard hyphen prevents text from splitting between two lines.

To prevent the hyphen character from breaking a line, press ⌘-Shift-hyphen.

Chapter 30

Ten Features You Don't Use but Paid for Anyway

*W*ord comes with many more features than you'll ever use. There are definitely more than ten and probably several dozen that I've never heard of. Some people writing those massive "complete" Word tomes have been known to disappear into a room and not emerge for months — or years! Indeed, I seriously doubt whether people who know everything about Word keep their sanity.

This chapter lists ten of the more interesting features that you bought when you paid for Word. (I'm not even bothering to mention some of the things that Microsoft lets you do with Word, such as embed sounds, movies, and other cute but useless things.) You probably didn't know that these goodies existed. That's OK — they're a bit technical to work with. This chapter covers each one briefly, but don't expect to learn how to use any of the paid-for-but-ignored features.

Annotation

If you're reading someone else's work, and you want to make a comment about it but don't want to make any changes, you can include an annotation. You can insert a comment ("Charles, it cannot both be the 'best of times' and 'worst of times.' Try to add more clarity to your writing.") in such a way that it won't print. The Annotation command is found in the Insert menu. You won't be able to see an annotation unless you choose View⇨Annotations.

Table of Contents

Years ago, compiling a table of contents could make a grown human of the masculine gender cry. (The task never had the same effect on my wife, but I guess not much is daunting after childbirth.) Who in their right mind would want to type in all those names and all those dots, and then figure out what page everything is on? (And there's not even a coach standing by reminding you to breathe.) Word, man, that's who!

If you have been careful with your styles (see Chapter 14 to learn about styles), inserting a table of contents is a sure bet. Well, almost. Choose Insert⇨Index and Tables and then click on the Table of Contents tab. Word looks through your entire document and takes everything that has been tagged with a style of Heading (followed by some number), determines what page it's on, and builds the table of contents for you.

Sounds like fun? Yeah, but it's complex to set up. If you didn't do this when you created your document, you may as well do it the old-fashioned way, weeping bitterly and all that.

Hyphenation

Hyphenation is an automatic feature that splits long words at the end of a line to make the text fit better on the page. Most people leave hyphenation off because all those broken words tend to slow down the pace at which people read. If you want to hyphenate a document, however, choose Tools⇨Hyphenation. Continuously jab the Help key when you need help.

Index

This is an interesting feature, but it's complicated to use. The Index and Tables command in the Insert menu (click on the Index tab) marks a piece of text that you want to include in an index. For example, you can tag a word for inclusion as an index entry. Then, using other commands too complicated to mention here, you can ask Word to generate an automatic index at the end of the document. This feature is a handy thing to have, but it takes time to learn, and you often don't need a full index for that five-page letter to Mom.

Cross-Reference

Choosing Insert⇨Cross-reference enables you to insert a "Refer to Chapter 99, Section Z" type of thing into your document. This feature works because you've taken the Krell brain booster and now have an IQ that can be expressed only in scientific notation. Fortunately, you also may have used the Heading style to mark text in your document that you want to cross-reference (you must do so for the Cross-reference command to work). A cross-reference includes a page-number reference that Word updates should you overhaul your document.

Macro

A *macro* is a little program that someone has written to do some neat thing in Word. There is a whole special programming language devoted to macros; therefore, writing macros is a job for the truly advanced or insane.

A *macro* is basically a shortcut. You can create a macro that automatically records something in your document, a set of commands, or anything that you normally have to repeat over and over. Macros automate the process. In Word, macros do more and comprise an actual programming language that you can use to extend Word's capabilities. This is heady, technical stuff that's getting harder to take with each version of Word. In fact, detailed books are devoted to the subject. If your name is Bill Gates, you should buy one to check it out.

Math

Why hasn't it ever dawned upon Word designers that math and English are two separate subjects for a reason? I mean, math and English are always taught as separate courses. The math and English parts of the SAT are separate — including the scores. So who needs a math function in a word processor? I don't know. Even if you did, it's still easier to calculate the numbers by using your desk calculator and typing them in manually.

To use the Math command, you must first put your data in a table. Then highlight the row or column that you want computed. Choose Table⇨Formula. Word suggests a formula type, or you can tell it what you want done with the numbers. On second thought, I guess this woulda been kinda handy during algebra class. Anyway, Word puts the answer wherever you left the insertion pointer.

Outlining

 Outlining in Word isn't as bad as outlining in other word processors, but it's still like another complete program that you have to learn before you can try it. To switch on Word's outline feature — and begin a long series of head pains — choose View⇨Outline. (Or just click the Outline button, in the lower-left corner of the screen.) This command activates Outline mode: your ruler is replaced, your text looks different, and every aspirin manufacturer enjoys an increased stock value. (My advice: Don't try outlining unless you have some serious time to kill.)

Random Statistics

This feature is something that you never use because it is a very unpopular thing. Besides, it is a royal pain in the digit. Word tracks all sorts of statistics about your document. To see them, choose File⇨Summary Info. Yuck! That would be bad enough, but now click on the Statistics button. Yoikles! Word tells you all sorts of things about your document, such as how many words it contains. Writers who are paid by the word use this feature to make sure that they get their full load in. This features can also give you a good idea of how "big" your document is, but this is all really silly stuff.

Repagination Nonsense

In the beginning, Word was a mere DOS application (and a slow one at that). To make the program faster, Microsoft left out a bunch of features that were standard in most word processors. One of those features was *repagination*, or the capability of the word processor to automatically insert page breaks on-screen (those dotted lines of death). In Word for the Macintosh, present version, repagination is done automatically. However (to be compatible I suppose), a Repaginate command still exists. Choose Tools⇨Options and click on the General tab. There you can turn off Background Repagination.

Chapter 31

Ten Shortcut Keys Worth Remembering

*T*his is sacrilege! You are forbidden — *forbidden* — to use the keyboard on your Macintosh! Shame on you!

Seriously, you can do lots of interesting things with the keyboard, things that can be done quite rapidly and without breaking off any nails. Although Word has a whole armada of key combinations, only a handful are worth knowing. This chapter contains the best, a shade more than ten. I'm confident that you'll grow fond of them in time.

Besides, the guy who invented the mouse doesn't even profit from it. He's an academic, so it's the intellectual property (or whatever that lame excuse is called) of Stanford University. But now he's a regular on late-night TV, where he tells us how for 20 years people thought that the mouse was an impractical and eccentric tool and would never take off for real computer use. He encourages the ingenious among us to invent and not be discouraged. He says that he doesn't even mind not profiting from the mouse because his whole point was to fill a need in the computer industry. Because the creation is the thing. Kinda gives you warm fuzzies, huh?

Strange, WordPerfect-esque Function Keys

Thank goodness this program isn't WordPerfect. Those folks have lots of function keys, all of them required just to work the program. In Word, using the function keys is optional, so why bother?

Actually, you may want to try hanging out with four of the function keys; No handy mnemonics here: You just have to get used to them.

F12, the Save As key

Pressing F12 is the same as choosing File⇨Save As. So why bother?

Shift-F3, the Switch Case key combo

To change the case of your text between all caps, lowercase, and mixed case, mark the text as a block and then press Shift-F3 until the text looks the way you want.

Shift-F4, the Repeat Find key combo

Find a bit of text. Great! Want to find it again? Pressing Shift-F4 makes Word look again and you don't even have to visit the Find dialog box a second time.

Shift-F5, the "Take me back to where I was" key combo

It's easy to get lost in Word. If you just pressed ⌘-End for no apparent reason (throwing the cursor to the end of your document), press the timesaving Shift-F5 to get back to where you were.

The Document Keys

Word has four handy — and mnemonic! — key combinations that you can press to do things with documents:

⌘-N: New

⌘-O: Open

⌘-S: Save

⌘-P: Print

The fifth document key is not mnemonic:

⌘-W: Close

I suppose that's *W* for *Window,* as in "Close the Window, I'm not paying to (heat/cool) the wild outdoors!" Please remember that ⌘-C is not the Close shortcut key; *C* is for *Copy* (see the following section). Drat! We need a larger alphabet.

Did you ever notice that the first letters of the first three commands in the File menu spell NOW? Is this some kind of subliminal message?

Save! Save! Save! Always save your document. Get in the habit of pressing ⌘-S often as you work.

The Kindergarten Keys: Cut, Copy, Paste

When you're working with blocks, three shortcut keys come in most handy:

⌘-X: Cut

⌘-C: Copy

⌘-V: Paste

To use these keys, first highlight a block. Then press ⌘-X to cut the block or ⌘-C to copy. Move the toothpick cursor to where you want the block pasted and press ⌘-V. Refer to Chapter 6 for more information on playing with blocks.

The Undo-Redo Keys

The ⌘-Z key is Word's Undo key. Pressing it will undo just about anything Word can do; you can even undo what was done before that, too.

If you need to redo something — that is, un-undo — you can press ⌘-Y.

Word's Undo command is very un-Macintosh. You cannot press ⌘-Z twice to undo and then redo something. Instead, you undo the last two things you did. Remember that ⌘-Y is redo in Word.

Text Formatting Keys

You can use these four shortcut keys — either as you type or on a marked block of text — to affect character formatting:

    ⌘-B: Bold

    ⌘-I: Italics

    ⌘-U: Underline

    ⌘-spacebar: Normal

Press ⌘-B when you want unbolded text made bold. Or if the text is already bold, you can mark it as a block and press ⌘-B to unbold the block. The same holds true with ⌘-I and italics.

Pressing ⌘-spacebar returns text to normal. So if you mark a block of text that has all sorts of crazy, mixed-up formatting, press ⌘-spacebar for an instant sea of sanity. Pressing ⌘-spacebar as you're entering text instantly switches off whatever formatting you're currently using.

Font Formatting Keys

Forget the Font dialog box. If you have enough spare memory cells after imbibing all that alcohol in college (or after reading the Mail Merge chapter), you can use these key combinations to ease text formatting:

    ⌘-Shift-F: Font

    ⌘-Shift-P: Font size

⌘-Shift-S: Style

⌘-Shift->: Make text bigger

⌘-Shift-<: Make text smaller

The ⌘-Shift-F, ⌘-Shift-P, and ⌘-Shift-S key combos highlight the corresponding list boxes on the Formatting toolbar. Type in the font name, size (in points, hence the *P*), or style that you want. This method may seem like quite a bit of work, but it is a quick way when you get the hang of it.

The ⌘-Shift->/< nonsense makes no sense. But sometimes it's fun to mess with the text size of a selected block by using those key combinations. It's much more visual than trying to mentally figure numbers in a dialog box.

Paragraph Formatting Keys

Insert the cursor in a paragraph (or mark the paragraph as a block) and then use one of the following key combinations to format it:

⌘-L: Left-justify

⌘-R: Right-justify

⌘-E: Center

⌘-J: Justify

⌘-1: Single-space

⌘-2: Double-space

⌘-5: $1^1/_2$ space

The oddball here is ⌘-E to center. Ack! Never mind. Just use the buttons on the Formatting toolbar. I actually used ⌘-2 to double-space a document the other day, though, which is why I'm listing it here.

Chapter 32

Ten Things Worth Remembering

● ●

In This Chapter

▶ Don't be afraid of your keyboard

▶ Have a supply of diskettes ready

▶ Keep printer paper, toner, and supplies handy

▶ Keep references handy

▶ Keep your files organized

▶ Remember ⌘-Z!

▶ Save your document often!

▶ Use AutoText for oft-typed stuff

▶ Use clever, memorable filenames

▶ Don't take it all too seriously

● ●

*T*here's nothing like finishing a book with a few, heartening words of good advice. As a Word novice, you need this kind of encouragement and motivation. Word can be unforgiving but not necessarily an evil place to work. This book shows you that it's also possible to have a lot of fun with Word and still get your work done. To help send you on your way, here are a few things worth remembering.

Don't Be Afraid of Your Keyboard

Try to avoid pressing Return repeatedly to start a new page, using the spacebar when the Tab key will do better, or manually numbering your pages. There's a handy Word command to do just about anything, but you'll never learn these commands if you're afraid to try them.

Have a Supply of Diskettes Ready

You need diskettes to use your computer, even if you have a hard drive! You need diskettes for backing up files and exchanging files with other people.

Keep a box or two of diskettes available. Always buy the proper size diskette for your Mac, either high- or low-density, though most Macs today can swallow high-density — "HD" — disks without choking.

Keep Printer Paper, Toner, and Supplies Handy

When you buy paper, buy a box. When you buy a toner cartridge or printer ribbon, buy two or three. Also keep a good stock of pens, paper, staples, paper clips, and all other office supplies (including diskettes) handy.

Keep References Handy

Word is a writing tool. As such, you need to be familiar with and obey the grammatical rules of your language. If that language happens to be English, then you have a big job ahead of you. Even though they're an electronic part of Word, I recommend that you keep a dictionary and a thesaurus handy. Strunk and White's *The Elements of Style* is also a great book for finding out where the apostrophes and commas go. If you lack these books, visit your local bookstore today. Plan on paying about $50 to stock up on quality references.

Keep Your Files Organized

Use subdirectories on your hard drive for storing your document files. Keep related documents together in the same subdirectory. You may need someone else's help to set up an organizational system. Refer to Chapters 18 and 24 for additional information.

Remember ⌘-Z!

⌘-Z is your Undo key combination. If you're typing away in Word, press ⌘-Z to undelete any text you may have mistakenly deleted. This key command works for individual letters, sentences, paragraphs, pages, and other large chunks of missing text.

Save Your Document Often!

Save your document to disk as soon as you get a few meaningful words down on-screen. Then save every so often after that. Even if you're using the Auto Save feature (discussed in Chapter 28), continue to manually save your document to disk: press ⌘-S.

Use AutoText for Oft-Typed Stuff

To quickly insert things that you type over and over, like your name and address, use a glossary entry. Type it in once and then define it as a glossary entry (choose Edit⇨Glossary). Then use a shortcut key to zap it in whenever you need it. See Chapter 13 for more about AutoText.

Use Clever, Memorable Filenames

A file named *Letter* is certainly descriptive, but what does it tell you? A file named *Letter to Mom* is even more descriptive but still lacks some information. A file *Mom's Letter #23* may indicate the 23rd letter you've written to Mom. Even better is *August's Letter to Mom*. You get the idea: Use creative and informative filenames.

If the name doesn't help you find what you want, refer to Chapter 18 for information on Word's Find File command, which can scope out any file on your Mac that contains some tidbit of text.

Don't Take It All Too Seriously

Computers are really about having fun. Too many people panic too quickly when they use a computer. Don't let it get to you! And please, please, don't reinstall Word to fix a minor problem. Anything that goes wrong has a solution. If the solution is not in this book, consult your guru. Someone is bound to help you out.

Index

Special Characters Index

• A •

Notes

Notes

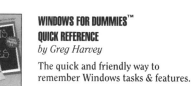

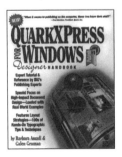

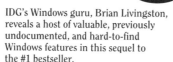

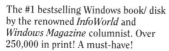

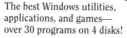

Order Form

Order Center: (800) 762-2974 (8 a.m.-5 p.m., PST, weekdays) **or (415) 312-0650**

For Fastest Service: Photocopy This Order Form and FAX it to: (415) 358-1260

Quantity	ISBN	Title	Price	Total

Shipping & Handling Charges

Subtotal	U.S.	Canada & International	International Air Mail
Up to $20.00	Add $3.00	Add $4.00	Add $10.00
$20.01-40.00	$4.00	$5.00	$20.00
$40.01-60.00	$5.00	$6.00	$25.00
$60.01-80.00	$6.00	$8.00	$35.00
Over $80.00	$7.00	$10.00	$50.00

In U.S. and Canada, shipping is UPS ground or equivalent.
For Rush shipping call (800) 762-2974.

Subtotal _____

CA residents add applicable sales tax _____

IN and MA residents add 5% sales tax _____

IL residents add 6.25% sales tax _____

RI residents add 7% sales tax _____

Shipping _____

Total _____

Ship to:

Name _____

Company _____

Address _____

City/State/Zip _____

Daytime Phone _____

Payment: ❑ Check to IDG Books (US Funds Only)   ❑ Visa   ❑ Mastercard   ❑ American Express

Card# _____ Exp._____ Signature_____

Please send this order form to: IDG Books, 155 Bovet Road, Suite 310, San Mateo, CA 94402.

Allow up to 3 weeks for delivery. Thank you!

IDG BOOKS WORLDWIDE REGISTRATION CARD

RETURN THIS REGISTRATION CARD FOR FREE CATALOG

Title of this book: **WORD 6 FOR MAC FOR DUMMIES**

My overall rating of this book: ❑ Very good [1] ❑ Good [2] ❑ Satisfactory [3] ❑ Fair [4] ❑ Poor [5]

How I first heard about this book:

❑ Found in bookstore; name: [6] _____   ❑ Book review: [7]

❑ Advertisement: [8]   ❑ Catalog: [9]

❑ Word of mouth; heard about book from friend, co-worker, etc.: [10]   ❑ Other: [11]

What I liked most about this book:

_____

_____

What I would change, add, delete, etc., in future editions of this book:

_____

_____

Other comments:

_____

Number of computer books I purchase in a year: ❑ 1 [12] ❑ 2-5 [13] ❑ 6-10 [14] ❑ More than 10 [15]

I would characterize my computer skills as: ❑ Beginner [16] ❑ Intermediate [17] ❑ Advanced [18] ❑ Professional [19]

I use ❑ DOS [20] ❑ Windows [21] ❑ OS/2 [22] ❑ Unix [23] ❑ Macintosh [24] ❑ Other: [25]_____

(please specify)

I would be interested in new books on the following subjects:

(please check all that apply, and use the spaces provided to identify specific software)

❑ Word processing: [26]   ❑ Spreadsheets: [27]

❑ Data bases: [28]   ❑ Desktop publishing: [29]

❑ File Utilities: [30]   ❑ Money management: [31]

❑ Networking: [32]   ❑ Programming languages: [33]

❑ Other: [34]

I use a PC at (please check all that apply): ❑ home [35] ❑ work [36] ❑ school [37] ❑ other: [38] _____

The disks I prefer to use are ❑ 5.25 [39] ❑ 3.5 [40] ❑ other: [41]_____

I have a CD ROM: ❑ yes [42]   ❑ no [43]

I plan to buy or upgrade computer hardware this year: ❑ yes [44]   ❑ no [45]

I plan to buy or upgrade computer software this year: ❑ yes [46]   ❑ no [47]

Name: _____ Business title: [48] _____ Type of Business: [49] _____

Address (❑ home [50] ❑ work [51] /Company name: _____)

Street/Suite# _____

City [52]/State [53]/Zipcode [54]: _____ Country [55] _____

❑ **I liked this book!** You may quote me by name in future
IDG Books Worldwide promotional materials.

My daytime phone number is _____

IDG BOOKS

THE WORLD OF
COMPUTER
KNOWLEDGE

❏ **YES!**
Please keep me informed about IDG's World of Computer Knowledge.
Send me the latest IDG Books catalog.